KANJI FROM ZERO!

Revision 2

George Trombley

Yukari Takenaka

Kanako Hatanaka

Justin McGowan

Kanji From Zero! Book 1
Proven Methods to Learn Kanji with Integrated Workbook

PREFACE

Kanji From Zero! is a Japanese kanji book series built on the idea that learning kanji shouldn't be mechanical and shouldn't only be about learning the readings of each kanji. The relationship to Japanese culture and the way kanji is integrated into Japanese life is key in establishing a strong foothold in integrating kanji into your Japanese fluency!

DEDICATION

This book is dedicated to and made for those who want to truly learn Japanese: Japanese culture lovers, Japanese language learners, Japanese drama watchers, Japanese beginners, JPOP music fans, Japanese anime watchers, Japanese manga readers, people of Japanese heritage connecting to their history, and, last but not least, anyone planning travel to Japan!

This began as a project to create a better book to learn kanji. It's not enough to merely learn how to read kanji. Kanji, like the members of a JPOP group or the characters of an *anime*, have unique personalities and quirks to be explored.

So many kanji books are merely reference materials listing every kanji, their readings, and maybe a few words. This barely scratches the surface of the amazing discoveries awaiting you when you fully grasp the connection kanji has with Japan and its culture. The entire *Kanji From Zero!* team wishes you success.

DISTRIBUTION

Distributed in the UK & Europe by:
Bay Foreign Language Books Ltd.
Unit 4, Kingsmead, Park Farm, Folkestone, Kent. CT19 5EU, Great Britain
sales@baylanguagebooks.co.uk

Distributed in the USA & Canada by:
From Zero LLC.
10624 S. Eastern Ave. #A769
Henderson, NV 89052, USA
sales@fromzero.com

COPYRIGHT

Kanji From Zero! 1
-- Table of Contents --

We love book reviews!

Reviews help! Not only do they help spread the word, they also help us to improve the book. Please visit any of the major book seller websites and post a review of *Kanji From Zero!* We are fanatical about making the best books for students who don't have access to a Japanese teacher. Your reviews help make new books possible!

You can help with feedback!

If you love, hate, or are confused about any concept in this book, please email us at feedback@fromzero.com. With your feedback we can improve future editions.

Also, don't forget to watch the HUNDREDS of videos available at our YouTube channel: http://www.youtube.com/yesjapan.

ありがとうございました！

Special thanks to our team!

Steven Golding
Sarah Dunlap
Frank Lin
Willow Hutchinson
Jesse Goodburne

MVP Award

Steven Golding

Steven went above and beyond our expectations in dedicating
time and energy to making *Kanji From Zero!* as error free as possible.

A | Kanji Basics

A | Kanji Basics かんじの きほん

● **A-1. Why kanji are important**

Welcome to Kanji from Zero, and congratulations for coming this far in your quest to learn Japanese. Many students ask, "Is it really necessary to learn kanji?" The answer is *yes*.

Kanji are not just phonetic symbols like hiragana and katakana. Each kanji has meaning. By learning kanji you will be able to make sense of how words are related to each other, and your ability to understand Japanese will increase substantially as you learn new characters.

For example, the kanji 食 can be read as しょく or た, depending on the word. The kanji 食 means "food," and words with this kanji in them tend to have meanings related to food. Even if you didn't know the word, you would know that it is related to food if this kanji were in it.

Consider the following words that use this kanji:

食堂	しょくどう	cafeteria
食卓	しょくたく	dinner table
食欲	しょくよく	appetite
食品	しょくひん	food products
夕食	ゆうしょく	dinner
食中毒	しょくちゅうどく	food poisoning
夜食	やしょく	midnight snack

As you can see, all of the words have 食 in them and are somehow related to food.

● A-2. Listening for kanji

Kanji are great because they give you a level of comprehension not available from hiragana and katakana alone. For example, if you hear the word にほんしょく, even though you have never heard the word before, you might be able to understand what it means based on the kanji you have already "heard."

Because you know that にほん means Japan, and you know that しょく is one of the readings for the kanji "food," you could assume that the word means "Japanese food."

Of course, it is possible that the しょく portion of にほんしょく was not the kanji for food but the kanji for color, 色, which can also be read as しょく. You can rule out other kanji possibilities by the context of the conversation.

Knowing how words are written in kanji helps comprehension because you can guess what something means based on what the possible kanji are.

Learning kanji is not as easy as learning hiragana or katakana, but the benefits of knowing kanji far outweigh the effort required to learn them.

● A-3. Different readings

Unlike hiragana and katakana, kanji almost always have more than one reading. The best way to learn the different readings is to learn a word that uses that particular reading. The kanji section of the lesson will provide you with sample words for each reading.

There are two types of readings:

くんよみ is the Japanese reading of the kanji. It is normally unique to the Japanese language.

おんよみ is the Chinese reading of the kanji. If you ever study Chinese, you will notice the similarity in the way the kanji is read in both languages.

However, since nearly all Japanese おんよみ readings originate from an older version of Chinese, sometimes the おんよみ of the kanji sounds *nothing* like it does in Chinese.

● A-4. ふりがな

Throughout this book you will see small hiragana characters above kanji words just like it shows below. These are commonly referred to as ふりがな. ふりがな is not a new way of writing, it's just normal ひらがな used to help the reader properly read the kanji.

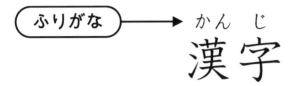

ふりがな is commonly used when the reading of the kanji is unusual or difficult. Also you will see ふりがな in まんが (comic books) and books targeted for elementary school students.

ふりがな is also used in song lyrics, poems, or any printed material where either the kanji is read with a unique reading or when the kanji isn't commonly known.

● A-5. おくりがな

Hiragana that follows the kanji is referred to as おくりがな.

おくりがな is used to conjugate verbs and adjectives. The conjugation of a verb or adjective will NEVER be written in kanji. As a matter of fact, particles are also never written in kanji.

● A-6. Reading instinct

Many students struggle with kanji because they are not sure whether the kanji in the word should be read with the おんよみ (Chinese reading) or くんよみ (Japanese reading). But you shouldn't be too hard on yourself if you make a mistake, since even Japanese people mistakenly read kanji from time to time.

Although there is no foolproof way to know which reading to use, you will usually be correct if you follow these simple guidelines:

1. When kanji is combined with ひらがな in a word, use くんよみ.
2. If a word has two or more kanji in a row and no hiragana, use おんよみ.
3. When kanji is all by itself, the くんよみ reading is most common.

Use Japanese Reading くんよみ

つき ひかり 月 の 光	Kanji with hiragana BETWEEN them are normally read as くんよみ.
み もの 見 る 物	Single kanji, and when part of a verb, are almost always くんよみ.
くるま 車	When referring to a kanji, they are often referred by their くんよみ when the くんよみ is an independent word.

Use Chinese Reading おんよみ

げっ こう 月 光	Kanji used together WITHOUT hiragana are almost always read as おんよみ.
けん ぶつ 見 物	Words with two or more kanji are called じゅくご and tend to be read with おんよみ.
れんしゅう 練 習 する	する verbs tend to be made with じゅくご and read as おんよみ.

● A-7. The power of knowing kanji

If you can learn to utilize your kanji knowledge with new words, your Japanese comprehension will increase exponentially. Let's look at a scenario where you hear a familiar word with the sound きょく in it.

Part 1:

These next three kanji all share the same sound. You don't have to learn these kanji, but instead focus on the concept of "referring" to kanji.

Kanji with same reading of きょく		
pole	station, department, office	song, tune
極	局	曲
きょく	きょく	きょく

Part 2:

After you study Japanese for a while, you will know MANY words, and some of those words will have the sound きょく in them.

south pole	drug store	new song
南極	薬局	新曲
なん・きょく	やっ・きょく	しん・きょく

Part 3:

Now you hear a word that you have never heard before:

ゆうびんきょく

Part 4:

Let's assume that you already know the word ゆうびん which means "mail", but you don't know which きょく is in ゆうびんきょく . You can ask your Japanese friend which きょく they mean by asking like this:

なんきょく
1. 南極の「きょく」ですか？

   Is it the きょく from なんきょく？

やっきょく
2. 薬局の「きょく」ですか？

   Is it the きょく from やっきょく？

しんきょく
3. 新曲の「きょく」ですか？

   Is it the きょく from しんきょく？

Your friend will answer that it is:

やっきょく　きょく
4. 薬局の局です。

   It's the きょく from やっきょく.

Now you can reliably assume that ゆうびんきょく means "post office."
If they had said it was 新曲のきょく then you might think it's some sort of song about mail.

Knowing kanji gives you a built in database in your brain that lets you link up words in ways that you couldn't do without them. The context of the conversation PLUS knowing the possible kanji in the word will eventually allow you to know what a word means THE MOMENT you hear it.

A | How Kanji is introduced in this book

The following key shows the sections of each new kanji introduced.

	165. speak, word, language			14 画
くんよみ	かた（る、らう）			
おんよみ	ゴ			

talk, speak	language study	English	story
かた 語る	ご がく 語学	えい ご 英語	ものがたり 物語

New Kanji Key

A Kanji Stroke Order

B Kanji Number & English Meaning

C Stroke Count (画 is read as かく)

D The Official Kanji Readings

E Kanji Writing Practice Boxes

F Kanji Words

1

Kanji lesson 1:

一二三四五六

1 New Kanji あたらしい かんじ

Make sure you learn the correct stroke order. Correct stroke order will mean neater symbols when writing quickly. Also, take time to learn the words listed for each kanji – these will help you memorize the different readings.

一	**1. one**					1画
	くんよみ	ひと (つ)				
	おんよみ	イチ、イツ				
	一					

one	one thing	January	unification
いち	ひと	いちがつ	とういつ
一	一つ	一月	統一

二	**2. two**					2画
	くんよみ	ふた (つ)				
	おんよみ	二				
	二					

two	February	2nd of the month	two things
に	にがつ	ふつか	ふた
二	二月	二日	二つ

3. three　　3 画

くんよみ	みっ (つ)
おんよみ	サン

三

three	triangle	3rd of the month	three things
さん	さん かく	みっ か	みっ
三	三角	三日	三つ

4. four　　5 画

くんよみ	よん、よっ (つ)
おんよみ	シ

四

four	four o'clock	square	four things
よん、し	よ じ	し かく	よっ
四	四時	四角	四つ

5. five　　4 画

くんよみ	いつ (つ)
おんよみ	ゴ

五

five	5th day of month	five things	five minutes
ご	いつ か	いつ	ご ふん
五	五日	五つ	五分

6. six						4 画
くんよみ	むっ(つ)、むい					
おんよみ	ロク、ロッ					
六						

six	6th day of month	six things	600
ろく 六	むい か 六日	むっ 六つ	ろっぴゃく 六百

---

1 | Kanji Usage かんじの つかいかた

● **1-1. What is a stroke?**

A stroke begins when the pen (or any other writing device) comes in contact with the paper. The stroke ends when the pen separates from the paper.

● **1-2. Why use brushes to write?**

Traditionally, Japanese was written with brushes. This book – and almost any book that teaches Japanese writing – uses the brush-written style for the Japanese characters. The brush-written style best represents how the characters should be written.

● **1-3. Different types of brush strokes**

There are three types of strokes. For ease of understanding we have named them *fade out*, *dead stop* and *bounce fade*. Whether writing with a brush, pen, or pencil, make sure that you pay attention to the stroke type. This will ensure that your writing is neat and proper.

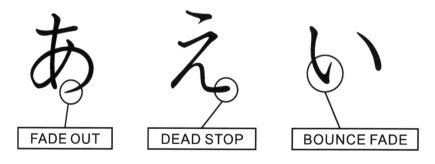

FADE OUT   DEAD STOP   BOUNCE FADE

If your teacher is Japanese you might hear the Japanese names of the stroke types:

fade out	dead stop	bounce fade
はらい	とめ	はね
（はらう）	（とめる）	（はねる）

● **1-4. Numbers in kanji versus "1, 2, 3…"**
In modern Japan, kanji numbers are not used as frequently as in the past. More commonly, numbers are written with Arabic numerals (1, 2, 3…). One factor that probably influenced this was the limitation of early computers.

Written Japanese employs many more characters than written English, and accordingly requires a more sophisticated computer code. It would have been more convenient to use Arabic numerals for computing, and the practice probably stuck.

100 yen	18 years old	3 o'clock
100 円	18 歳	3 時
百円	十八歳	三時
（ひゃく・えん）	（じゅう・はっ・さい）	（さん・じ）

Although there is still a place for kanji numbers in Japan, they aren't used as frequently today. In Japan today you will see the Arabic numbers you are used to on TV, clocks, license plates and just about anything that uses numbers. However, you do need to know the kanji used for numbers, since many words and phrases integrate these kanji into them.

Kanji numbers can still be found in magazines and newspapers where the writing is written vertically (up and down) and not horizontally (left to right).

1 | Words You Can Write かける ことば

In the "Words You Can Write" section we will introduce words that you can write using the new kanji introduced in the lesson.

If we haven't learned all of the kanji in the word, hiragana will be used instead of the unknown kanji. This is exactly how it is done in Japanese kanji drill books in Japan. Write each new word for practice.

一つ（ひとつ）1 thing

一	つ									

一時（いちじ）1 o'clock

一	じ									

二個（にこ）2 things

二	こ									

二つ（ふたつ）2 things

二	つ									

三日 (みっか) 3rd of month

三	か									

三個（さんこ）3 things

三	こ									

四日 (よっか) 4th of month

四	か									

四時 (よじ) 4 o'clock

四	じ								

五つ (いつつ) 5 things

五	つ								

五時 (ごじ) 5 o'clock

五	じ								

六日 (むいか) 6th of month

六	か								

1 | Stroke Order Check 書き順確認

Circle A or B whichever represents the correct stroke order for each Kanji.

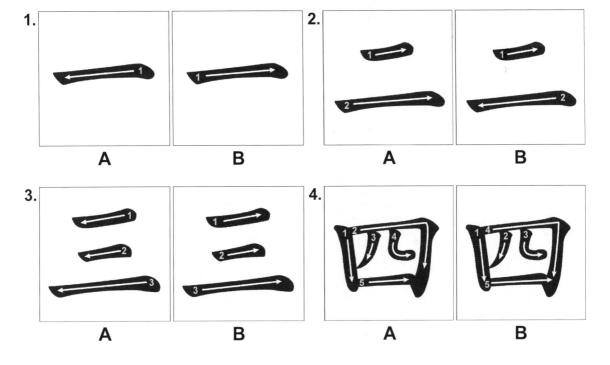

5.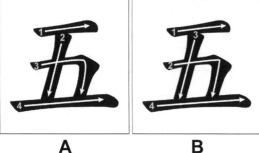

A   B

6.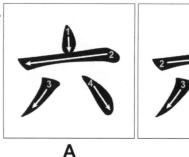

A   B

1 | Kanji meaning match

Write the following kanji next to its meaning: 二 六 五 一 四 三

1. ____ three

2. ____ one

3. ____ five

4. ____ two

5. ____ six

6. ____ four

1 | Fill in the kanji

Fill in the appropriate kanji in the blanks for each sentence.

ろく よん　　 ご

1. あした ____じ____じゅう____ふんに おきます。
   I will wake up tomorrow at 6:45.

さん　　　　　　　に

2. かみが ____まいと えんぴつが____ほん あります。
   I have 3 pieces of paper and 2 pencils.

に　　 みっ　　 よ

3. ____がつ____かの____じに いきます。
   I will go on February 3rd at 4 o'clock.

4. おとうさんは ＿＿＿じゅう＿＿＿さいです。

      ろく   いっ

My father is 61 years old.

5. まいにち、ビールを ＿＿＿ぽんしか のみません。

                    いっ

I only drink one beer every day.

6. にほんに ともだちが ＿＿＿ にん います。

                    ご

I have 5 friends in Japan.

7. ＿＿＿ じ＿＿＿じゅっぷんごろ きます。

   に   よん

They will come around 2:40.

1 | Kanji matching

Draw a line to connect each kanji with only one of its ON or KUN readings.

六・	・よん
二・	・ご
一・	・ひと
四・	・みっ
三・	・むい
五・	・ふた

1 | Answer Key 答え合わせ

Stroke order check (answers)

1. B 2. A 3. B 4. A 5. A 6. B

Kanji meaning match (answers)

1. 三 three   2. 一 one   3. 五 five

4. 二 two   5. 六 six   6. 四 four

Fill in the kanji (answers)

1. あした 六じ四じゅう五ふんに おきます。

2. かみが 三まいと えんぴつが 二ほん あります。

3. 二がつ三かの四じに いきます。

4. おとうさんは 六じゅう一さいです。

5. まいにち、ビールを 一ぽんしか のみません。

6. にほんに ともだちが 五にん います。

7. 二じ四じゅっぷんごろ きます。

Kanji matching (answers)

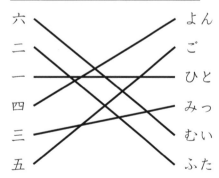

六　　　　　　よん
二　　　　　　ご
一　　　　　　ひと
四　　　　　　みっ
三　　　　　　むい
五　　　　　　ふた

2

Kanji lesson 2:

七八九十百千

2 | New Kanji あたらしい かんじ

Make sure you learn the correct stroke order. Correct stroke order will mean neater symbols when writing quickly. Also, take time to learn the words listed for each kanji – these will help you memorize the different readings.

---

7. seven　　　　　　　　　　　　　　　　**2画**

くんよみ	なな、なの
おんよみ	シチ

七

seven	7th day of the month	July	seven o'clock
なな	なの か	しちがつ	しちじ
七	七日	七月	七時

---

8. eight　　　　　　　　　　　　　　　　**2画**

くんよみ	や、やっ、よう
おんよみ	ハチ

八

eight	8th day of the month	eight things	August
はち	よう か	やっ つ	はちがつ
八	八日	八つ	八月

9. nine   2画

くんよみ	ここの (つ)		
おんよみ	キュウ、ク		

九							

nine	nine things	90	September
きゅう	ここの	きゅうじゅう	く　がつ
九	九つ	九十	九月

10. ten   2画

くんよみ	とお、と		
おんよみ	ジュウ、ジッ		

十							

10	October	ten times	10th of the month
じゅう	じゅうがつ	じゅっかい	とお　か
十	十月	十回	十日

11. hundred (100)   6画

くんよみ	none		
おんよみ	ヒャク		

百							

100	600	300 yen	department store
ひゃく	ろっぴゃく	さんびゃくえん	ひゃっかてん
百	六百	三百円	百貨店

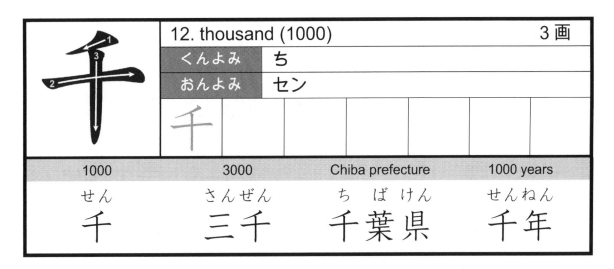

	12. thousand (1000)						3画
	くんよみ	ち					
	おんよみ	セン					
	千						

1000	3000	Chiba prefecture	1000 years
せん	さんぜん	ち　ば　けん	せんねん
千	三千	千葉県	千年

2 | Kanji Usage かんじの つかいかた

● **2-1. Combining kanji to make じゅくご**

じゅくご means "compound kanji." Any word composed of two or more kanji is considered じゅくご. Many times, when two kanji are combined, the second kanji's reading is slightly modified by adding だくてん to the reading. For example, the word 花火 (はな・び) has the kanji 火 (ひ) in it, but it is read as び. This happens with many じゅくご, so it should be the first thing you do when guessing the reading of a word.

Here is a summarization of this rule:

> When kanji are combined into じゅくご, often the reading of the second kanji is modified by adding だくてん to the first hiragana.

たんじょう　　　　　ひ　　　　たんじょうび
誕生 ＋ 日 ＝ 誕生日
birth　　　＋　　day　　＝　　birthday

⬤ **2-2. How should 十 be read when in other words?**
Officially when the kanji 十 is used in words like, 十本 (10 bottles etc.),
十分 (10 minutes), and 十回 (10 times), the correct reading is じっ.

10 minutes	10 long cylindrical objects
十分 じっ・ぷん	十本 じっ・ぽん
10 times	**10 cups (of something)**
十回 じっ・かい	十杯 じっ・ぱい

However, in actual Japanese speaking, you will often hear it sound like
じゅっ instead of じっ. This is common in the Tokyo area and due to
Tokyo's influence on all of Japan, it has spread to other parts, so many
people consider じゅっ to also be correct.

10 minutes	10 long cylindrical objects
十分 じゅっ・ぷん	十本 じゅっ・ぽん
10 times	**10 cups (of something)**
十回 じゅっ・かい	十杯 じゅっ・ぱい

While じゅっ is commonly used throughout Japan, children are marked
wrong when using じゅっ and will be told to use じっ in school. For the rest
of this series we will follow Japanese official school guidelines and use じっ.
Even though some Japanese people might consider it wrong. ☺

● 2-3. Soft sounds versus strong sounds (十)

Continuing what was discussed in the last section, it's important to remember that 十 can also be read as じゅう. The reading changes depending on the sound that follows.

When 十 is followed by "strong sounds" starting with K, P, T, and S it's read as じっ.

じっ / じゅっ when used with strong sounds	
10 letters	**10 copies (books, prints etc.)**
十通 じっ・つう	十冊 じっ・さつ
10 small round objects (generic)	**10 heads (of cattle etc.)**
十個 じっ・こ	十頭 じっ・とう

However, it's important to note that when 十 is followed by all other sounds such as M, D, B, N, and F etc it's pronounced じゅう.

じゅう when used with soft sounds	
10 thin flat objects	**10 machines (cars, computers etc.)**
十枚 じゅう・まい	十台 じゅう・だい
10 times (X 10)	**number 10 (#10)**
十倍 じゅう・ばい	十番 じゅう・ばん

2 | **Words You Can Write かける ことば**

Write each word in the open boxes. Kanji we haven't learned will be in hiragana.

七つ （ななつ） 7 things

七	つ									

七日 （なのか） 7th of month

七	か									

八つ （やっつ） 8 things

八	つ									

八日 （ようか） 8th of month

八	か									

九つ （ここのつ） 9 things

九	つ									

九十 （きゅうじゅう） 90

九	十									

十二 （じゅうに） 12

十	二									

十日 （とおか） 10th of month

十	か									

三百 (さんびゃく) 300

三	百								

百個 (ひゃっこ) 100 items

百	こ								

四千 (よんせん) 4,000

四	千								

三千 (さんぜん) 3,000

三	千								

2 | Fill in the Kanji

Fill in the appropriate kanji in the blanks for each sentence.

　　　じゅう　よ

1. にほんに ＿＿＿ ＿＿＿ねんかん、いました。
   I was in Japan for 14 years.

　　　に　じゅう

2. ＿＿＿ ＿＿＿ ねんまえに アメリカに きました。
   I came to America 20 years ago.

　　　ご　　　よう　　　しち

3. ＿＿＿がつ＿＿＿かの＿＿＿じに きて ください。
   Please come May 8th at 7 o'clock.

はちじゅうさん

4. おばあさんは ＿＿ ＿＿ ＿＿さい です。
My grandmother is 83 years old.

きゅうせん はっぴゃく

5. このシャツは ＿＿ ＿＿ ＿＿ ＿＿ えん です。
This shirt is 9,800 yen.

し ち   ろっ

6. ひとが＿＿ にんと ねこが＿＿ぴき います。
There are 7 people and 6 cats.

に せんきゅうひゃく

7. チケットを＿＿ ＿＿ ＿＿ ＿＿ まい かいます。
I will buy 2,900 tickets.

2 | Kanji meaning match

Write the following kanji next to its meaning: 六 十 百 三 千 七 四 八 九

1. ＿＿ ten   2. ＿＿ three   3. ＿＿ thousand

4. ＿＿ hundred   5. ＿＿ six   6. ＿＿ four

7. ＿＿ seven   8. ＿＿ nine   9. ＿＿ eight

2 | Stroke order check

Circle A or B whichever represents the correct stroke order for each kanji.

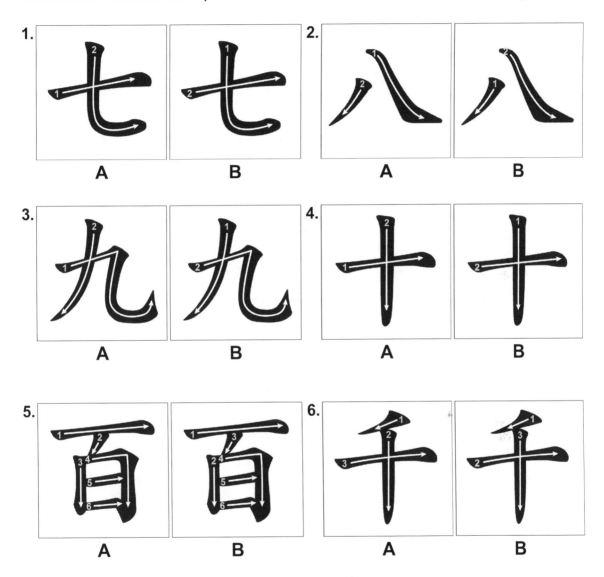

2 | Kanji matching

Draw a line to connect each kanji with only one of its ON or KUN readings.

七 ・　　　　　・ く
百 ・　　　　　・ と　お
一 ・　　　　　・ い　つ
九 ・　　　　　・ ひ　ゃ　く
十 ・　　　　　・ せ　ん
千 ・　　　　　・ し
八 ・　　　　　・ し　ち　ん
三 ・　　　　　・ さ　ん
四 ・　　　　　・ よ　う

2 | Answer Key 答え合わせ

Fill in the kanji (answers)

1. にほんに 十四 ねんかん、いました。

2. 二十 ねんまえに アメリカに きました。

3. 五 がつ 八 かの 七 じに きて ください。

4. おばあさんは 八十三 さい です。

5. このシャツは 九千八百 えん です。

6. ひとが 七 にんと ねこが 六 ぴき います。

7. チケットを 二千九百 まい かいます。

Kanji meaning match (answers)

1. 十 ten
2. 三 three
3. 千 thousand
4. 百 hundred
5. 六 six
6. 四 four
7. 七 seven
8. 九 nine
9. 八 eight

Stroke order check (answers)

1. A 2. B 3. B 4. A 5. A 6. B

Kanji matching (answers)

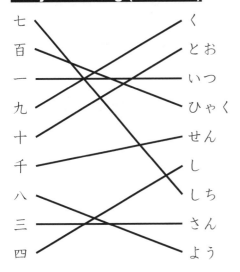

3 Kanji Lesson 3:
日月火水木金土
13-19

3 New Kanji あたらしい かんじ

Make sure you learn the correct stroke order. Correct stroke order will mean neater symbols when writing quickly. Also, take time to learn the words listed for each kanji – these will help you memorize the different readings.

日	13. day			4 画
	くんよみ	ひ、か		
	おんよみ	ニチ、ジツ		
	日			

day	a period of 10 days	day off, holiday	Sunday
ひ	とお か かん	きゅうじつ	にちよう び
日	十日間	休 日	日曜日

月	14. moon			4 画
	くんよみ	つき		
	おんよみ	ゲツ、ガツ		
	月			

moon	New Year's	Monday	this month
つき	しょうがつ	げつよう び	こんげつ
月	正 月	月曜日	今 月

15. fire		4 画
くんよみ	ひ	
おんよみ	カ	

火						

fire	Tuesday	fireworks	a fire
ひ	か よ う び	は な び	か じ
火	火曜日	花火	火事

16. water		4 画
くんよみ	みず	
おんよみ	スイ	

水						

water	light blue color	Wednesday	Mercury (planet)
みず	みずいろ	すいよう び	すいせい
水	水色	水曜日	水星

17. tree, wood		4 画
くんよみ	き、こ	
おんよみ	ボク、モク	

木						

tree, wood	Thursday	grove of trees	potted plant
き	も く よう び	こ だ ち	う え き
木	木曜日	木立	植木

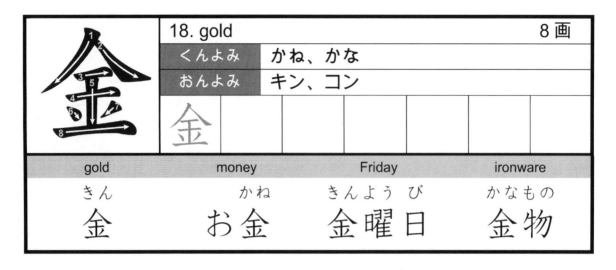

18. gold				8 画
くんよみ	かね、かな			
おんよみ	キン、コン			

gold	money	Friday	ironware
きん	かね	きんようび	かなもの
金	お金	金曜日	金物

19. soil, earth				3 画
くんよみ	つち			
おんよみ	ト、ド			

soil, earth	Saturday	land	red clay
つち	どようび	とち	あかつち
土	土曜日	土地	赤土

3 | Kanji Usage かんじの つかいかた

● **3-1. Font differences for kanji**

The font in this book showing stroke order shows the second stroke of 日 (ひ) as a *bounce fade*. However, it should actually be written as a *dead stop*. Just like English, Japanese fonts distort letters for style purposes.

Different font samples for 日

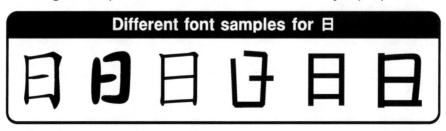

● 3-2. Kanji and the planets

You may have noticed that some of the example words in this section are planets. The second kanji in these words is the kanji for star, which is 星 (ほし). It is interesting to note that planet Earth doesn't have 星 in it, but instead uses the kanji for "sphere." Here is a list of all the planets and dwarf planets:

English	Kanji	Kana	Kanji breakdown
Mercury	水星	すいせい	water planet
Venus	金星	きんせい	metal planet
Earth	地球	ちきゅう	earth sphere
Mars	火星	かせい	fire planet
Jupiter	木星	もくせい	wood planet
Saturn	土星	どせい	soil planet
Uranus	天王星	てんのうせい	heaven king planet
Neptune	海王星	かいおうせい	ocean king planet
The dwarf planets			
Pluto	冥王星	めいおうせい	dark king planet
Ceres	N/A	セレス	N/A
Eris	N/A	エリス	N/A
Haumea	N/A	ハウメア	N/A
Makemake	N/A	マケマケ	N/A
Sedna	N/A	セドナ	N/A

Note: We have chosen to include recently discovered planets such as Eris (2005) and Sedna (2003) in order to have an accurate list. Also, it's interesting to see that the more recently discovered planets do not have kanji assigned to them. Despite Ceres being discovered in 1801, even before Neptune, it doesn't have kanji. In China, Ceres is written as 穀神星, however Japan never adopted a kanji for this dwarf planet (asteroid).

Unfortunately, for kanji lovers such as myself, new Japanese words are often "borrowed" from English and are only written in katakana. These borrowed words are called 外来語 (がいらいご), which ironically, is written in kanji. ☺

● **3-3. The kanji for "Japan" (日本)**
The kanji for Japan doesn't actually contain any of the official readings listed in this and most books. Over time some words such as 日本 have changed from one reading to another, and this leads to unofficial readings being used.

To make it just a bit more interesting, 日本 can be read in two different ways.

Japan	Japan
日本	日本
に・ほん	にっ・ぽん

So which one should I use??
Japan itself has not officially decided which version of 日本 to use. According to research by NHK (Japan Broadcasting Corporation) 61% of people read 日本 as にほん and 37% as にっぽん. The data shows that younger people tend to use にほん.

にっぽん is often used in the names of official instituions such as 日本銀行 (にっぽんぎんこう) the Bank of Japan and even NHK, the originator of the research cited above, 日本放送協会 (にっぽん・ほうそう・きょうかい) uses にっぽん in its name.

---

3 | **Words You Can Write かける ことば**

四日 （よっか） 4th of month

四	日								

八日 （ようか） 8th of month

八	日								

十月（じゅうがつ）October

十	月								

六月（ろくがつ）June

六	月								

月曜日（げつようび）Monday

月	よ	う	日				

火曜日（かようび）Tuesday

火	よ	う	日				

水曜日（すいようび）Wednesday

水	よ	う	日				

木曜日（もくようび）Thursday

木	よ	う	日				

金曜日（きんようび）Friday

金	よ	う	日				

土曜日（どようび）Saturday

土	よ	う	日				

日曜日（にちようび）Sunday

日	よ	う	日				

3 | Fill in the Kanji

Fill in the appropriate kanji in the blanks for each sentence.

かね
1. お ＿＿＿ が ありますか。

　　　　　ご　せん　さん　びゃく
はい、＿＿＿ ＿＿＿ ＿＿＿ ＿＿＿ えん あります。
Do you have money? Yes, I have 5,300 yen.

　　ろく　がつ　なの　か　　　に
2. ＿＿＿ ＿＿＿ ＿＿＿ ＿＿＿に ＿＿＿ ほんに いきます。
I will go to Japan on June 7.

　　　　か　　　　び　　　よ
3. ＿＿＿ よう＿＿＿は ＿＿＿じから しごと です。
Tuesday, I work from 4 o'clock.

　　　　　　　き　　　に　じゅっ
4. あそこに ＿＿＿ が＿＿＿ ＿＿＿ ぽん、あります。
There are 20 trees over there.

　　みず　よっ
5. ＿＿＿ を＿＿＿つと メニューを おねがいします。
I would like 4 waters and a menu please.

　　　　　　　げつ　　　び　　とお　か
6. らいしゅうの ＿＿＿ よう＿＿＿は ＿＿＿ ＿＿＿です。
Monday of next week is the 10th.

3 | Kanji matching

Draw a line to connect each kanji with only one of its ON or KUN readings.

日 •	• もく
六 •	• にち
木 •	• ち
土 •	• ひゃく
千 •	• すい
月 •	• ろく
金 •	• かね
火 •	• つち
水 •	• つき
百 •	• ひ

3 | Kanji meaning

Write the following kanji next to its meaning: 七 日 月 火 水 木 金 土 五

1. ____ moon

2. ____ soil, earth

3. ____ water

4. ____ day

5. ____ five

6. ____ gold

7. ____ tree, wood

8. ____ fire

9. ____ seven

3 | Stroke Order Check

Circle A or B whichever represents the correct stroke order for each kanji.

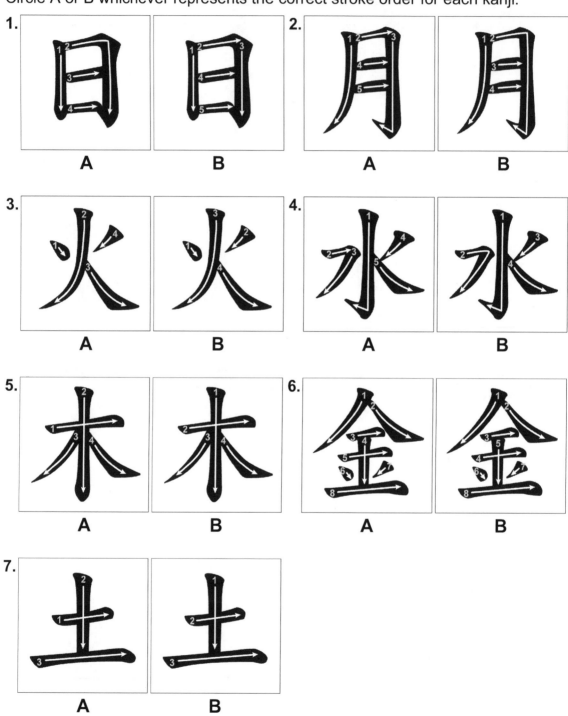

3 | Answer Key 答え合わせ

Fill in the kanji (answers)

1. お 金 が ありますか。はい 五千三百 えん あります。

2. 六月七日 に 日 ほんに いきます。

3. 火 よう 日 は 四 じから しごと です。

4. あそこに 木 が 二十 ぽん、あります。

5. 水 を 四 つと メニューを おねがいします。

6. らいしゅうの 月 よう 日 は 十日 です。

Kanji meaning (answers)

1. 月 moon　　2. 土 soil, earth　　3. 水 water

4. 日 day　　5. 五 five　　6. 金 gold

7. 木 tree, wood　　8. 火 fire　　9. 七 seven

Kanji matching (answers)

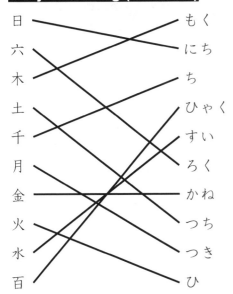

Stroke order check (answers)

1. A　2. B　3. B　4. B　5. A　6. B　7. A

4

Kanji lesson 4:

20-24

休上下左右

4 | New Kanji あたらしい かんじ

Make sure you learn the correct stroke order. Correct stroke order will mean neater symbols when writing quickly. Also, take time to learn the words listed for each kanji – these will help you memorize the different readings.

---

20. rest, day off, holiday   6 画

くんよみ	やす(む)
おんよみ	キュウ

休

day off, holiday	to take a break	a break	summer vacation
やす	やす	きゅうけい	なつやす
休み	休む	休憩	夏休み

---

21. up, above   3 画

くんよみ	うえ、うわ、かみ のぼ(る)、あ(げる、がる)
おんよみ	ジョウ、ショウ

上

up, above	to ascend, to climb	to go up	elegant
うえ	のぼ	あ	じょうひん
上	上る	上がる	上品

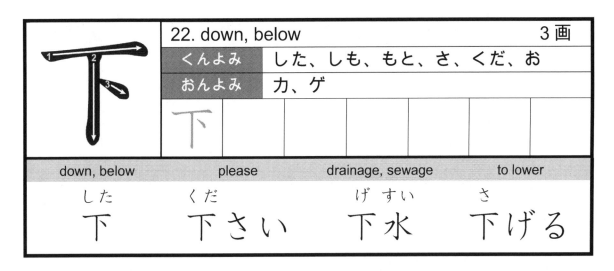

22. down, below　　3画

| くんよみ | した、しも、もと、さ、くだ、お |
| おんよみ | カ、ゲ |

下

down, below	please	drainage, sewage	to lower
した	くだ	げ すい	さ
下	下さい	下水	下げる

23. left　　5画

| くんよみ | ひだり |
| おんよみ | サ |

左

left	upper left	left and right	left turn
ひだり	ひだりうえ	さゆう	させつ
左	左上	左右	左折

24. right　　5画

| くんよみ | みぎ |
| おんよみ | ウ、ユウ |

右

right	lower right	right-handed	right turn
みぎ	みぎした	みぎ き	う せつ
右	右下	右利き	右折

4 | Kanji Usage かんじの つかいかた

● 4-1. Kanji memory techniques and mnemonics

It's often said that kanji are "pictographs." Indeed they were often created by putting certain parts together to tell a story. It's easy to see how some kanji evolved from a simplistic picture.

Some kanji look like a simplified picture.	
sun, day	**eye**
日	目
looks like a simple sun	looks like a simple eye (vertical)
tree	**mouth**
木	口
looks like a tree	looks like a square mouth

However, it's not the case that all kanji are easily figured out by looking at them as a pictographs.

Some kanji are not easily viewed as a pictograph without historical context.			
departure	**enter**	**child**	**father**
出	入	子	父
8-bit race car?	tent? wishbone?	3 with a line?	X with eyebrows?
left	**right**	**four**	**five**
左	右	四	五
lean over an anvil?	lean over a mouth?	*four* has 5 strokes, *five* has 4! hmm	

Entire books have been dedicated to teaching mnemonics to help remember the meaning of each kanji. Sometimes a mnemonic can be so good that everyone who learns it can benefit from it. For example, in this lesson we learn 休 which means "rest."

The first part of 休 is a "squished" version of person (人) and the second part is a tree (木). So you can imagine a person leaning on a tree to rest.

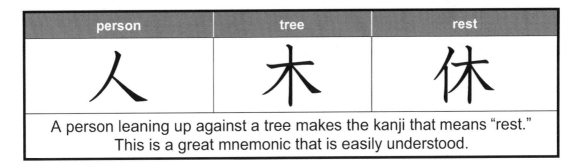

person	tree	rest
人	木	休

A person leaning up against a tree makes the kanji that means "rest." This is a great mnemonic that is easily understood.

Mnemonics like this can be a great help for remembering the kanji. It can even help you remember how to write the kanji. If kanji were all ACTUALLY pictographs, or if they were all designed using logical parts of smaller kanji this method would work very well. However, the parts of each kanji, also called radicals, are often chosen simply because the sound matches the word and has nothing to do with the actual meaning of the part.

Mnemonics are personal
We feel that the mnemonics created for some kanji are often more tedious to remember than actually just learning a few words related to each kanji. Mnemonics are far more powerful, and stick easier, when you have created them on your own, using your own criteria.

This being the case, we will use mnemonics sparingly in this book, however we 100% encourage you to try to come up with small stories to memorize the meaning of each kanji. The mnemonic you invent often will only make sense to you, but that's okay since what works for one person as a memory technique often doesn't make sense to others.

● 4-2. Words using opposing kanji

Using the kanji from this lesson, you can make two very useful じゅくご.

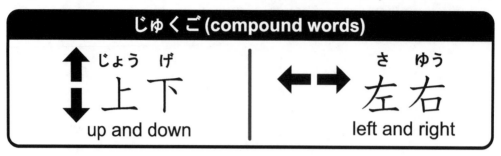

じゅくご (compound words)

上下
up and down

左右
left and right

● 4-3. Memorizing 左 (left) and 右 (right) stroke order

You may have noticed that the kanji for "left" and "right" are very similar EXCEPT for their stroke order.

Getting the stroke order wrong will not be accepted on the Kanji Proficiency Test (Kanji Kentei). If you memorize the next phrase, you shouldn't have any more trouble remembering the stroke order:

> **Downright Leftovers!**

The kanji for "right" starts with the stroke going **down**, and the kanji for "left" starts with the horizontal line going **over** to the right.

● 4-4. Which one is left and which one is right?

Students often mistake the kanji for "right" and "left" since they are similar. There is a sneaky way to remember which one is which. This trick involves using the katakana ロ (ro). Since the katakana ロ starts with an "R" sound, it is easy to remember that the kanji with the small ロ in it means "**r**ight."

The kanji for *right* has a katakana ロ (ro) in it. Use this to distinguish it from the kanji for *left*. *Ro* starts with *R* for *right*.

4 | **Words You Can Write かける ことば**

休む（やすむ）to rest

休	む								

休日（きゅうじつ）holiday

休	日								

上る（のぼる）to ascend, to climb

上	る								

上下（じょうげ）up and down

上	下								

左右（さゆう）left and right

左	右								

水上（すいじょう）aquatic

水	上								

左上（ひだりうえ）upper left

左	上								

右下（みぎした）bottom right

右	下								

下水 （げすい） drainage, sewage

下	水								

下さい （ください） please

下	さ	い							

4 | Fill in the Kanji

Fill in the appropriate kanji in the blanks for each sentence.

き　　し　た　　　　じゅう

1. ＿＿＿の ＿＿＿に ひとが ＿＿＿ にん います。

There are 10 people underneath the tree.

じゅう いち がつ みっ　か　　やす

2. ＿＿＿ ＿＿＿ ＿＿＿ ＿＿＿ ＿＿＿は＿＿＿みです。

November 3rd is a vacation.

ど　　　　び　　じゅう　に

3. ＿＿＿ よう＿＿＿は ＿＿＿ ＿＿＿じに ひるごはんを たべる。

I will eat lunch at 12 o'clock on Saturday.

うえ　　　　　　よん じゅう

4. テーブルの ＿＿＿ に かみが＿＿＿ ＿＿＿ まい あります。

There are 40 pieces of paper on top of the table.

ひだ り　　　　　　　む っ

5. ＿＿＿ に いすが ＿＿＿つ あります。

There are six chairs on the left.

じょう　げ　さ　ゆう　　　　　　く だ

6. ＿＿＿ ＿＿＿ ＿＿＿ ＿＿＿を よくみて＿＿＿さい。

Please look carefully up, down, left, and right.

　　　　きん　　　び　　やす　　　　　くだ
7. らいしゅうの____ よう ____に ____まないで____さい。
　　Please don't take the day off next Friday.

4 | Kanji meaning match

Write the following kanji next to its meaning: 日 上 金 左 休 下 右 火 九

1. ____ down

2. ____ nine

3. ____ gold

4. ____ right

5. ____ day

6. ____ left

7. ____ up

8. ____ rest

9. ____ fire

4 | Kanji matching

Draw a line to connect each kanji with one of its ON or KUN readings.

左　・　　　　　・みず
上　・　　　　　・みぎ
水　・　　　　　・もく
休　・　　　　　・はち
月　・　　　　　・ひだり
右　・　　　　　・つき
四　・　　　　　・した
下　・　　　　　・じょう
木　・　　　　　・よん
八　・　　　　　・やす

4 | Stroke Order Check

Circle A or B whichever represents the correct stroke order for each kanji.

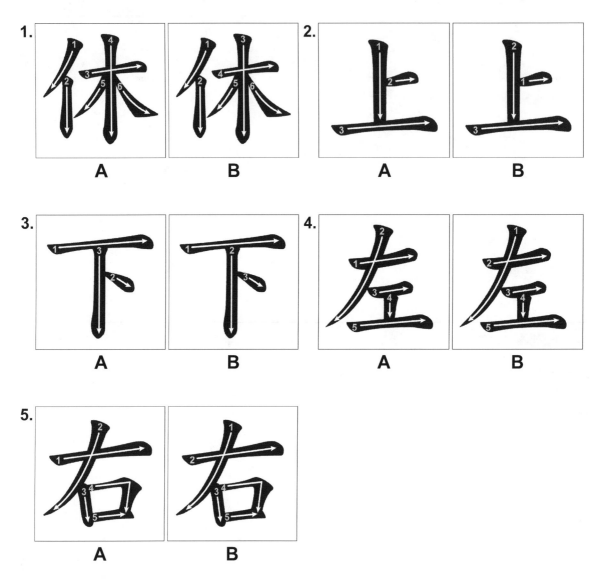

4 | Answer Key 答え合わせ

Fill in the kanji (answers)

1. 木の下に ひとが 十にん います。

2. 十一月三日は 休み です。

3. 土よう日は 十二じに ひるごはんを たべる。

4. テーブルの 上に かみが 四十まい あります。

5. 左に いすが 六つ あります。

6. 上下左右を よくみて 下さい。

7. らいしゅうの 金よう日に 休まないで 下さい。

Kanji meaning match (answers)

1. 下 down	2. 九 nine	3. 金 gold
4. 右 right	5. 日 day	6. 左 left
7. 上 up	8. 休 rest	9. 火 fire

Kanji matching (answers)

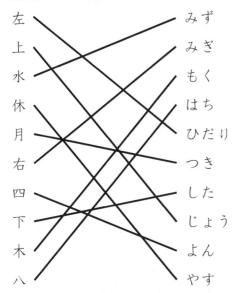

左　　　　　　みず
上　　　　　　みぎ
水　　　　　　もく
休　　　　　　はち
月　　　　　　ひだり
右　　　　　　つき
四　　　　　　した
下　　　　　　じょう
木　　　　　　よん
八　　　　　　やす

Stroke order check (answers)

1. A　2. A　3. B　4. A　5. B

5

Kanji lesson 5:

大中小円人目

5 | New Kanji あたらしい かんじ

Make sure you learn the correct stroke order. Correct stroke order will mean neater symbols when writing quickly. Also, take time to learn the words listed for each kanji – these will help you memorize the different readings.

大	25. big			3 画
	くんよみ	おお(きい)		
	おんよみ	ダイ、タイ		
	大			

big	main street	college	terrible, disastrous
おお	おおどお	だいがく	たいへん
大きい	大通り	大学	大変

中	26. inside, in			4 画
	くんよみ	なか		
	おんよみ	チュウ		
	中			

inside, in	junior high school	on duty	the middle, center
なか	ちゅうがっこう	しごとちゅう	ちゅうしん
中	中学校	仕事中	中心

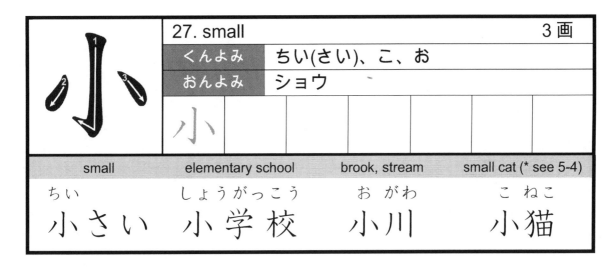

27. small			3 画
くんよみ	ちい(さい)、こ、お		
おんよみ	ショウ		

small	elementary school	brook, stream	small cat (* see 5-4)
ちい	しょうがっこう	お がわ	こ ねこ
小さい	小学校	小川	小猫

28. circle, yen, round			4 画
くんよみ	まる(い)		
おんよみ	エン		

round	100 yen	strong yen v's other currencies	half circle, semicircle
まる	ひゃくえん	えんだか	はんえん
円い	百円	円高	半円

29. person, people			2 画
くんよみ	ひと		
おんよみ	ジン、ニン		

person, people	Japanese person	human	lover
ひと	に ほんじん	にんげん	こいびと
人	日本人	人間	恋人

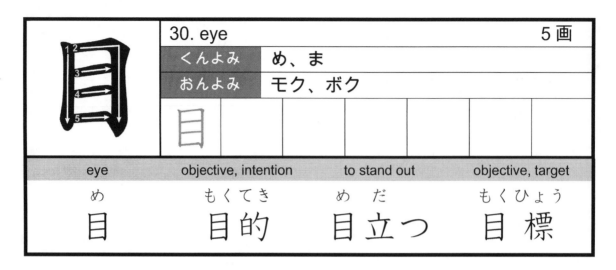

eye	objective, intention	to stand out	objective, target
め 目	もくてき 目的	め だ 目立つ	もくひょう 目標

5	**Kanji Usage かんじの つかいかた**

● **5-1. Kanji in Japanese schools (what they learn and when)**
You might be surprised that if you learn all the kanji in this book you will know as much as a typical Japanese student who has graduated the 2nd grade.

Grade	Kanji Learned
Elementary School Grade 1	80
Elementary School Grade 2	160
Elementary School Grade 3	200
Elementary School Grade 4	200
Elementary School Grade 5	185
Elementary School Grade 6	181
Total Kanji Learned in Elementary School	1006

After graduating elementary school, Japanese students will know all of the "educational kanji" 教育漢字 (きょういくかんじ), which consists of 1006 kanji. Compared to what we learn in the USA and other English speaking countries this might seem overwhelming, but don't let this discourage you because if 120 million Japanese people can do it, so can you!

● **5-2. Common mistake with 人 (person) versus 入 (enter)**

We haven't learned 入 (enter) yet, but as you can see it looks similar to 人 (person). If you use them at the wrong time the meaning of the word can change dramatically.

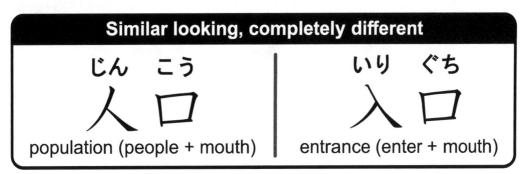

Similar looking, completely different

じん　こう	いり　ぐち
人口	入口
population (people + mouth)	entrance (enter + mouth)

● **5-3. Same kanji twice in one word using 々 (くりかえし)**

Get ready to learn something really cool! There are times when the same kanji can be in a word twice and be read in different ways each time. You already learned one word that does this with 日曜日 (にち・よう・び) which means "Sunday." But sometimes a kanji repeats all by itself. Often, the spot for the repeated kanji uses the 々 (くりかえし) character, which literally means "repetition." 々 becomes the repeated kanji and takes on its reading.

Repeating kanji	English	Notes
日々 (ひび)	every day, daily	
日にち (ひにち)	the # of days, date	often 2nd kanji is hiragana to avoid confusion
中々 (なかなか)	very, considerably	normally written as なかなか
一々 (いちいち)	one-by-one	
人々 (ひとびと)	people	
月々 (つきづき)	monthly	
九々 (くく)	multiplication table	normally written as 九九

● 5-4. Small cats VS kittens (小)

Although this might sound like the title of one of the greatest anime ever made and released from Ghibli studios, it's an important point of discussion.

The kanji 子 is taught in lesson 7, and means "child." It's easy to confuse it with 小 because they both can be read as こ.

small	child
小	子
こ	こ

There is a key difference though.

(小) These are small animals. They can be babies or fully grown.	
small cat	**small dog**
小猫	小犬
こ・ねこ	こ・いぬ
small cow	**small pig**
小牛	小豚
こ・うし	こ・ぶた

(子) These are baby / non-adult animals. The can be big or small.	
kitten	**puppy**
子猫	子犬
こ・ねこ	こ・いぬ
calf	**piglet**
子牛	子豚
こ・うし	こ・ぶた

5 | **Words You Can Write かける ことば**

百円（ひゃくえん）100 yen

百	円								

千円（せんえん）1000 yen

千	円								

右目（みぎめ）right eye

右	目								

左目（ひだりめ）left eye

左	目								

大きい（おおきい）big

大	き	い					

小さい（ちいさい）small

小	さ	い					

大学（だいがく）college

大	が	く					

五十円（ごじゅうえん）50 yen

五	十	円					

一日目（いちにちめ）the first day

一	日	目					

二日目（ふつかめ）the second day

二	日	目										

五百人（ごひゃくにん）500 people

五	百	人										

日ほん人（にほんじん）Japanese person

日	ほ	ん	人							

5 | Fill in the Kanji

Fill in the appropriate kanji in the blanks for each sentence.

だい　　　みっ

1. あした、____ がくで ____ つのクラスが あります。
Tomorrow, I have three classes at college.

なか　ちい　　　　　ふた

2. へやの ____ に ____さいテーブルが____つ あります。
There are two small tables in the room.

おお　　　　　　ろっぴゃく えん

3. ____きいりんごは ____ ____ ____です。
The big apple is 600 yen.

ひと　さんじゅっ

4. あのおんなの ____ は____ ____ さいだと ききました。
I heard that woman is 30 years old.

みぎ め

5. いつも ウィンクは ____ ____でします。
I always wink with my right eye.

ひと　　に　じゅう　ご　にん

6. このクラスに ＿＿＿が ＿＿＿ ＿＿＿ ＿＿＿ ＿＿＿います。

　　In this class there are 25 people.

ちゅう　　　　　　ご

7. いまは しごと ＿＿＿ だから、＿＿＿じに あいましょう。

　　I am in the middle of work now, so let's meet at 5 o'clock.

5 | Stroke Order Check

Circle A or B whichever represents the correct stroke order for each kanji.

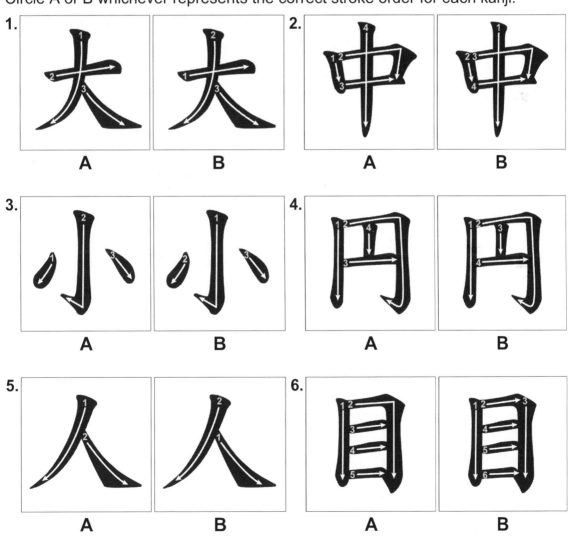

1. A　　B
2. A　　B
3. A　　B
4. A　　B
5. A　　B
6. A　　B

5 | Kanji matching

Draw a line to connect each kanji with one of its readings.

中 •   • した
目 •   • なか
小 •   • すい
上 •   • しょう
円 •   • にん
水 •   • め
人 •   • えん
日 •   • じょう
下 •   • おお
大 •   • にち

5 | Kanji meaning

Write the following kanji next to its meaning: 人 千 目 右 大 小 円 左 中

1. ____ right   2. ____ small   3. ____ eye

4. ____ inside   5. ____ person   6. ____ thousand

7. ____ big   8. ____ round   9. ____ left

5 | Answer Key 答え合わせ

Fill in the kanji (answers)

1. あした、 大 がくで 三 つのクラスが あります。

2. へやの 中 に 小 さいテーブルが 二 つ あります。

3. 大 きいりんごは 六百円 です。

4. あのおんなの 人 は 三十 さいだと ききました。

5. いつも ウィンクは 右目 で します。

6. このクラスに 人 が 二十五人 います。

7. いまは しごと 中 だから、 五 じに あいましょう。

Stroke order check (answers)

1. B   2. A   3. B   4. B   5. A   6. A

Kanji matching (answers)

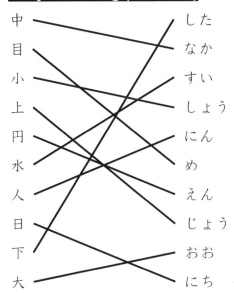

中	した
目	なか
小	すい
上	しょう
円	にん
水	め
人	えん
日	じょう
下	おお
大	にち

Kanji meaning match (answers)

1. 右 right
2. 小 small
3. 目 eye
4. 中 inside
5. 人 person
6. 千 thousand
7. 大 big
8. 円 round
9. 左 left

SR Super Review 1

SR1 | Kanji selection

Select the best kanji to fill in the blank in each sentence.

1. 日よう日より、＿＿＿よう日の ほうが いそがしいです。
   A. 百　　　　　B. 目　　　　　C. 月　　　　　D. 四

2. きょう、おひるごはんに ＿＿＿円 つかいました。
   A. 金　　　　　B. 千　　　　　C. 大　　　　　D. 木

3. いもうとは とても＿＿＿さくて、かわいいです。
   A. 大　　　　　B. 小　　　　　C. 人　　　　　D. 右

4. ＿＿＿みの日は、土よう日と 日よう日です。
   A. 木　　　　　B. 水　　　　　C. 六　　　　　D. 休

SR1 | Kanji reading

Select the best reading for the underlined kanji.

1. わたしは 右目より 左目の ほうが いいです。
   A. いし　　　　B. ひだり　　　C. くち　　　　D. みぎ

2. よしださんは、あの目の 大きい人 ですか。
   A. おお　　　　B. だい　　　　C. ちい　　　　D. おう

3. 火よう日は しごとが ありますが、木よう日は ありませんよ。
   A. き　　　　　B. きん　　　　C. か　　　　　D. もく

4. 百円だまが 八まい あります。
   A. ろく　　　　B. はち　　　　C. きゅう　　　D. なな

SR1	Compound kanji word puzzle

Fill in the correct kanji based on the list below the puzzle.

1)	2)	3)
4)		
5)		6)
7)		8)

Down ↓
1) left and right
3) sewage
5) 500
6) 4000
Left to Right →
1) upper left
2) up and down
4) right eye
5) fifth day of the month
7) 100 yen
Right to Left ←
6) fourth day of the month
8) 1000 yen

SR1 | Answer Key 答え合わせ

Kanji selection (answers)

1. C – 月曜日
   <ruby>月曜日<rt>げつようび</rt></ruby>

   Monday is busier than Sunday.

2. B – 千円
   <ruby>千円<rt>せんえん</rt></ruby>

   Today, I used 1000 yen for lunch.

3. B – 小さくて
   <ruby>小<rt>ちい</rt></ruby>さくて

   My younger sister is very small and cute.

4. D – 休み
   <ruby>休<rt>やす</rt></ruby>み

   My days off are Saturday and Sunday.

Kanji reading (answers)

1. D – 右目
   <ruby>右目<rt>みぎめ</rt></ruby>

   My left eye is better than my right eye.

2. A – 大きい
   <ruby>大<rt>おお</rt></ruby>きい

   Is Yoshida-san that person with the big eyes?

3. D – 木曜日
   <ruby>木曜日<rt>もくようび</rt></ruby>

   I have work on Tuesday but I don't have any on Thursday.

4. B – 八枚
   <ruby>八枚<rt>はちまい</rt></ruby>

   I have eight 100 yen coins.

Compound kanji word puzzle (answers)

左	上	下
右	目	水
五	日	四
百	円	千

6

Kanji lesson 6:

耳口手足力

6 | New Kanji あたらしい かんじ

Make sure you learn the correct stroke order. Correct stroke order will mean neater symbols when writing quickly. Also, take time to learn the words listed for each kanji – these will help you memorize the different readings.

31. ear			6 画
くんよみ	みみ		
おんよみ	ジ		
耳			

ear	tinnitus, ear-ringing	ear and nose doctor	ear infection
みみ	みみ な	じ び か	ちゅう じ えん
耳	耳鳴り	耳鼻科	中耳炎

32. mouth			3 画
くんよみ	くち		
おんよみ	コウ、ク		
口			

mouth	entrance	tone of voice	population
くち	い ぐち	く ちょう	じんこう
口	入り口	口調	人口

33. hand 4 画

くんよみ	て、た
おんよみ	シュ

手

hand	Karate (empty hand)	handshake	reins (for horses etc.)
て	から て	あく しゅ	た づな
手	空手	握手	手綱

34. foot (leg 脚) 7 画

くんよみ	あし、た
おんよみ	ソク

足

leg, foot	to have enough	3 pairs (shoes etc)	excursion
あし	た	さん そく	えん そく
足	足りる	三足	遠足

35. power, energy 2 画

くんよみ	ちから
おんよみ	リョク、リキ

力

power, energy	physical work	electric power	rickshaw
ちから	ちから し ごと	でん りょく	じん りき しゃ
力	力仕事	電力	人力車

6 | Kanji Usage かんじの つかいかた

● 6-1. Kanji on your body

You already know that kanji are often based on picture representations of their meanings. The kanji for 1, 2, and 3 are perfect examples of how the kanji were created with deep thought: 一, 二, 三 are pretty easy to grasp.

Kanji on your hand!

But, if I told you that there is a kanji visible on everyone's body you might not believe me – if you look at the palm of your right hand, you will notice a rough version of the kanji for "hand." Of course it isn't going to be a perfect copy of the kanji, but you can see where it comes from.

● 6-2. Is it a leg or a foot???

In Japanese あし means foot, feet, leg and legs, which can cause some confusion if your feet hurt. あしが いたいです after all can mean "my feet hurt" or "my leg hurts." Luckily there is a way to distinguish your feet from your legs. Even though the sound is the same for feet and legs the kanji are different. 脚 (あし) means "leg, legs" and 足 (あし) means "foot, feet."

● 6-3. Kanji as pictographs

Unlike the kana, which are phonetic sounds without meaning, kanji are pictographs which are designed as pictures of the word they represent.

Some books go out of their way to put a picture to every kanji introduced to help a student learn. But often the connection is forced and makes it harder to remember the kanji.

However, many of the simple kanji (with limited strokes) perfectly represent their meaning as a picture.

6 | Words You Can Write かける ことば

人口 （じんこう） population

人	口										

左手 （ひだりて） left hand

左	手										

右手 （みぎて） right hand

右	手										

左足 （ひだりあし） left foot

左	足										

右足 （みぎあし） right foot

右	足										

一足 （いっそく） one pair (footwear)

一	足										

一口 （ひとくち） one bite, mouthful

一	口										

手口 （てぐち） modus operandi, criminal technique, trick

手	口										

手すり（てすり）handrail

手	す	り										

足首（あしくび）ankle

足	く	び										

足りる（たりる）to be enough

足	り	る										

手紙（てがみ）letter

手	が	み										

体力（たいりょく）stamina, physical strength

た	い	力										

人力車（じんりきしゃ）rick-shaw

人	力	し	ゃ									

6 | Fill in the Kanji

Fill in the appropriate kanji in the blanks for each sentence.

　　　　て　　あし　おお

1. わたしの ＿＿＿ と＿＿＿は ＿＿＿ きいです。
   My hands and feet are big.

　　　　ぐち　　　　　　ひと　よ　にん

2. あのいり ＿＿＿ のまえに ＿＿＿ が ＿＿＿ ＿＿＿ います。
   There are four people in front of that entrance over there.

て   すい   び
3. から ____ のクラスは ____ よう____ です。
My karate class is Wednesday.

みぎ あし   ちから
4. ____ ____が いたいです。 ____ が ありません。
My right foot hurts. It doesn't have any power.

みみ   ちい
5. わたしのいぬは ____が ____さい です。
My dog's ears are small. / My dog, its ears are small.

ひだり   さん ぜん えん
6. ____ のメロンは ____ ____ ____です。
The melon on the left is 3000 yen.

じん こう   せん に ひゃく   にん
7. とうきょうの____ ____は ____ ____ ____ まん____ ぐらいです。
The population of Tokyo is about 12,000,000 people.

6 | Kanji meaning

Write the following kanji next to its meaning: 火 手 口 力 百 大 耳 金 足

  1. ____ fire   2. ____ 100   3. ____ big

  4. ____ mouth   5. ____ hand   6. ____ foot

  7. ____ ear   8. ____ gold   9. ____ power

6 | Stroke Order Check

Circle A or B whichever represents the correct stroke order for each kanji.

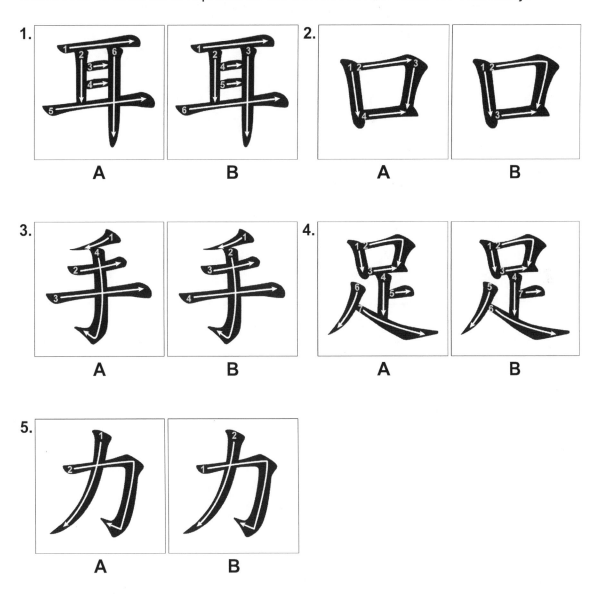

6 | Kanji matching

Draw a line to connect each kanji with only one of its ON or KUN readings.

耳 ・   ・ あ し き
足 ・   ・ つ し ゅ
人 ・   ・ し か ん
三 ・   ・ な ち と
口 ・   ・ さ く
月 ・   ・ ひ
小 ・   ・ こ り
手 ・   ・ り ょ く
中 ・   ・ み み
力 ・

6 Answer Key 答え合わせ

Fill in the kanji (answers)

1. わたしの 手 と 足 は 大 きいです。

2. あのいり 口 のまえに 人 が 四人 います。

3. から 手 のクラスは 水 よう 日 です。

4. 右足 が いたいです。 力 が ありません。

5. わたしのいぬは 耳 が 小 さい です。

6. 左 のメロンは 三千円 です。

7. とうきょうの 人口 は 千二百 まん 人 ぐらいです。

Kanji meaning match (answers)

1. 火 fire   2. 百 100   3. 大 big

4. 口 mouth   5. 手 hand   6. 足 foot

7. 耳 ear   8. 金 gold   9. 力 power

Stroke order check (answers)
1. A   2. B   3. A   4. A   5. B

Kanji matching (answers)

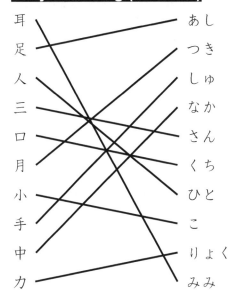

7 Kanji lesson 7: 36-40
立男女子生

7 | New Kanji あたらしい かんじ

Make sure you learn the correct stroke order. Correct stroke order will mean neater symbols when writing quickly. Also, take time to learn the words listed for each kanji – these will help you memorize the different readings.

立	36. stand up, rise			5画
	くんよみ	た(つ)		
	おんよみ	リツ、リュウ		
	立			

to stand	independence	private (i.e. school)	beginning of autumn
た 立つ	どくりつ 独立	し りつ 私立	りっしゅう 立秋

男	37. boy, man			7画
	くんよみ	おとこ		
	おんよみ	ダン、ナン		
	男			

man	male	boy	first born son
おとこ 男	だんせい 男性	おとこ こ 男の子	ちょうなん 長男

38. girl, woman　　3画

くんよみ	おんな、め
おんよみ	ジョ、ニョ、ニョウ

女

woman	female	girl	goddess
おんな	じょせい	おんな　こ	め　がみ
女	女性	女の子	女神

39. child　　3画

くんよみ	こ
おんよみ	シ、ス

子

child	child; children	adopted child	folding Japanese fan
こ	こ　ども	よう　し	せん　す
子	子供	養子	扇子

40. to live, raw　　5画

くんよみ	い(きる、かす)、う(む、まれる) は(える、やす)、き、なま
おんよみ	セイ、ショウ

生

raw	to live	to grow	teacher
なま	い	は	せんせい
生	生きる	生える	先生

7 | Kanji Usage かんじの つかいかた

● 7-1. Power in the rice fields

Later we learn the kanji 田 for "rice field" which sort of looks like a simple rice field would. The kanji for "man" is made by putting "power" in the rice field.

● 7-2. Kanji tongue twister

Here is a simple yet famous Japanese tongue twister that uses the kanji 生(なま), and it goes like this:

なまむぎ なまごめ なまたまご
生麦 生米 生卵

The translation is simple: "Raw wheat, raw rice, raw eggs." Try saying it fast five times in a row!

● 7-3. Kanji in Japanese first names

You can often tell if a person is male or female just by the last kanji in their first name. Some of the kanji you already know.

Boy Kanji	Meaning	Notes
男 (お)	man	
夫 (お)	husband, man	
一 (いち)	one	first born boys
二 (じ)	two	second born boys
秀 (ひで)	excel, surpass	
介 (すけ)	mediate	

Sample Boy Names

光男 (みつお)　　　　　　　　健一 (けんいち)
正一 (まさいち)　　　　　　　譲二 (じょうじ)
正秀 (まさひで)　　　　　　　幸秀 (ゆきひで)
大介 (だいすけ)　　　　　　　雄介 (ゆうすけ)

Girl Kanji	Meaning	Notes
子 (こ)	child	
美 (み)	beauty	
香 (か)	fragrance	
恵 (え)	favor, blessing	
里 (り)	parent's home	

Sample Girl Names

洋子 (ようこ)　　　　　　　久美子 (くみこ)
由美 (ゆみ)　　　　　　　　真奈美 (まなみ)
由香 (ゆか)　　　　　　　　恵梨香 (えりか)
理恵 (りえ)　　　　　　　　由香里 (ゆかり)

7 | Words You Can Write かける ことば

立つ（たつ）to stand

立	つ								

子女（しじょ）sons and daughters, girl

子	女								

三女（さんじょ）third daughter

三	女								

人生（じんせい）life (as in "my life")

人	生							

一生 (いっしょう) whole life, a lifetime

一	生								

男女 (だんじょ) men and women, both sexes

男	女								

生きる（いきる）to live

生	き	る							

男の人 (おとこのひと) man

男	の	人							

女の子 (おんなのこ) girl

女	の	子							

子供 (こども) child, children

子	ど	も							

目立つ (めだつ) to stand out

目	立	つ							

先生 (せんせい) teacher

せ	ん	生							

一人っ子 (ひとりっこ) an only child

一	人	っ	子					

一年生 （いちねんせい） 1st year student

一	ねん	生										

小学生 （しょうがくせい） elementary student

小	が	く	生									

中学生 （ちゅうがくせい） junior high student

中	が	く	生									

大学生 (だいがくせい) college student

大	が	く	生									

7 | Fill in the Kanji

Fill in the appropriate kanji in the blanks for each sentence.

　　　ぐち　　　　　こ　　　　　ちい

1. やま ＿＿＿さんの ＿＿＿どもは ＿＿＿さくて、かわいいです。
   Yamaguchi-san's child is small and cute.

　　　　　しょう　　　　　　ご　　　せい

2. ゆかちゃんは ＿＿＿ がっこう＿＿＿ねん＿＿＿です。
   Yuka is a 5th grade elementary student.

　　　おんな　ひと　　　　　　　　め　だ

3. あの ＿＿＿ の ＿＿＿は きれいだから、＿＿＿＿＿ちます。
   That woman over there is pretty so she stands out.

せい　　　　　うえ　　た
4. せん ____ が つくえの____ で ____たないでと いいました。
The teacher said not to stand on top of the desk.

だい　　せい　ろく がつ　　　　　やす
5. ____ がく ____ は ____ ____から なつ ____み です。
College students have summer vacation from June.

ちゅう　　　　　おお
6. あの ____ がっこうは ____ きいですね。
That junior high school over there is big.

ぐち　　おとこ ひと　　た
7. えきの で____ で ____ の____ が ____っています。
There is a man standing at the exit of the station.

7 | Kanji matching

Draw a line to connect each kanji with only one of its ON or KUN readings.

女 ・　　　　　・き
立 ・　　　　　・だん
木 ・　　　　　・なま
男 ・　　　　　・じゅう
土 ・　　　　　・つち
五 ・　　　　　・おんな
子 ・　　　　　・りつ
七 ・　　　　　・こ
生 ・　　　　　・しち
十 ・　　　　　・ご

7 | Kanji meaning

Write the following kanji next to its meaning: 女 右 生 手 口 子 立 男 足

1. ____ foot   2. ____ man   3. ____ right

4. ____ mouth   5. ____ to live   6. ____ girl

7. ____ hand   8. ____ child   9. ____ to stand

7 | Stroke Order Check

Circle A or B whichever represents the correct stroke order for each kanji.

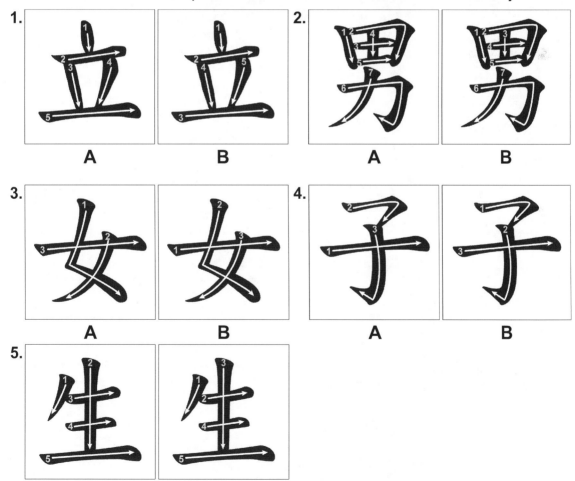

7 | Answer Key 答え合わせ

Fill in the kanji (answers)

1. やま口さんの 子どもは 小さくて、かわいいです。

2. ゆかちゃんは 小がっこう五ねん生です。

3. あの 女の人は きれいだから、目立ちます。

4. せん生が つくえの上で 立たないでと いいました。

5. 大がく生は 六月から なつ休みです。

6. あの 中がっこうは 大きいですね。

7. えきの で口で 男の人が 立っています。

Kanji matching (answers)

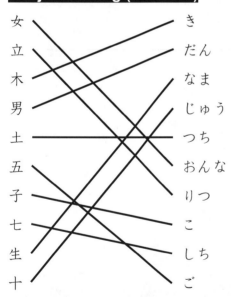

女　　　　　き
立　　　　　だん
木　　　　　なま
男　　　　　じゅう
土　　　　　つち
五　　　　　おんな
子　　　　　りつ
七　　　　　こ
生　　　　　しち
十　　　　　ご

Kanji meaning match (answers)

1. 足 foot	2. 男 man	3. 右 right
4. 口 mouth	5. 生 to live	6. 女 girl
7. 手 hand	8. 子 child	9. 立 to stand

Stroke order check (answers)

1. A   2. B   3. A   4. B   5. B

8

Kanji lesson 8:

天空気雨山川

8 | New Kanji あたらしい かんじ

Make sure you learn the correct stroke order. Correct stroke order will mean neater symbols when writing quickly. Also, take time to learn the words listed for each kanji – these will help you memorize the different readings.

天	41. heaven			4 画
	くんよみ	あめ、あま		
	おんよみ	テン		
	天			

heaven	weather	the Milky Way	genius
てん 天	てん き 天気	あま　　がわ 天の川	てんさい 天才

空	42. sky, empty, vacant			8 画
	くんよみ	そら、あ(く)、から、あき		
	おんよみ	クウ		
	空			

sky	airport	vacant house	empty
そら 空	くうこう 空港	あ　　や 空き家	から 空

43. spirit, mood　　　　6画

くんよみ	none
おんよみ	キ、ケ

気

spirit, mood	stamina, vigor, health	air	indication
き	げん き	くう き	け はい
気	元気	空気	気配

44. rain　　　　8画

くんよみ	あめ、あま
おんよみ	ウ

雨

rain	rain clouds	rainy weather	amount of rain
あめ	あまぐも	う てん	う りょう
雨	雨雲	雨天	雨量

45. mountain　　　　3画

くんよみ	やま
おんよみ	サン

山

mountain	mountain climbing	Mt. Fuji	volcano
やま	やまのぼ	ふ じ さん	か ざん
山	山登り	富士山	火山

川	46. river			3 画
	くんよみ	かわ		
	おんよみ	セン		
	川			

river	brook, stream	upper reaches of a river	rivers; river system
かわ	お がわ	かわかみ	か せん
川	小川	川上	河川

8	**Kanji Usage かんじの つかいかた**

● 8-1. The "rain" radical (雨) あめかんむり

After you get through the basic characters, you will start to see simple kanji being used as parts of other kanji. These are called "radicals." When a radical is on top of the kanji it's called a かんむり. The word かんむり means "crown" in Japanese. So you can imagine the radical is the crown of the Kanji.

The "rain" radical, called あめかんむり, is used to make many other kanji.

Look at the various kanji that contain the あめかんむり radical for "rain":

cloud	snow	thunder	electricity
雲	雪	雷	電
くも	ゆき	かみなり	でん(き)

● 8-2. Kanji of the soul and spirit (気)

気 is used in many Japanese phrases and common words in Japanese.

Phrase	Meaning	Literally means
気を付ける	to be careful	put on your spirit
気のせい	in one's imagination	fault of your spirit
気に入る	to favor / like	enter your spirit
気の毒	to be sorry for, unfortunate	poison of the spirit
気にする	to be concerned with~	put in your spirit
気がする	to have a feeling that~	put in your spirit
気が狂う	to go crazy	spirit goes crazy

● 8-3. This kanji is available (空)

空 means "empty" or "vacant" so it's used with words that mean "available".

taxi for hire (empty + car)	available room (empty + room)
空車 くう・しゃ	空室 くう・しつ

an empty stomach (empty + stomach)	space, room (empty + space)
空腹 くう・ふく	空間 くう・かん

vacant seat, vacancy (empty + seat)	blank space (empty + white)
空席 くう・せき	空白 くう・はく

● 8-4. Reading the air? (空)

If a person is clueless to something that is obvious then they are "unable to read the air" of the room.

> かれ　　くうき　　よ
> 彼は空気が読めないです。
> He is clueless. / He has no idea.

While we are here, why don't we learn some other good words that use 空.

air force	vacant land, empty lot
空軍	空き地
くう・ぐん	あき・ち

empty bottle	empty can
空き瓶	空き缶
あき・びん	あき・かん

vacuum (empty of matter)	blue sky
真空	青空
しん・くう	あお・ぞら

night sky	starry sky
夜空	星空
よ・ぞら	ほし・ぞら

8 | Words You Can Write かける ことば

天気 （てんき） weather

空気 （くうき） air

空手 （からて） karate (martial arts)

雨天 （うてん） rainy weather

大気 （たいき） atmosphere (of Earth)

火山 （かざん） volcano

小川 （おがわ） stream, brook

人気 （にんき） popular

雨水 （あまみず） rain water

小雨（こさめ）light rain, drizzle (not a common reading of 雨)

小	雨									

大雨（おおあめ）heavy rain

大	雨									

空耳（そらみみ）mishearing (of a word)

空	耳									

天国（てんごく）heaven

天	ご	く							

天の川（あまのがわ）Milky Way

天	の	川						

8 | Fill in the Kanji

Fill in the appropriate kanji in the blanks for each sentence.

　　てん　き　　　　　　やま

1. ＿＿＿ ＿＿＿がいいです。＿＿＿に ハイキングに いきましょう。
   The weather is good. Let's go hiking in the mountains.

　　　あめ　　　　　　　　　かわ　みず

2. ＿＿＿が たくさんふったから、＿＿＿の ＿＿＿が おおいですね。
   Because it rained a lot, there is a lot of water in the river.

　　くう　き　　　　　　　あま　がわ

3. ＿＿＿ ＿＿＿が きれいだから、＿＿＿ の＿＿＿が よくみえる。
   Because the air is clean, you can see the Milky Way well.

みぎ   ふた   め   やま   さん

4. ____ から ____つ ____の____が ふじ____です。
The second mountain from the right is Mt. Fuji.

げつ   び   き

5. ____ よう____は いつも げん____ じゃないです。
I am never energetic on Mondays.

そら   いつ

6. ____ に ほしが ____つ しか みえません。
I can only see five stars in the sky.

ろく にん   こ   かわ

7. ____ ____の ____どもと ____で ピクニックをしました。
I had a picnic at the river with six children.

8 | Kanji matching

Draw a line to connect each kanji with only one of its ON or KUN readings.

気 ・   ・ てん
川 ・   ・ りつ
男 ・   ・ かわ
天 ・   ・ あ ま
月 ・   ・ や ま
立 ・   ・ が つ
空 ・   ・ き
山 ・   ・ み ず
雨 ・   ・ そ ら
水 ・   ・ お と こ

8 | Kanji meaning

Write the following kanji next to its meaning: 生 百 川 金 山 空 天 雨 気

1. ____ mood

2. ____ life

3. ____ sky

4. ____ heaven

5. ____ river

6. ____ mountain

7. ____ 100

8. ____ rain

9. ____ Gold

8 | Stroke Order Check

Circle A or B whichever represents the correct stroke order for each kanji.

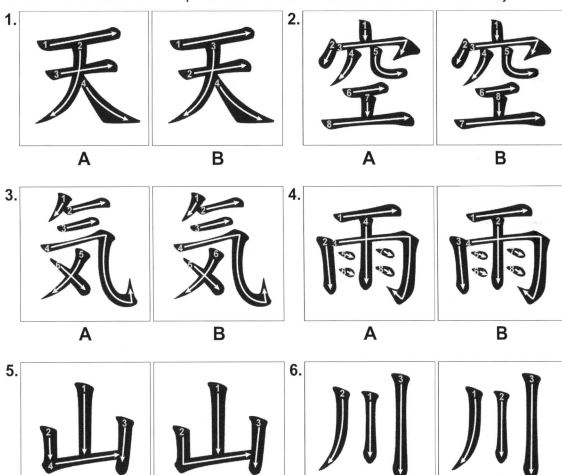

1. A B

2. A B

3. A B

4. A B

5. A B

6. A B

8 | Answer Key 答え合わせ

Fill in the kanji (answers)

1. 天気がいいです。山に ハイキングに いきましょう。

2. 雨が たくさんふったから、川の 水が おおいですね。

3. 空気が きれいだから、天の川が よくみえる。

4. 右から 二つ目の山が ふじ山です。

5. 月よう日は いつも げん気じゃないです。

6. 空に ほしが 五つ、しか みえません。

7. 六人の 子どもと 川で ピクニックをしました。

Kanji matching (answers)

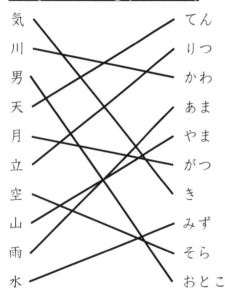

気　　　　てん
川　　　　りつ
男　　　　かわ
天　　　　あま
月　　　　やま
立　　　　がつ
空　　　　き
山　　　　みず
雨　　　　そら
水　　　　おとこ

Kanji meaning match (answers)

1. 気 mood
2. 生 life
3. 空 sky
4. 天 heaven
5. 川 river
6. 山 mountain
7. 百 100
8. 雨 rain
9. 金 gold

Stroke order check (answers)

1. B   2. A   3. A   4. A   5. B   6. B

9

Kanji lesson 9:

林森石花犬虫町

9 | New Kanji あたらしい かんじ

Make sure you learn the correct stroke order. Correct stroke order will mean neater symbols when writing quickly. Also, take time to learn the words listed for each kanji – these will help you memorize the different readings.

	47. woods, forest			8 画
	くんよみ	はやし		
	おんよみ	リン		
	林			

woods, forest	mountain forest	apple	planted forest (man-made)
はやし 林	さんりん 山林	りんご 林檎	じんこうりん 人工林

	48. forest, woods			12 画
	くんよみ	もり		
	おんよみ	シン		
	森			

forest, woods	Aomori Prefecture	in the forest	forest; woods
もり 森	あおもりけん 青森県	もり　なか 森の中	しんりん 森林

49. stone — 5 画

くんよみ	いし
おんよみ	セキ、シャク、コク

stone	jewel stone	magnet	stone materials
いし	ほうせき	じしゃく	せきざい
石	宝石	磁石	石材

50. flower — 7 画

くんよみ	はな
おんよみ	カ

flower	fireworks	spark	flower bed
はな	はなび	ひばな	かだん
花	花火	火花	花壇

51. dog — 4 画

くんよみ	いぬ
おんよみ	ケン

dog	doghouse	pet dog	cuspid tooth (canine)
いぬ	いぬごや	あいけん	けんし
犬	犬小屋	愛犬	犬歯

52. bug, insect			6 画
くんよみ	むし		
おんよみ	チュウ		

虫

bug, insect	cavity, bad tooth	caterpillar	harmful bug
むし	むし ば	け むし	がいちゅう
虫	虫歯	毛虫	害虫

53. town			7 画
くんよみ	まち		
おんよみ	チョウ		

町

town	downtown	outskirts of town	head of town
まち	した まち	まちはず	ちょうちょう
町	下町	町外れ	町長

9 | Kanji Usage かんじの つかいかた

● 9-1. Doubling and tripling of kanji

Some kanji don't leave a lot to the imagination. Simply by repeating the kanji we get new words in the same category, or with a similar scope.

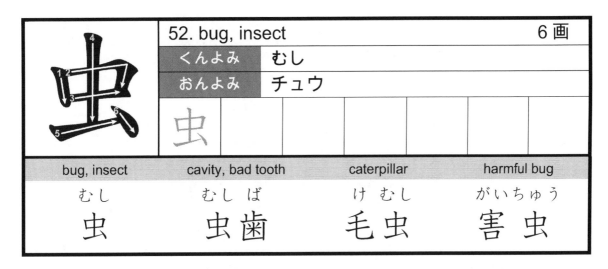

tree	woods	forest
木	林	森
き	はやし	もり

sun, sunshine	crystal
日	晶
ひ	(すい)しょう

fire	flame, blaze
火	炎
ひ	ほのお

woman	wicked, seduce
女	姦
おんな	カン

● 9-2. The "tree / wood" radical きへん

The kanji for tree 木 is a common radical called きへん for many kanji that are related to trees and wood.

desk	pillow *	root (of plant)	village
机	枕	根	村
つくえ	まくら	ね	むら

* 枕 (まくら)

Pillows in ancient China, where kanji originates, used to be made of wood with the purpose of just supporting the head instead of being soft.

● 9-3. Small changes, big difference

Kanji can sometimes look very similar to other kanji with only a minor change. Initially this can be challenging, but over time you will learn to be aware of the small differences.

right	stone
右	石
みぎ	いし

big	thick, fat	dog
大	太	犬
おお(きい)	ふと(い)	いぬ

9 | Words You Can Write かける ことば

山林 （さんりん）mountain forest

山	林										

森林 （しんりん）woodland

森	林										

花火 （はなび）fireworks

花	火										

子犬（こいぬ）puppy

子	犬								

火花（ひばな）spark

火	花								

下町（したまち）downtown

下	町								

毛虫（けむし）caterpillar

け	虫								

虫歯（むしば）tooth cavity

虫	ば								

小石（こいし）small stone, pebble

小	石								

森の中（もりのなか）in the forest

森	の	中							

生け花（いけばな）flower arrangement

生	け	花							

9 │ Fill in the Kanji

Fill in the appropriate kanji in the blanks for each sentence.

もり　　はやし　　なか

1. ＿＿ や ＿＿ の＿＿は あつくないです。

It's not hot in places like the woods or the forest.

おお　　　いし　　むっ

2. あそこに ＿＿ きい＿＿ が＿＿つ あります。

There are 6 big stones over there.

ちい　　むし　　　　　　した

3. ＿＿ さい＿＿ が つくえの＿＿に います。

There is a small bug under the desk.

に　　　　こ　　　　はな び　　だい

4. ＿＿ ほんの＿＿ どもは ＿＿ ＿＿が ＿＿すき です。

Children of Japan love fireworks.

まち　　に せん さん

5. この ＿＿ に ＿＿ ＿＿ ＿＿ねんから すんでいます。

I have lived in this town since 2003.

こ　いぬ　じっ

6. ＿＿ ＿＿が ＿＿ぴき います。

There are 10 puppies.

いぬ　　め　　　　　　　みみ

7. わたしの＿＿は ＿＿ が あおくて、＿＿ が グレー です。

My dog's eyes are blue and his ears are gray.

9 | Kanji matching

Draw a line to connect each kanji with one of its ON or KUN readings.

林 ·	· はな
千 ·	· じょ
花 ·	· もり
石 ·	· ちょう
女 ·	· せん
森 ·	· いぬ
犬 ·	· いし
耳 ·	· みみ
虫 ·	· はやし
町 ·	· むし

9 | Kanji meaning

Write the following kanji next to its meaning: 森 休 犬 虫 左 町 林 石 花

1. ____ flower

2. ____ woods

3. ____ left

4. ____ dog

5. ____ forest

6. ____ day off

7. ____ bug

8. ____ stone

9. ____ town

9 | Stroke Order Check

Circle A or B whichever represents the correct stroke order for each kanji.

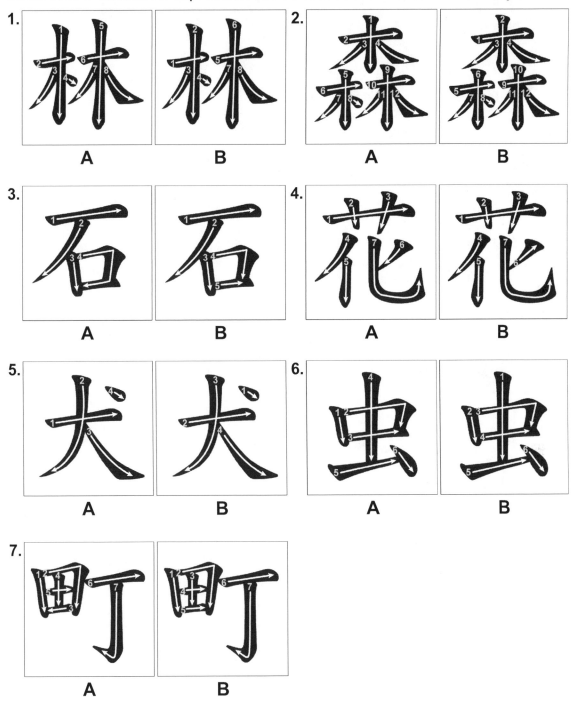

9 | Answer Key 答え合わせ

Fill in the kanji (answers)

1. 森や林の中は あつくない です。

2. あそこに 大きい石が 六つ、あります。

3. 小さい虫が つくえの下に います。

4. 日ほんの子どもは 花火が 大すき です。

5. この町に 二千三ねんから、すんでいます。

6. 子犬が 十ぴき、います。

7. わたしの犬は 目が あおくて、耳がグレー です。

Kanji meaning match (answers)

1. 花 flower   2. 林 woods   3. 左 left

4. 犬 dog   5. 森 forest   6. 休 day off

7. 虫 bug   8. 石 stone   9. 町 town

Kanji matching (answers)

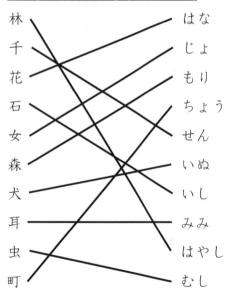

林		はな
千		じょ
花		もり
石		ちょう
女		せん
森		いぬ
犬		いし
耳		みみ
虫		はやし
町		むし

Stroke order check (answers)

1. B   2. B   3. B   4. A   5. A   6. A   7. B

10 Kanji lesson 10: 村田夕赤青白見

10 New Kanji あたらしい かんじ

Make sure you learn the correct stroke order. Correct stroke order will mean neater symbols when writing quickly. Also, take time to learn the words listed for each kanji – these will help you memorize the different readings.

54. village — 7 画

くんよみ	むら
おんよみ	ソン

village	villager	mountain village	village chief
むら	むらびと	さんそん	そんちょう
村	村人	山村	村長

55. rice paddy, field — 5 画

くんよみ	た
おんよみ	デン

rice paddy, field	Akita prefecture	water filled paddy	oil field
た	あきたけん	すいでん	ゆでん
田んぼ	秋田県	水田	油田

56. evening　　3画

くんよみ	ゆう
おんよみ	セキ

夕 | | | | | |

evening	setting sun	dinner	last night
ゆうがた 夕方	ゆうひ 夕日	ゆうしょく 夕食	ゆう 夕べ

57. red　　7画

くんよみ	あか
おんよみ	セキ、シャク

赤 | | | | | |

red	in the red, in debt	red tide	the equator
あか 赤	あかじ 赤字	あかしお 赤潮	せきどう 赤道

58. blue　　8画

くんよみ	あお
おんよみ	セイ、ショウ

青 | | | | | |

blue	green light	young man	blue sky
あお 青	あおしんごう 青信号	せいねん 青年	あおぞら 青空

59. white			5画
くんよみ	しろ		
おんよみ	ハク、ビャク		

white	interesting	confession	caucasian
しろ	おもしろ	こくはく	はくじん
白	面白い	告白	白人

60. to look			7画
くんよみ	み		
おんよみ	ケン		

to look	to show	study by observation	sample
み	み	けんがく	みほん
見る	見せる	見学	見本

10 | Kanji Usage かんじの つかいかた

● 10-1. Colorful expressions

尻が青い – Your butt is blue.
しり　あお

This phrase is similar to the English phrase, "You are wet behind the ears." It refers to someone who is inexperienced. Japanese and other Asian people are often born with Mongolian spots 蒙古斑 (もうこはん) which look similar to bluish bruises on their body. These spots can be on any part of the body but are most common on the butt. Over time, the spots disappear. So a younger person would still have a "blue butt" and therefore be considered inexperienced.

赤の他人 - A complete stranger

他人 (たにん) means "stranger." Instead of 赤 (あか) meaning "red" in this case, it means "completely" or "obvious." A similar phrase is 真っ赤な嘘 (まっかなうそ) which means an "obvious lie."

白い目で見る – To look at with white eyes

When someone looks at you with white eyes, it means they are not looking at you directly so that the whites of their eyes are visible. They are upset with you so they won't properly look at you. It is similar to looking at someone with cold eyes in English.

● 10-2. Japanese name origins

Before the Meiji Era it was forbidden for anyone who was not a samurai to have a last name. This left 90% of the population without a last name. In the 1870's the laws changed, requiring families to have a last name.

Village priests helped determine the last names, but due to the overwhelming number of names required, they were often forced to choose random combinations of different kanji based on where the family lived.

Priests often unknowingly assigned the same characters to multiple families and this resulted in several non-related families having the same last name.

Name	Meaning	Name	Meaning
田村	rice paddy village	村上	above the village
田中	center of the paddy	中田	inside the paddy
村田	rice paddy in the village	中村	inside the village
青木	green (blue) tree	村中	center of village
林	woods	森	forest
石川	stone river	山田	mountain paddy
川田	river paddy	小川	stream (small river)
木村	tree village	山口	base of mountain
小林	small woods	山下	below the mountain

10 | Words You Can Write かける ことば

山村 （さんそん） mountain village

山	村										

水田 （すいでん） flooded paddy

水	田										

夕べ （ゆうべ） evening

夕	べ										

夕日 （ゆうひ） setting sun

夕	日										

空白 （くうはく） blank space

空	白										

見る （みる） to see

見	る										

赤い （あかい） red

赤	い										

青い （あおい） blue

青	い										

青空 (あおぞら) blue sky

青	空									

月見 (つきみ) moon viewing

月	見									

七夕 (たなばた) Tanabata (festival) * this reading is unique

七	夕									

白人 (はくじん) white person, Caucasian

白	人									

花見 (はなみ) cherry blossom viewing

花	見									

田んぼ (たんぼ) rice paddy

田	ん	ぼ							

見せる (みせる) to show

見	せ	る							

青森けん (あおもりけん) Aomori prefecture (in northern Japan)

青	森	け	ん						

赤ちゃん (あかちゃん) baby

赤	ち	ゃ	ん				

10 | Fill in the Kanji

Fill in the appropriate kanji in the blanks for each sentence.

　　　　むら　　ひと　　よん ひゃく にん
1. その ＿＿ に＿＿ が ＿＿ ＿＿ ＿＿ います。
   There are 400 people in that village.

　　　に　　　　　　すい でん
2. ＿＿ ほんには ＿＿ ＿＿ が たくさん あります。
   In Japan there are a lot of water-filled paddies.

　　やま　　うえ　　あか ゆう ひ
3. ＿＿ の＿＿ の ＿＿い＿＿ ＿＿ が きれい ですね。
   The red sunset above the mountain sure is pretty.

　　あお　　そら　　しろ　　　　　なな
4. ＿＿ い＿＿ に ＿＿い くもが ＿＿つ あります。
   There are 7 white clouds in the blue sky.

　　　　　はく じん　　おんな　　こ
5. あの ＿＿ ＿＿ の ＿＿ の＿＿ は だれ ですか。
   Who is that white girl? (Caucasian)

　　　た　　　　　　　　　しろ　あか　はな
6. ＿＿ んぼのよこに、＿＿ と＿＿の ＿＿ が あります。
   There are white and red flowers next to the paddy.

　　　ど　　　び　　やす　　　　　　　み
7. ＿＿ よう＿＿ は ＿＿み です。えいがが＿＿ たい です。
   Saturday is my day off. I want to see a movie.

10 | Kanji matching

Draw a line to connect each kanji with only one of its ON or KUN readings.

赤 ・　　　・ ゆう
田 ・　　　・ た
足 ・　　　・ そん
白 ・　　　・ せき　き
百 ・　　　・ あ　お
見 ・　　　・ ひゃく
目 ・　　　・ め
青 ・　　　・ しろ　ろく
村 ・　　　・ そく　くん
夕 ・　　　・ けん

10 | Kanji meaning

Write the following kanji next to its meaning: 赤 四 田 夕 白 右 村 見 青

1. ___ evening

2. ___ village

3. ___ to look

4. ___ right

5. ___ white

6. ___ four

7. ___ blue

8. ___ red

9. ___ rice paddy

10 | Stroke Order Check

Circle A or B whichever represents the correct stroke order for each kanji.

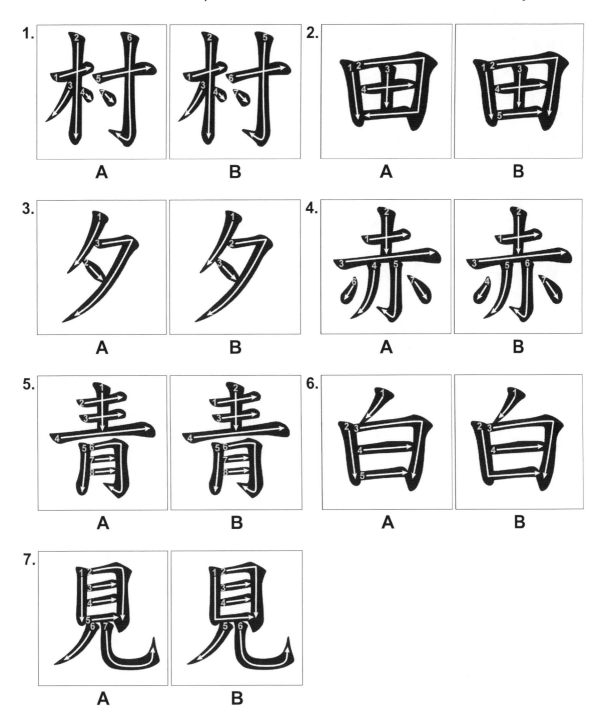

10 | Answer Key 答え合わせ

Fill in the kanji (answers)

1. その 村 に 人 が 四百人 います。

2. 日 ほんには 水田 が たくさん あります。

3. 山 の 上 の 赤い 夕日 が きれい ですね。

4. 青 い 空 に 白 いくもが 七 つ あります。

5. あの 白人 の 女 の 子 はだれ ですか。

6. 田 んぼのよこに、白 と 赤 の 花 が あります。

7. 土 よう 日 は 休 み です。えいがが 見 たい です。

Kanji matching (answers)

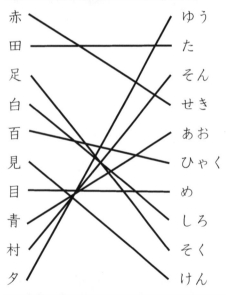

赤　　　　ゆう
田　　　　た
足　　　　そん
白　　　　せき
百　　　　あお
見　　　　ひゃく
目　　　　め
青　　　　しろ
村　　　　そく
夕　　　　けん

Kanji meaning match (answers)

1. 夕 evening　　2. 村 village　　3. 見 to look

4. 右 right　　5. 白 white　　6. 四 four

7. 青 blue　　8. 赤 red　　9. 田 rice paddy

Stroke order check (answers)

1. A　2. B　3. B　4. A　5. B　6. A　7. A

SR | Super Review 2

SR2 | Kanji selection

Select the best kanji to fill in the blank in each sentence.

1. あの白い＿＿＿は だれの ですか。
   A. 右　　　　　　B. 犬　　　　　　C. 金　　　　　　D. 水

2. きょうは天気がよくて、空が＿＿＿い ですね。
   A. 赤　　　　　　B. 円　　　　　　C. 青　　　　　　D. 雨

3. 女の子より男の子のほうが ＿＿＿が あります。
   A. 火　　　　　　B. 気　　　　　　C. 足　　　　　　D. 力

4. うちの犬は＿＿＿きくて うるさいです。
   A. 大　　　　　　B. 中　　　　　　C. 小　　　　　　D. 火

SR2 | Kanji reading

Select the best reading for the underlined kanji.

1. わたしの子は 耳が とても 大きい です。
   A. あし　　　　　B. て　　　　　　C. みみ　　　　　D. くち

2. わたしのむすこは 二千五年に 生まれました。
   A. う　　　　　　B. い　　　　　　C. は　　　　　　D. せい

3. グラスが 空ですね。もっとのみますか。
   A. そら　　　　　B. くう　　　　　C. から　　　　　D. あき

4. おばあちゃんは 生け花をべんきょう しています。
   A. か　　　　　　B. ばな　　　　　C. はな　　　　　D. ぱな

SR2 | Compound kanji word puzzle

Fill in the correct kanji based on the list below the puzzle.

1)	2)	3)
4)		
5)	6)	7)
		8)

Down ↓
2) air
3) hands and legs
5) thermal power
7) brook, stream

Left to Right →
1) blue sky
2) karate
4) weather
5) spark

Right to Left ←
6) fireworks
8) down stream

SR2 | Answer Key 答え合わせ

Kanji selection (answers)

1. B – 犬
   いぬ

   Whose is that white dog?

2. C – 青い
   あお

   Today the weather is good and the sky is blue.

3. D – 力
   ちから

   Boys have more power than girls. (This is slightly sexist… sorry!)

4. A – 大
   おお

   Our dog is big and loud.

Kanji reading (answers)

1. C – 耳
   みみ

   My child's ears are very big.

2. A – 生まれました
   う

   My son was born in 2005.

3. C – 空
   から

   Your glass is empty. Will you drink more?

4. B – 生け花
   い ばな

   Grandmother is studying flower arrangement.

Compound kanji word puzzle (answers)

青	空	手
天	気	足
火	花	小
力	下	川

11

Kanji lesson 11:

出入先早本文

11 | New Kanji あたらしい かんじ

Make sure you learn the correct stroke order. Correct stroke order will mean neater symbols when writing quickly. Also, take time to learn the words listed for each kanji – these will help you memorize the different readings.

	61. leave, come out						5 画
	くんよみ	で(る)、だ(す)					
	おんよみ	シュツ、スイ					
	出						

to come out, to leave	to put out, to send	departure	receipts, expenditures
で 出る	だ 出す	しゅっぱつ 出発	すいとう 出納

	62. enter						2 画
	くんよみ	い(れる)、はい(る)					
	おんよみ	ニュウ					
	入						

to enter, to join	to put in	entrance	hospitalization
はい 入る	い 入れる	い　ぐち 入り口	にゅういん 入院

先

63. ahead, previous, prior			6 画
くんよみ	さき		
おんよみ	セン		

先

tip, future, priority	finger tip	teacher	last month
さき	ゆびさき	せんせい	せんげつ
先	指先	先生	先月

早

64. early, fast			6 画
くんよみ	はや(い)		
おんよみ	ソウ、サッ		

早

early, fast	fast talking	right away	early morning
はや	はやくち	さっそく	そうちょう
早い	早口	早速	早朝

本

65. origin, book			5 画
くんよみ	もと		
おんよみ	ホン		

本

book	Japan	3 cylindrical objects	Yamamoto (last name)
ほん	にほん	さんぼん	やまもと
本	日本	三本	山本

文	66. sentence					4 画
	くんよみ	ふみ				
	おんよみ	ブン、モン、モ				
	文					

sentence	grammar	letter (of alphabet)	phrase, complaint
ぶん 文	ぶんぽう 文法	もじ 文字	もんく 文句

11 | Kanji Usage かんじの つかいかた

● **11-1. Knowing a word meaning based on the kanji**
Each kanji in a word has meaning and じゅくご (compound kanji words) are often created by building a mini story based on the kanji used. Often, words are easier to learn if you know the kanji used to create them.

teacher (prior + birth)	premature birth (early + give birth)
先生 せん・せい	早産 そう・ざん

entrance (enter + opening)	exit (depart + opening)
入口 いり・ぐち	出口 で・ぐち

fast talking (fast + mouth)	last month (prior + moon)
早口	先月
はや・くち	せん・げつ

adult (big + person)	dwarf (small + person)
大人	小人
お・とな	こ・びと

● **11-2. How did Japan get its name?**

Some words are put together with seemingly unrelated kanji, however, historically they often have significance.

Japan (sun + origin)	Word Origin
日本 にほん or にっぽん	Japan was given its current name by China. Japan is located to the east of China where the sun rises. Therefore, because of its location in relation to China, Japan became "origin of the sun." This is also why Japan is often called the land of the rising sun.

11 | Words You Can Write かける ことば

出る（でる）to exit, leave

出る								

出す（だす）to put out

出す								

出口 （でぐち） exit

出	口										

入る （はいる） to enter

入	る										

入力（にゅうりょく） to input (data into a form or computer)

入	力										

先生 （せんせい） teacher

先	生									

先月 （せんげつ） last month

先	月									

早い （はやい） early

早	い									

日本 （にほん） Japan

日	本									

見本 （みほん） sample

見	本									

三本 （さんぼん） three cylindrical objects

三	本								

例文（れいぶん） example sentence

れ	い	文							

入れる（いれる） to put inside

入	れ	る							

入り口（いりぐち） entrance

入	り	口							

11 | Fill in the Kanji

Fill in the appropriate kanji in the blanks for each sentence.

　　せん せい　　はや く ち

1. ＿＿＿ ＿＿＿は ＿＿＿ ＿＿＿ことばを いいました。
   The teacher said a tongue twister.

　　　　　　こ　　　　　　　　　し　 が つ　ちゅう　　せい

2. ゆみ ＿＿＿ ちゃんは、＿＿＿ ＿＿＿に ＿＿＿ がく＿＿＿に なります。
   Yumiko will become a junior high student in April.

　　せん　　　　　　もく　　　び　　　　　　　　　だ

3. ＿＿＿ しゅうの ＿＿＿ よう＿＿＿に しゅくだいを＿＿＿しました。
   I turned in my homework last Thursday.

　　に　 ほん　　ぶん

4. ＿＿＿ ＿＿＿ ごの＿＿＿ は むずかしい ですね。
   Japanese sentences sure are difficult.

　　で　 ぐち　　　　　　　　　　　　みぎ

5. ＿＿＿ ＿＿＿は あのエスカレーターの＿＿＿ に あります。
   The exit is to the right of that escalator.

にち　　はち　　　　　　　で
6. まい ＿＿＿ 、＿＿＿ じに いえを ＿＿＿ます。
   I leave home every day at 8 o'clock.

はや　　　だい
7. ＿＿＿く 、＿＿＿ がくに いきたい です。
   I want to go to college soon.

11 | Kanji meaning

Write the following kanji next to its meaning: 金 出 森 入 先 町 早 本 文

1. ＿＿＿ sentence   2. ＿＿＿ book   3. ＿＿＿ town

4. ＿＿＿ to leave   5. ＿＿＿ money   6. ＿＿＿ prior, previous

7. ＿＿＿ early   8. ＿＿＿ forest   9. ＿＿＿ to enter

11 | Kanji matching

Draw a line to connect each kanji with only one of its ON or KUN readings.

早 ・   ・ で
手 ・   ・ そう
下 ・   ・ ぶん
出 ・   ・ さき
先 ・   ・ じん
木 ・   ・ もく
入 ・   ・ にゅう
本 ・   ・ しゅ
人 ・   ・ ほん
文 ・   ・ か

11 | Stroke Order Check

Circle A or B whichever represents the correct stroke order for each kanji.

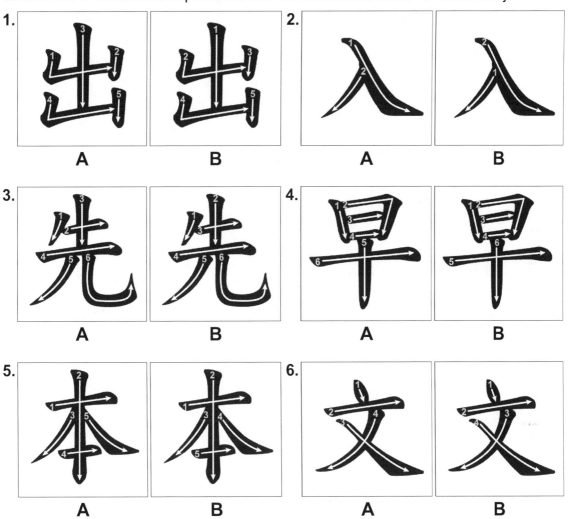

11 | Answer Key 答え合わせ

Fill in the kanji (answers)

1. 先生は 早口 ことばを いいました。

2. ゆみ子ちゃんは、四月に 中がく生に なります。

3. 先しゅうの 木よう日に しゅくだいを 出しました。

4. 日本ごの 文は むずかしい ですね。

5. 出口は あのエスカレーターの 右に あります。

6. まい日、八じに いえを 出ます。

7. 早く 、大がくに いきたい です。

Kanji meaning match (answers)

1. 文 sentence	2. 本 book	3. 町 town
4. 出 to leave	5. 金 money	6. 先 prior, previous
7. 早 early	8. 森 forest	9. 入 to enter

Kanji matching (answers)

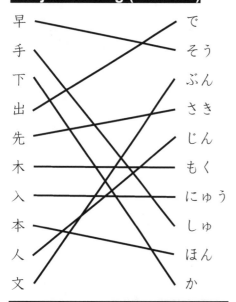

早　　　で
手　　　そう
下　　　ぶん
出　　　さき
先　　　じん
木　　　もく
入　　　にゅう
本　　　しゅ
人　　　ほん
文　　　か

Stroke order check (answers)

1. B　2. B　3. A　4. B　5. B　6. B

12

Kanji lesson 12:

名字学校正年王

12 | New Kanji あたらしい かんじ

Make sure you learn the correct stroke order. Correct stroke order will mean neater symbols when writing quickly. Also, take time to learn the words listed for each kanji – these will help you memorize the different readings.

名	**67. name**			**6画**
	くんよみ	な		
	おんよみ	メイ、ミョウ		
	名			

name	famous	last name	nickname
な まえ	ゆうめい	みょうじ	な
名前	有名	名字	あだ名

字	**68. letter, character**			**6画**
	くんよみ	あざ		
	おんよみ	ジ		
	字			

letter, character	Kanji, Chinese character	lower case letter	larger section (of village)
じ	かんじ	こ も じ	おおあざ
字	漢字	小文字	大字

69. study of, learning — 8 画

くんよみ	まな(ぶ)
おんよみ	ガク

学

to learn	student	college	year in school
まな	がくせい	だいがく	がくねん
学ぶ	学生	大学	学年

70. school — 10 画

くんよみ	none
おんよみ	コウ

校

school	high school	school principal	gate, entrance to school
がっこう	こうこう	こうちょう	こうもん
学校	高校	校長	校門

71. correct — 5 画

くんよみ	ただ(しい)、まさ
おんよみ	セイ、ショウ

正

correct	dreams that come true	correct answer	New Year's
ただ	まさゆめ	せいかい	しょうがつ
正しい	正夢	正解	正月

年	**72. year, age**					6 画
	くんよみ	とし				
	おんよみ	ネン				
	年					

year, age	the elderly	one year	several years
ねん 年	としよ 年寄り	いちねん 一年	すうねん 数年

王	**73. king**					4 画
	くんよみ	none				
	おんよみ	オウ				
	王					

king	prince	princess	Pluto (dwarf planet)
おうさま 王様	おうじ 王子	おうじょ 王女	めいおうせい 冥王星

12 | Kanji Usage かんじの つかいかた

● **12-1. First name / Last Name**

In Japan, the "last name" is always said first. This is why a person's "first name" in Japanese is made with the characters 名前, which literally means "before the name."

name (name + prior)	last name (name + character)
名前 な・まえ	名字 みょう・じ

● **12-2. The study of things 学**

Fields of study will almost always end with 学.

科学 (science)

数学 (math)

語学 (language study)

文学 (literature)

物理学 (physics),

生物学 (biology)

天文学 (astronomy)

心理学 (psychology)

There are also a lot of school related words containing 学.

入学 (entering a school)

退学 (dropping out of school)

独学 (self study)

停学 (suspension from school)

通学 (commuting to school)

留学 (to study abroad)

---

12 | Words You Can Write かける ことば

名字 (みょうじ) last name

名	字								

文字 (もじ) letter, character

文	字								

学校 (がっこう) school

学	校								

学生（がくせい）student

学年（がくねん）grade, year

五年（ごねん）5 years

女王（じょおう）queen

正月（しょうがつ）New Year's

名前（なまえ）name

小学校（しょうがっこう）elementary school

正しい（ただしい）correct

12 | Fill in the Kanji

Fill in the appropriate kanji in the blanks for each sentence.

に　ほん　　だい　がく　せい

1. ＿＿＿ ＿＿＿ の＿＿＿ ＿＿＿ ＿＿＿は よく アルバイトを します。
Japanese college students often work part time jobs.

ただ　　　　　じ　　　　　　くだ

2. ＿＿＿ しい かん＿＿＿ を かいて＿＿＿さい。
Please write the correct kanji.

まち　ちゅう がっ こう　　ここの

3. この ＿＿＿ に ＿＿＿ ＿＿＿ ＿＿＿ が ＿＿＿ つ あります。
There are nine junior high schools in this town.

しろ　はな　な　　　　　　　くだ

4. その ＿＿＿ い＿＿＿ の＿＿＿まえを おしえて＿＿＿さい。
Please tell me the name of that white flower.

やま　だ　　　　なな ねん　　　　むら

5. ＿＿＿ ＿＿＿ さんは ＿＿＿ ＿＿＿まえに この＿＿＿に きました。
Mr. Yamada came to this village 7 years ago.

しょう がく せい

6. わたしの いもうとは ＿＿＿ ＿＿＿ ＿＿＿ です。
My younger sister is an elementary school student.

ねん　　しょう がつ　てん き

7. きょ＿＿＿の お ＿＿＿ ＿＿＿は、＿＿＿ ＿＿＿が わるかった です。
The weather last New Year's was bad.

12 | Kanji meaning

Write the following kanji next to its meaning: 年 名 雨 字 水 学 正 王 校

1. ____ school

2. ____ rain

3. ____ to learn

4. ____ name

5. ____ letter

6. ____ correct

7. ____ king

8. ____ year, age

9. ____ water

12 | Kanji matching

Draw a line to connect each kanji with only one of its ON or KUN readings.

王 ・   ・な ま
正 ・   ・え ん
生 ・   ・じ
年 ・   ・り き
円 ・   ・こ う
名 ・   ・お う
校 ・   ・が く
字 ・   ・め い
学 ・   ・し ょ う
力 ・   ・ね ん

12 | Stroke Order Check

Circle A or B whichever represents the correct stroke order for each kanji.

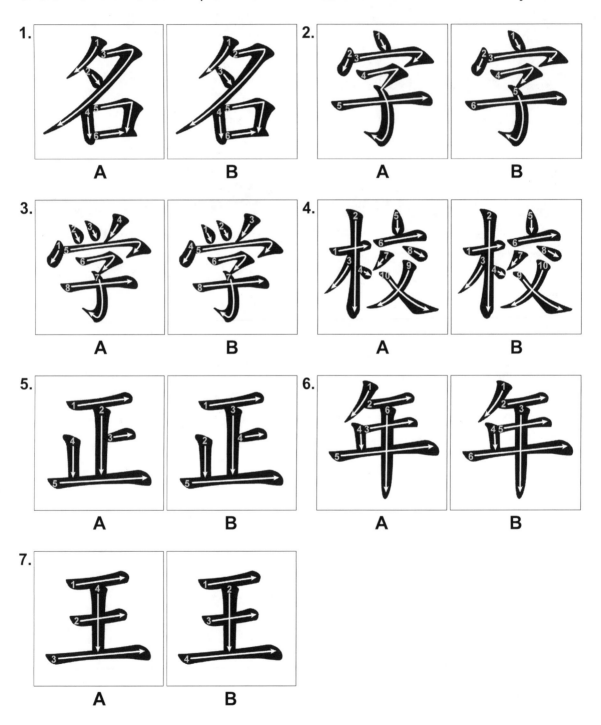

12 | Answer Key 答え合わせ

Fill in the kanji (answers)

1. 日本 の 大学生 は よく アルバイト を します。

2. 正 しい かん 字 を かいて 下 さい。

3. この 町 に 中学校 が 九 つ あります。

4. その 白 い 花 の 名 まえ を おしえて 下 さい。

5. 山田 さんは 七年 まえに この 村 に きました。

6. わたし のいもうとは 小学生 です。

7. きょ 年 の お 正月 は、 天気 が わるかった です。

Kanji meaning match (answers)

1. 校 school　　　　2. 雨 rain　　　　3. 学 to learn
4. 名 name　　　　5. 字 letter　　　　6. 正 correct
7. 王 king　　　　8. 年 year, age　　　9. 水 water

Kanji matching (answers)

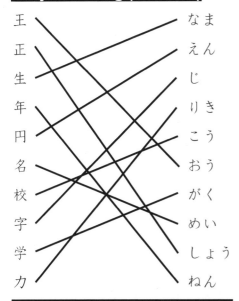

王　　　　　　なま
正　　　　　　えん
生　　　　　　じ
年　　　　　　りき
円　　　　　　こう
名　　　　　　おう
校　　　　　　がく
字　　　　　　めい
学　　　　　　しょう
力　　　　　　ねん

Stroke order check (answers)

1. B　2. B　3. B　4. A　5. A　6. A　7. B

13 Kanji lesson 13: 音糸車貝玉草竹

74-80

13 | New Kanji あたらしい かんじ

Make sure you learn the correct stroke order. Correct stroke order will mean neater symbols when writing quickly. Also, take time to learn the words listed for each kanji – these will help you memorize the different readings.

音	**74. sound**			9 画
	くんよみ	おと、ね		
	おんよみ	オン、イン		
	音			

sound	music	true feelings	vowel
おと	おんがく	ほん ね	ぼ いん
音	音楽	本音	母音

糸	**75. thread, string**			6 画
	くんよみ	いと		
	おんよみ	シ		
	糸			

thread, string	knitting yarn	fluff, piece of thread, lint	cotton thread
いと	け いと	いと	めんし
糸	毛糸	糸くず	綿糸

車	76. car						7 画
	くんよみ	くるま					
	おんよみ	シャ					
	車						

car, wheel	train	garage, carport	wheel
くるま	でんしゃ	しゃこ	しゃりん
車	電車	車庫	車輪

貝	77. shell						7 画
	くんよみ	かい					
	おんよみ	none					
	貝						

shell	outer shell	shellfish	spiral shell
かい	かいがら	かいるい	まきがい
貝	貝殻	貝類	巻貝

玉	78. ball						5 画
	くんよみ	たま					
	おんよみ	ギョク					
	玉						

ball, sphere	onion	polka dots	100 yen coin
たま	たま	みずたま	ひゃくえんだま
玉	玉ねぎ	水玉	百円玉

草	79. grass							9 画
	くんよみ	くさ						
	おんよみ	ソウ						
	草							

grass	gesture, behavior	Japanese footwear	weed
くさ	し ぐさ	ぞう り	ざっそう
草	仕草	草履	雑草

竹	80. bamboo							6 画
	くんよみ	たけ						
	おんよみ	チク						
	竹							

bamboo	bamboo shoots	stilts	bamboo (woods)
たけ	たけ こ	たけうま	ちくりん
竹	竹の子	竹馬	竹林

13 | Kanji Usage かんじの つかいかた

● **13-1. Best invention since the wheel (車)**
When words end in 車 they are often related to a mode of transportation.

じ どうしゃ
自動車 (automobile)

しょうぼうしゃ
消防車 (fire truck)

じ てんしゃ
自転車 (bicycle)

でんしゃ
電車 (train)

きゅうきゅうしゃ
救急車 (ambulance)

さんりんしゃ
三輪車 (tricycle)

If the word isn't a mode of transportation it is normally related to the actions of a mode of transportation.

発車 (departure of train)　停車 (stopping of train)
はっしゃ　　　　　　　　　　　　　ていしゃ

乗車 (taking a train)　　　下車 (getting off a train)
じょうしゃ　　　　　　　　　　　げ しゃ

* These are also used for cars and busses etc.

There are also some words that end with 車 that have nothing to do with transportation, but have rotating parts instead.

歯 車 (gear)　　　　　　風車 (windmill)
は ぐるま　　　　　　　　　ふうしゃ

● **13-2. The red thread of fate 運命の赤い糸**
うんめい　あか　いと

This is the equivalent of a "soul mate". A red thread is tied to the pinky finger of the girl and the thumb of the boy who are soulmates. If you meet someone that your friends think match you perfectly they might say:

赤い糸がつながっている！
あか　いと
You are connected with the red thread.

In Japanese culture, the gesture of raising the pinky means "girlfriend" or "lover" and a raised thumb means "boyfriend."

It's also not a coincidence that these same gestures are used in Japanese sign language.

A raised pinky also signifies a "promise" in Japan, so it's more common nowadays that the red thread is between pinkies to show the promise made to each other.

13 | Words You Can Write かける ことば

毛糸（けいと）knitting yarn

け	糸								

水玉 (みずたま) polka dots

水	玉								

草花 (くさばな) flowering plant

草	花								

音楽 (おんがく) music

音	が	く					

電車 (でんしゃ) train

で	ん	車					

百円玉 (ひゃくえんだま) 100 yen coin

百	円	玉					

貝殻 (かいがら) outer shell

貝	が	ら					

竹の子 (たけのこ) bamboo shoots

竹	の	子					

13 | Fill in the Kanji

Fill in the appropriate kanji in the blanks for each sentence.

くるま　　なか　　　おん

1. ＿＿＿ の ＿＿＿ で ＿＿＿がくを ききます。
   I listen to music in the car.

おお　　　　まち　　　　しゃ　くるま　おと

2. ＿＿＿きい＿＿＿ は でん＿＿＿や ＿＿＿ の＿＿＿が うるさいです。
   In big cities, train and car noises are annoying.

あか　　かい　　よっ　　　　しろ　　かい　いつ　　み

3. ＿＿＿い＿＿＿を＿＿＿つと、＿＿＿い＿＿＿を＿＿＿つ、＿＿＿つけた。
   I found 4 red shells and 5 white shells.

ひゃく　えん　だま　　　　　　　　した　　み

4. ＿＿＿ ＿＿＿ ＿＿＿が つくえの＿＿＿ に ＿＿＿つかりました。
   A 100 yen coin was found under the desk.

ご　がつ　　　く さ　　き

5. ＿＿＿＿＿＿ は、＿＿＿や＿＿＿のいろが きれいです。
   In May, the color of the grass and trees is pretty.

あお　みず たま　　　　　ろく　せん えん

6. ＿＿＿い＿＿＿ ＿＿＿のシャツは、＿＿＿ ＿＿＿ ＿＿＿です。
   The blue polka-dot shirt is 6000 yen.

ち く　りん　　たけ　　こ

7. ＿＿＿ ＿＿＿で ＿＿＿の＿＿＿を さがしました。
   I looked for bamboo shoots in the bamboo woods.

13 | Kanji meaning

Write the following kanji next to its meaning: 玉 文 糸 貝 草 虫 車 竹 音

1. ＿＿＿ shell

2. ＿＿＿ bamboo

3. ＿＿＿ sentence

4. ＿＿＿ thread, string

5. ＿＿＿ sound

6. ＿＿＿ grass

7. ＿＿＿ ball

8. ＿＿＿ bug

9. ＿＿＿ car

13 | Kanji matching

Draw a line to connect each kanji with only one of its ON or KUN readings.

貝 ・   ・ くもく

目 ・   ・ んおん

見 ・   ・ うけん

車 ・   ・ さおう

音 ・   ・ いく

竹 ・   ・ しゃか

草 ・   ・ けた

糸 ・   ・ といい

玉 ・   ・ またた

王 ・   ・

13 | Stroke Order Check

Circle A or B whichever represents the correct stroke order for each kanji.

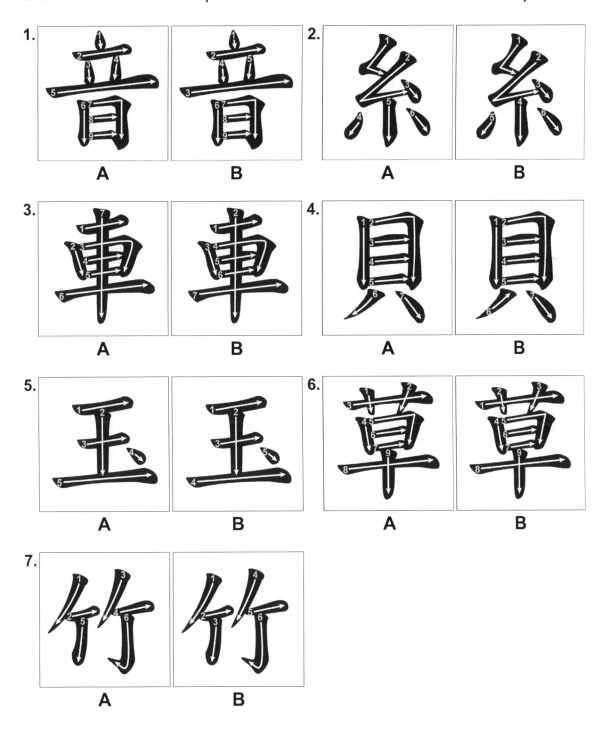

1.　　A　　B

2.　　A　　B

3.　　A　　B

4.　　A　　B

5.　　A　　B

6.　　A　　B

7.　　A　　B

13 | Answer Key 答え合わせ

Fill in the kanji (answers)

1. 車 の 中 で 音 がくを ききます。

2. 大 きい 町 は でん 車 や 車 の 音 が うるさいです。

3. 赤 い 貝 を 四 つと、白 い 貝 を 五 つ、見 つけた。

4. 百円玉 が つくえの 下 に 見 つかりました。

5. 五月 は、草 や 木 のいろが きれいです。

6. 青 い 水玉 のシャツは、六千円 です。

7. 竹林 で 竹 の 子 を さがしました。

Kanji meaning match (answers)

1. 貝 shell
2. 竹 bamboo
3. 文 sentence
4. 糸 thread, string
5. 音 sound
6. 草 grass
7. 玉 ball
8. 虫 bug
9. 車 car

Kanji matching (answers)

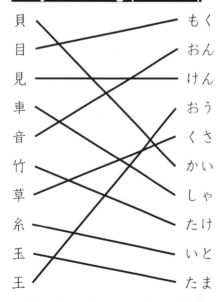

Stroke order check (answers)

1. A   2. B   3. A   4. A   5. B   6. B   7. B

14

Kanji lesson 14:

遠近強弱高楽

14 | New Kanji あたらしい かんじ

Make sure you learn the correct stroke order. Correct stroke order will mean neater symbols when writing quickly. Also, take time to learn the words listed for each kanji – these will help you memorize the different readings.

---

81. far	13 画
くんよみ	とお(い)
おんよみ	エン

far	go for an outing	an excursion	long distance
とお	とおで	えんそく	えんきょり
遠い	遠出	遠足	遠距離

---

82. near, approach, recent	7 画
くんよみ	ちか(い)
おんよみ	キン

close, near	shortcut	recently, most recent	neighborhood
ちか	ちかみち	さいきん	きんじょ
近い	近道	最近	近所

83. strong, strengthen   11画

| くんよみ | つよ(い、まる、める)、し(いる) |
| おんよみ | キョウ、ゴウ |

強 | | | | | | |

strong	to impose	study	force, overbearing
つよ	し	べんきょう	ごういん
強い	強いる	勉強	強引

84. weak   10画

| くんよみ | よわ(い、る、まる、める) |
| おんよみ | ジャク |

弱 | | | | | | |

weak	coward	weak point	strength and weaknesses
よわ	よわむし	じゃくてん	きょうじゃく
弱い	弱虫	弱点	強弱

85. high   10画

| くんよみ | たか(い、まる、める) |
| おんよみ | コウ |

高 | | | | | | |

high, expensive	high-valued yen	high school	high speed
たか	えんだか	こうこう	こうそく
高い	円高	高校	高速

楽	86. enjoyable, comfort, ease			13 画
	くんよみ	たの(しい、しむ)		
	おんよみ	ラク、ガク		
	楽			

enjoyable	to enjoy oneself	music	comfortable
たの	たの	おんがく	きらく
楽しい	楽しむ	音楽	気楽

14 | Kanji Usage かんじの つかいかた

● **14-1. Why does each kanji have multiple ways to read it?**

Prior to Chinese characters being imported into Japan, the Japanese language, at the time called 和語 (わご), had no existing writing system. Existing Japanese words were mapped to the new Chinese characters.

For example: the word "mountain" in native Japanese is YAMA, since Japanese had no writing system they simply connected the existing word to the closest Chinese character. For YAMA, this was the character 山, which was originally read as SAN in Chinese at the time of import.

To further complicate things, in later years different dialects of Chinese were also added, leading to even more readings. Also, in order to accommodate the many Japanese regional dialects, other readings were added. This has led to some kanji characters having multiple くんよみ (native Japanese readings) and multiple おんよみ (imported Chinese readings).

Some kanji, such as 校 (こう) and 王 (おう), only have Chinese readings. Later on, we will learn about original Japanese kanji that don't exist in China.

Additionally, many new words were added to Japanese from the original Chinese as needed. This is similar to how, in modern times, many new words are borrowed from English and added to Japanese.

● **14-2. Getting the most out of (高)**
高 (こう) is used to mean "high" in many words.

<ruby>高<rt>こう</rt></ruby>カロリー   high calorie

<ruby>高<rt>こう</rt>画<rt>が</rt>質<rt>しつ</rt></ruby>   high resolution (photo etc.)

<ruby>高<rt>こう</rt>出<rt>しゅつ</rt>力<rt>りょく</rt></ruby>   high output

<ruby>高<rt>こう</rt>温<rt>おん</rt>度<rt>ど</rt></ruby>   high temperature

<ruby>高<rt>こう</rt>血<rt>けつ</rt>圧<rt>あつ</rt></ruby>   high blood pressure

高速 high speed	
こうそくどうろ 高速道路 freeway, highway, expressway	こうそくてつどう 高速鉄道 high speed rail, rapid transit

高層 multi storied	
こうそう 高層ビル skyscraper	こうそうたいき 高層大気 upper atmosphere

高齢 old age, advanced age	
こうれいしゃ 高齢者 old person	こうれいしゅっさん 高齢出産 late childbearing

14 | Words You Can Write かける ことば

遠い（とおい）far

遠	い								

遠足（えんそく）an excursion

遠	足								

遠出（とおで）an outing

遠	出								

近い（ちかい）close

近	い								

強い（つよい）strong

強	い								

強引（ごういん）forceful

強	引								

強気（つよき）self assured

強	気								

弱い（よわい）weak

弱	い								

弱虫（よわむし）coward, weakling

弱	虫								

高い（たかい）expensive, tall

高	い										

高校（こうこう）high school

高	校										

音楽（おんがく）music

音	楽										

楽しい（たのしい）enjoyable

楽	し	い									

14 | Fill in the Kanji

Fill in the appropriate kanji in the blanks for each sentence.

　　がっこう　　　　　　えんそく

1. ＿＿＿ ＿＿＿のともだちと ＿＿＿ ＿＿＿に いきたい です。
   I want to go on an outing (excursion) with my school friends.

　　　　　　　　　とお　　　　　くるま　に

2. おばあちゃんのうちは ＿＿＿ いです。 ＿＿＿ で＿＿＿じかん です。
   Grandma's house is far. It's two hours by car.

　　た　なか　　　　　　つよ　き

3. ＿＿＿ ＿＿＿ さんは いつも＿＿＿ ＿＿＿ですね。
   Takana-san is always self assured.

　　　　　きん　　　きょう

4. さい ＿＿＿ 、べん ＿＿＿ する じかんが ありません。
   Recently, I don't have time to study.

5.
きょうは ____ おんが ____ い ですね。

き　　　たか

The temperature sure is hot today.

6.
いまのしごとは、とても____ ____ ですよ。

き　らく

My current job is very comfortable.

7.
わたしは けいさんに ____いけど さくぶんに ____い です。

よわ　　　　　　　つよ

I am weak with calculations but I am strong with compositions.

---

14 | Kanji matching

Draw a line to connect each kanji with only one of its ON or KUN readings.

楽 •　　　　　• きん
高 •　　　　　• らく
草 •　　　　　• えん
遠 •　　　　　• よわ
弱 •　　　　　• きょう
文 •　　　　　• な
強 •　　　　　• こう
近 •　　　　　• ぶん
正 •　　　　　• しょう
名 •　　　　　• そう

14 | Kanji meaning

Write the following kanji next to its meaning: 遠 青 近 竹 強 弱 糸 高 楽

1. ____ high

2. ____ thread

3. ____ far

4. ____ enjoyable

5. ____ bamboo

6. ____ close

7. ____ weak

8. ____ strong

9. ____ blue

14 | Stroke Order Check

Circle A or B whichever represents the correct stroke order for each kanji.

1.

A   B

2.

A   B

3.

A   B

4.

A   B

5.

A   B

6.

A   B

14 | Answer Key 答え合わせ

Fill in the kanji (answers)

1. 学校 のともだちと 遠足 にいきたい です。

2. おばあちゃんのうちは 遠 いです。 車 で 二 じかん です。

3. 田中 さんはいつも 強気 ですね。

4. さい 近 、べん 強 するじかんが ありません。

5. きょうは 気 おんが 高 い ですね。

6. いまのしごとは、とても 気楽 ですよ。

7. わたしは けいさんに 弱 いけど さくぶんに 強 い です。

Kanji meaning match (answers)

1. 高 high
2. 糸 thread
3. 遠 far
4. 楽 enjoyable
5. 竹 bamboo
6. 近 close
7. 弱 weak
8. 強 strong
9. 青 blue

Kanji matching (answers)

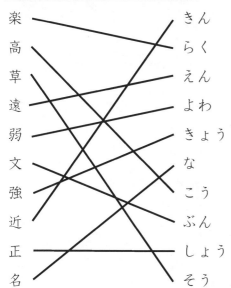

楽	きん
高	らく
草	えん
遠	よわ
弱	きょう
文	な
強	こう
近	ぶん
正	しょう
名	そう

Stroke order check (answers)

1. A 2. A 3. A 4. A 5. A 6. A

15

Kanji lesson 15:

87-92

親新古多少明

---

15 | New Kanji あたらしい かんじ

Make sure you learn the correct stroke order. Correct stroke order will mean neater symbols when writing quickly. Also, take time to learn the words listed for each kanji – these will help you memorize the different readings.

親	**87. parent, intimate**			16 画
	くんよみ	おや、した(しい、しむ)		
	おんよみ	シン		
	親			

parent	close, familiar	kind	close friend
おや	した	しんせつ	しんゆう
親	親しい	親切	親友

新	**88. new, fresh, novel**			13 画
	くんよみ	あたら(しい)、あら(た)、にい		
	おんよみ	シン		
	新			

new	newly	newspaper	new year
あたら	あら	しんぶん	しんねん
新しい	新たに	新聞	新年

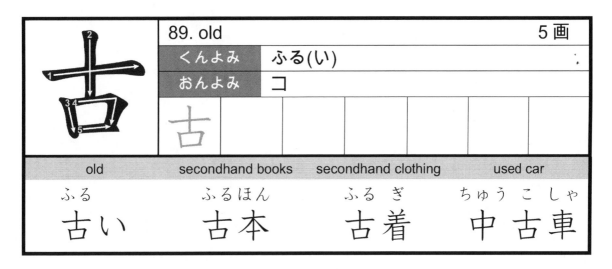

89. old			5 画
くんよみ	ふる(い)		
おんよみ	コ		

old	secondhand books	secondhand clothing	used car
ふる	ふるほん	ふるぎ	ちゅうこしゃ
古い	古本	古着	中古車

90. many, much, multiple			6 画
くんよみ	おお(い)		
おんよみ	タ		

many	more than average	probably	more or less
おお	おお	たぶん	たしょう
多い	多め	多分	多少

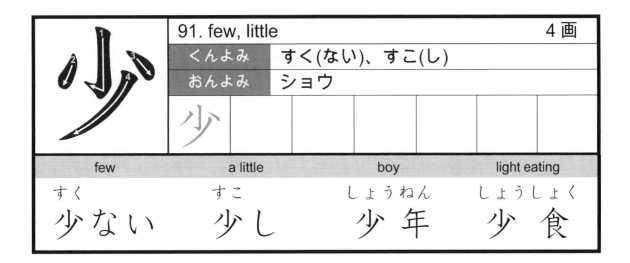

91. few, little			4 画
くんよみ	すく(ない)、すこ(し)		
おんよみ	ショウ		

few	a little	boy	light eating
すく	すこ	しょうねん	しょうしょく
少ない	少し	少年	少食

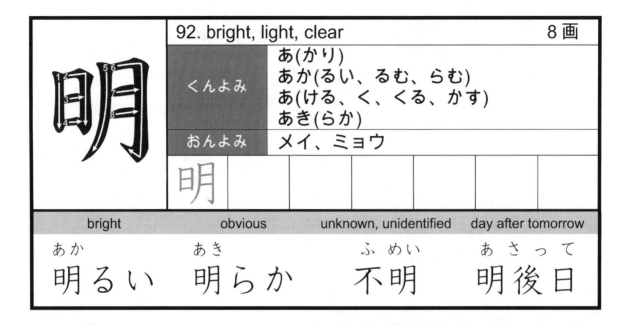

92. bright, light, clear					8画
くんよみ	あ(かり) あか(るい、るむ、らむ) あ(ける、く、くる、かす) あき(らか)				
おんよみ	メイ、ミョウ				
明					

bright	obvious	unknown, unidentified	day after tomorrow
あか 明るい	あき 明らか	ふめい 不明	あさって 明後日

---

15 | Kanji Usage かんじの つかいかた

● **15-1. Opposites attract in compound kanji**

Often, two kanji with opposite meanings are contained in compound words.

きょう じゃく **強弱** degree of strength, stress (of sound) (strong + weak)	た しょう **多少** somewhat, a little (many + few)

えいご　　はな　　とききょうじゃく　いしき　　はな　　　　しぜん
1.　英語を話す時 強 弱 を意識して話せばより自然に

き
聞こえます。

You will sound more natural if you pay attention to English stressing when you speak English.

きょうじゃく　　かんち
2.　あるスマホはタッチの 強 弱 を感知できます。

Some smartphones are able to sense touch strength.

3. 多少の誤差は仕方ないです。
<small>た しょう ご さ し かた</small>

Small measurement errors can't be helped.

4. 会議に多少遅れるかもしれないです。
<small>かい ぎ た しょうおく</small>

I might be a little late for the meeting.

えん きん 遠近	しろ くろ 白黒
far and near, perspective (far + close)	black and white, right and wrong, settle, make clear (white + black)

5. 私のメガネは遠近レンズが入っています。
<small>わたし えんきんれ ん ず はい</small>

My eyeglasses use a progressive lens (perspective lens).

6. この絵は遠近感があっていいですね。
<small>え えんきんかん</small>

This painting is nice since it has a sense of perspective.

7. 白黒テレビの時代が懐かしいです。
<small>しろくろ じ だい なつ</small>

The era of black and white television is nostalgic.

8. どちらが正しいか白黒をつけよう。
<small>ただ しろくろ</small>

Let's make it clear which is correct.

だん じょ 男女	せい し 生死
men and women, both sexes (man + woman)	life and death (birth + death)

9. この公園のトイレは男女に分かれていません。
The toilets in this park aren't separated into men and women.

10. 同じ仕事で女性の 給料 が男性より低い時は
男女差別だと思う人が多いです。
Many people think when a woman's salary is lower than a man's, for the same work, it's gender discrimination.

11. 医者は生死に関わるミスを防がなければならない。
Doctors must avoid life (and death) threatening mistakes.

12. 自分の生死は自分で判断出来るものではない。
Your own life and death isn't something you can decide by yourself.

手足	天下
hands and feet, limbs (hand + foot)	whole world, whole country, under the sun (heaven + below)

13. 変な位置で寝て手足がしびれました。
I slept in a strange position and my hands and feet went numb.

14. 彼は手足が不自由だ。
His hands and feet are disabled (impaired).

15. 日本のお米は天下一美味しいです。
Japanese rice is the most delicious in the whole world.

16. 日本の戦国時代に織田信長は天下を取りました。
During Japan's war period, Nobunaga Oda took control of the entire country.

● **15-2. Same kanji different reading (明日)**

Kanji can sometimes be read different ways. Neither way is wrong, but sometimes the nuance and meaning can change. Knowing which way something is read is based on the surrounding context.

tomorrow (more written)	tomorrow (more spoken)	tomorrow (most polite)
明日	明日	明日
あ・す	あした	みょう・にち

nowadays, in this day and age	today	good afternoon
今日	今日	今日は
こん・にち	きょう	こん・にち・は(わ)

15 | Words You Can Write かける ことば

親友 （しんゆう) best friend

親	友									

新年 （しんねん) new year

新	年									

古い （ふるい) old

古	い									

古本（ふるほん）used book

古	本										

多少（たしょう）more or less

多	少										

多い（おおい）many

多	い										

少し（すこし）a little bit

少	し										

少年（しょうねん）boy, juvenile, young boy

少	年										

明日（あした・あす）tomorrow

明	日										

親しい（したしい）intimate, close

親	し	い						

新しい（あたらしい）new

新	し	い						

明るい（あかるい）bright

明	る	い						

15 | Fill in the Kanji

Fill in the appropriate kanji in the blanks for each sentence.

　　おや　　　　　　　　　　づよ

1. ＿＿＿ がいるから、こころ＿＿＿い です。

Because my parents are around, I am reassured.

　　しん ねん　 ふる

2. ＿＿＿ ＿＿＿に ＿＿＿い おてらに いきました。

In the new year I went to some old temples.

　　　　　　　に　ほん　　　　　　　　　　おお

3. きょうの＿＿＿ ＿＿＿ ごの しゅくだいは ＿＿＿い ですね。

There is a lot of Japanese homework today.

　　あし　　　　　すこ

4. ＿＿＿くび が ＿＿＿ し いたい です。

My ankle hurts a little.

　　　　　　　あき　　　　せん せい

5. このばあいは＿＿＿ らかに ＿＿＿ ＿＿＿が わるい ですよ。

In this case, the teacher is obviously wrong.

　　　　　　　　た しょう　　らく

6. このごろ、しごとが＿＿＿ ＿＿＿ 、＿＿＿に なりました。

Recently, work has gotten a little comfortable (easy).

　　　　あたら　　　　　　　ちか

7. わたしの ＿＿＿ しいうちは、えきに＿＿＿ くて べんり です。

My new home, being close to the station, is convenient.

15 | Kanji meaning

Write the following kanji next to its meaning: 親 明 赤 少 早 多 古 町 新

1.____ new

2. ____ many

3. ____ bright

4. ____ parent

5. ____ few

6. ____ red

7. ____ old

8. ____ early

9. ____ town

15 | Kanji matching

Draw a line to connect each kanji with only one of its ON or KUN readings.

明 ・   ・ お や
多 ・   ・ こ う
親 ・   ・ め い
古 ・   ・ あ た ら
弱 ・   ・ え ん
校 ・   ・ お お
少 ・   ・ こ わ
新 ・   ・ よ く
字 ・   ・ す じ
遠 ・   ・ じ

15 | Stroke Order Check

Circle A or B whichever represents the correct stroke order for each kanji.

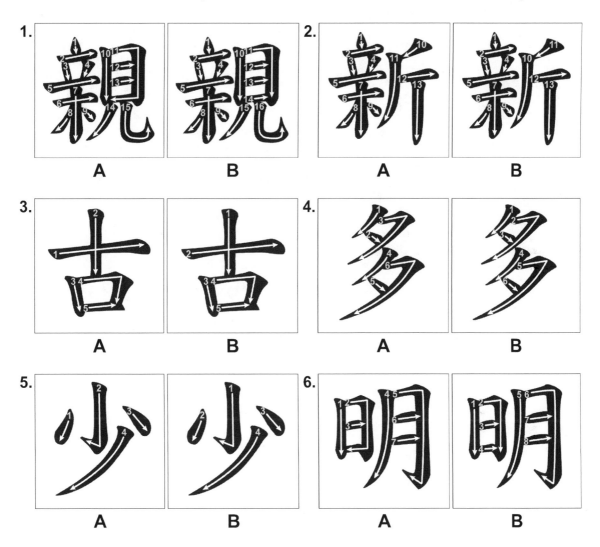

15 | Answer Key 答え合わせ

Fill in the kanji (answers)

1. 親 がいるから、こころ 強 い です。

2. 新年 に 古 いおてらに いきました。

3. きょうの 日本 ごのしゅくだいは 多 い ですね。

4. 足 くびが 少 し、いたい です。

5. このばあいは 明 らかに 先生 がわるい ですよ。

6. このごろ、しごとが 多少 、楽 に なりました。

7. わたしの 新 しいうちは、えきに 近 くてべんり です。

Kanji meaning match (answers)

1. 新 new   2. 多 many   3. 明 bright

4. 親 parent   5. 少 few   6. 赤 red

7. 古 old   8. 早 early   9. 町 town

Kanji matching (answers)

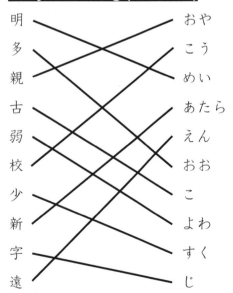

明	おや
多	こう
親	めい
古	あたら
弱	えん
校	おお
少	こ
新	よわ
字	すく
遠	じ

Stroke order check (answers)

1. B   2. A   3. A   4. B   5. B   6. B

SR Super Review 3

SR3 | Kanji selection

Select the best kanji to fill in the blank in each sentence.

1. わたしの名____は スミス です。
   A. 学　　　　　　B. 正　　　　　　C. 田　　　　　　D. 字

2. むすめは ことし、六____生に なります。
   A. 年　　　　　　B. 学　　　　　　C. 子　　　　　　D. 校

3. ここは____口 ですか。出口 ですか。
   A. 入　　　　　　B. 人　　　　　　C. 犬　　　　　　D. 下

4. わたしのちちは、強くて____しい人 です。
   A. 遠　　　　　　B. 楽　　　　　　C. 弱　　　　　　D. 明

SR3 | Kanji reading

Select the best reading for the underlined kanji.

1. わたしのあねは、高校生 です。
   A. たか　　　　　B. ちか　　　　　C. こう　　　　　D. ここ

2. ひろしくんは 文字を かいています。
   A. ぶん　　　　　B. も　　　　　　C. もん　　　　　D. ふみ

3. 夏休みに 海に いって、たくさん貝を ひろいました。
   A. め　　　　　　B. いし　　　　　C. かい　　　　　D. むし

4. わたしと おとうとは、年子 です。
   A. とし　　　　　B. ねん　　　　　C. どし　　　　　D. せい

SR3 | Compound kanji word puzzle

Fill in the correct kanji based on the list below the puzzle.

1)			2)
3)	4)	5)	
6)	7)	8)	
			9)

Down ↓

2) last name

3) three pairs (of socks/shoes)

5) literature

6) footsteps (sound)

7) polka dots

Left to Right →

1) Japanese person

4) small letter (of alphabet)

8) school

Right to Left ←

2) master, expert

9) 100 yen coin

SR3 | Answer Key 答え合わせ

Kanji selection (answers)

1. D – 名字
（みょうじ）

My last name is Smith.

2. A – 六年生
（ろくねんせい）

My daughter becomes a 6th grader this year.

3. A – 入口
（いりぐち）

Is this the entrance? Is it the exit?

4. C – 楽しい
（たの）

My father is strong and fun.

Kanji reading (answers)

1. C – 高校生
（こうこうせい）

My older sister is a high school student.

2. B – 文字
（もじ）

Hiroshi is writing letters.

3. C – 貝
（かい）

On my summer vacation I went to the beach and picked up a lot of shells.

4. A – 年子
（としご）

My brother and I were born within one year of each other.

Compound kanji word puzzle (answers)

日	本	人	名
三	小	文	字
足	水	学	校
音	玉	円	百

16 Kanji lesson 16:
93-98

広太細丸長元

16 | New Kanji あたらしい かんじ

Make sure you learn the correct stroke order. Correct stroke order will mean neater symbols when writing quickly. Also, take time to learn the words listed for each kanji – these will help you memorize the different readings.

広	93. wide, broad, spread						5画
	くんよみ	ひろ(い、まる、める、がる、げる)					
	おんよみ	コウ					
	広						

spacious	to spread out	plaza	advertisement
ひろ	ひろ	ひろ ば	こうこく
広い	広がる	広場	広告

太	94. big, fat, thick						4画
	くんよみ	ふと(い、る)					
	おんよみ	タイ、タ					
	太						

think, fat	to get fat	sun	drum
ふと	ふと	たいよう	たい こ
太い	太る	太陽	太鼓

95. narrow, thin, fine　　11画

くんよみ	ほそ(い、る)、こま(か、かい)
おんよみ	サイ

fine, thin	small, minute, delicate	lonely	bacterium
ほそ 細い	こま 細かい	こころぼそ 心細い	さいきん 細菌

96. round, ball　　3画

くんよみ	まる、まる(い、める)
おんよみ	ガン

round, circular	round face	whole	log
まる 丸い	まるがお 丸顔	まる 丸ごと	まる た 丸太

97. long, far, chief　　8画

くんよみ	なが(い)
おんよみ	チョウ

long	height (people)	principal	merit
なが 長い	しんちょう 身長	こうちょう 校長	ちょうしょ 長所

元	98. origin, cause					4画
	くんよみ	もと				
	おんよみ	ゲン、ガン				
	元					

origin of fire	New Year's Day	energetic, vigor, healthy	local
ひ　もと	がんじつ	げん　き	じ　もと
火の元	元日	元気	地元

---

16 | Kanji Usage かんじの つかいかた

● **16-1. Things that have a past (元)**

元 is used in many common everyday words you will hear with friends or on the news.

ex-boyfriend	ex-girlfriend
元彼	元彼女
もと・かれ	もと・かのじょ

ex-wife	ex-husband
元妻	元夫
もと・つま	もと・おっと

ex-president	former prime-minister
元大統領	元首相
もと・だいとうりょう	もと・しゅしょう

● **16-2. The "thread" radical いとへん**

Kanji with the いとへん radical don't always seem to connect with "thread." Here are some common kanji and words using the いとへん radical.

thin, detailed	line, track

thin, detailed

ほそ
細い (thin)

こま
細かい (intricate)

しょうさい
詳細 (details)

line, track

せん い
線維 (fibers)

ち へいせん
地平線 (horizon)

でんせん
電線 (electric lines)

cotton

わたあめ
綿飴 (cotton candy)

めんぼう
綿棒 (cotton swab)

めんみつ
綿密 (detailed, thorough)

paper

かみぶくろ
紙袋 (paper bag)

て がみ
手紙 (letter, note)

よう し
用紙 (blank form)

picture, painting

え ほん
絵本 (picture book)

ぬ え
塗り絵 (coloring book)

え
絵はがき (pic. post card)

elementary, principle

そ ざい
素材 (materials)

よう そ
要素 (component)

す てき
素敵 (lovely, great)

purple, violet

むらさきいろ
紫色 (purple color)

し がいせん
紫外線 (ultra-violet rays)

ふかむらさき
深紫 (deep purple)

continue, series

れんぞく
連続 (consecutive)

ぞくへん
続編 (sequel)

つづ
続き (continuation)

green

りょくちゃ
緑茶 (green tea)

き みどり
黄緑 (yellow-green)

あおみどり
青緑 (blue-green)

class, grade, rank

こう きゅう
高級 (high class)

じょうきゅう
上級 (advanced)

しょきゅう
初級 (beginner)

● 16-3. Two types of round 丸い vs 円い

In lesson 5 we learned 円 which shares a reading with 丸. Both of these kanji can mean "round."

round	round
丸い	円い
まる・い	まる・い

There is a key difference though.

(円) Used for FLAT or 2D round objects		
round shape, circle	circumference	round table
円形	円周	円卓
えん・けい	えん・しゅう	えん・たく

(丸) Used for SPHERICAL or 3D objects		
bullet, shot, shell	buzz cut (haircut)	round pill
弾丸	丸刈り	丸薬
だん・がん	まる・がり	がん・やく

In some cases 丸 and 円 can both be used, if you occasionally mix up 丸 and 円 when the reading is まる don't worry… because you are JUST LIKE many Japanese people.

(丸) and (円) are often interchangeable	
round, circular	round face
円型/丸型	丸顔/円顔
まる・がた	まる・がお

● 16-4. Completely (丸)

丸 means "round" in many words but it is also used in other heavily used words that mean "completely" or "entirely."

(丸) Used to show ENTIRE periods of time	
a whole month	**an entire year**
丸一ヶ月	丸一年
まる・いっ・か・げつ	まる・いち・ねん
an entire day	**a complete hour**
丸一日	丸一時間
まる・いち・にち	まる・いち・じ・かん

(丸) Used to show words that indicate completeness	
completely revealed, exposed	**completely (adverb)**
丸出し	丸っきり
まる・だし	まる・っきり
complete ruin	**copying in entirety**
丸つぶれ	丸写し
まる・つぶれ	まる・うつし
rote memorization, rote learning	**full view, plain sight**
丸暗記	丸見え
まる・あんき	まる・みえ

BONUS: In the same way ships are often named *SS Minnow* with the "SS" in front of the boat name, Japanese often name boats with 丸 (まる) at the end.

BONUS #2: The red circle on the Japanese flag is called 日の丸 (ひのまる) and it means "the sun."

16 | Words You Can Write かける ことば

広い（ひろい）spacious, wide

広	い								

太い（ふとい）thick, fat

太	い								

太る（ふとる）to grow fat

太	る								

丸太（まるた）log

丸	太								

長い（ながい）long

長	い								

元日（がんじつ）New Year's Day

元	日							

元気（げんき）energetic, vigor, healthy

元	気							

広める（ひろめる）to broadcast, to spread around

広	め	る						

細かい（こまかい）small, minute, delicate

細	か	い						

丸ごと（まるごと）whole

丸	ご	と									

16 | Fill in the Kanji

Fill in the appropriate kanji in the blanks for each sentence.

あたら　　　　　　ひろ　　あか

1. わたしの ＿＿＿ しいいえは、＿＿＿くて ＿＿＿るい ですよ。
   My new house is spacious and bright.

ふと

2. たくさん たべると、＿＿＿ ってしまいます。
   If you eat a lot you will end up being fat.

こま　　　　　　　　　き　　　　くだ

3. ＿＿＿かいしごとだから、＿＿＿ を つけて＿＿＿さい。
   Since it's detailed work please be careful.

あか　　　　まる

4. あの ＿＿＿ ちゃんは ＿＿＿ がおで、とてもかわいいです。
   That baby is very cute because it has a round face.

やす　　なが

5. アメリカのなつ＿＿＿ みは ＿＿＿ くて いいですね。
   It's nice that American summer vacations are long.

まる　　　　た

6. ケーキを ＿＿＿ ごと ＿＿＿べてしまいました。
   I ended up eating the whole cake.

はや　げん　き　　　　くだ

7. ＿＿＿ く ＿＿＿ ＿＿＿に なって＿＿＿さい。
   Please get healthy soon.

16 | Kanji meaning

Write the following kanji next to its meaning: 広 貝 太 森 細 長 見 元 丸

1. ＿＿＿ round   2. ＿＿＿ narrow, thin   3. ＿＿＿ big, fat

4. ＿＿＿ long   5. ＿＿＿ to watch   6. ＿＿＿ forest

7. ＿＿＿ shell   8. ＿＿＿ wide, broad   9. ＿＿＿ the origin

16 | Kanji matching

Draw a line to connect each kanji with only one of its ON or KUN readings.

元 •	• まる
長 •	• ふ と ん
赤 •	• そ ん
丸 •	• げ ん
細 •	• け ん そ
太 •	• ほ そ
犬 •	• で
広 •	• せ き
村 •	• ち ょ う
出 •	• ひ ろ

16 | Stroke Order Check

Circle A or B whichever represents the correct stroke order for each kanji.

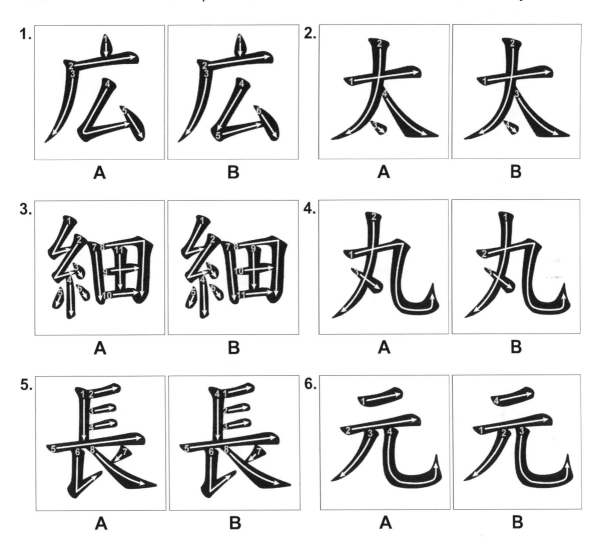

1. A   B
2. A   B
3. A   B
4. A   B
5. A   B
6. A   B

16 | Answer Key 答え合わせ

Fill in the kanji (answers)

1. わたしの 新 しいいえは、 広 くて 明 るい ですよ。

2. たくさんたべると、 太 ってしまいます。

3. 細 かいしごとだから、 気 をつけて 下 さい。

4. あの 赤 ちゃんは 丸 がおで、とてもかわいいです。

5. アメリカのなつ 休 みは 長 くていいですね。

6. ケーキを 丸 ごとたべてしまいました。

7. 早 く 元気 になって 下 さい。

Kanji meaning match (answers)

1. 丸 round
2. 細 narrow, thin
3. 太 big, fat
4. 長 long
5. 見 to watch
6. 森 forest
7. 貝 shell
8. 広 wide, broad
9. 元 the origin

Kanji matching (answers)

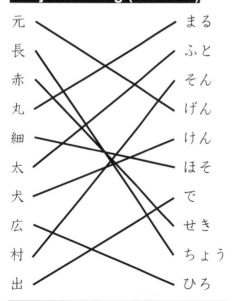

元　　　　　まる
長　　　　　ふと
赤　　　　　そん
丸　　　　　げん
細　　　　　けん
太　　　　　ほそ
犬　　　　　で
広　　　　　せき
村　　　　　ちょう
出　　　　　ひろ

Stroke order check (answers)

1. A　2. B　3. B　4. B　5. A　6. A

17

Kanji lesson 17:

99-104

通走歩行来帰

17 | New Kanji あたらしい かんじ

Make sure you learn the correct stroke order. Correct stroke order will mean neater symbols when writing quickly. Also, take time to learn the words listed for each kanji – these will help you memorize the different readings.

通	**99. pass, go to and from**			10 画
	くんよみ	とお(る、す)、かよ(う)		
	おんよみ	ツウ、ツ		
	通			

to commute	path	commuting to work	funeral wake
かよ	とお　みち	つうきん	つ　や
通う	通り道	通勤	通夜

走	**100. run**			7 画
	くんよみ	はし(る)		
	おんよみ	ソウ		
	走			

to run	runner	get-away, escape	substitute runner
はし	そうしゃ	とうそう	だいそう
走る	走者	逃走	代走

101. walk, step, rate — 8画

くんよみ	ある(く)、あゆ(む)
おんよみ	ホ、ブ、フ

歩

to walk	step, progress	pedestrian	a walk
ある 歩く	あゆ 歩み	ほ こうしゃ 歩行者	さん ぽ 散歩

102. go, do, conduct, stroke — 6画

くんよみ	い(く)、ゆ(く)、おこな(う)
おんよみ	コウ、ギョウ

行

to go	to perform	bank	line up, line
い 行く	おこな 行う	ぎんこう 銀行	ぎょうれつ 行列

103. come, next, since — 7画

くんよみ	く(る)、きた(る、す)
おんよみ	ライ

来

to come	next year	future	houseguest
く 来る	らいねん 来年	み らい 未来	らいきゃく 来客

帰	104. return		10 画
	くんよみ	かえ(す、る)	
	おんよみ	キ	

帰						

to return	the way back	returning home	return, comeback
かえ	かえ　みち	き たく	ふっ き
帰る	帰り道	帰宅	復帰

17 Kanji Usage かんじの つかいかた

● **17-1. Connecting with 通**

通 is used in many words that you might hear in conversation or on TV.

transmission, communication	normal
通信	普通
つう・しん	ふ・つう

interpreter, interpretation	notification
通訳	通知
つう・やく	つう・ち

common, general, usual	passage, pathway, aisle
通常	通路
つう・じょう	つう・ろ

● 17-2. The "crossroads" radical ぎょうにんべん

The ぎょうにんべん radical represents a "crossroads" and means "walking little by little." As stated before, knowing the radical alone, doesn't really help to immediately understand the underlying meaning of any character.

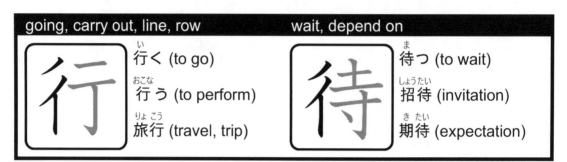

going, carry out, line, row

行く (to go)
行う (to perform)
旅行 (travel, trip)

wait, depend on

待つ (to wait)
招待 (invitation)
期待 (expectation)

behind, later

後ろ (behind, back)
後悔 (regret)
後半 (second half)

restore, revert, resume

復活 (revival)
往復 (round trip)
復習 (review)

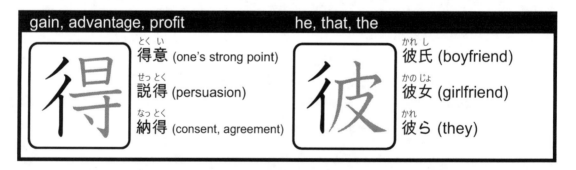

gain, advantage, profit

得意 (one's strong point)
説得 (persuasion)
納得 (consent, agreement)

he, that, the

彼氏 (boyfriend)
彼女 (girlfriend)
彼ら (they)

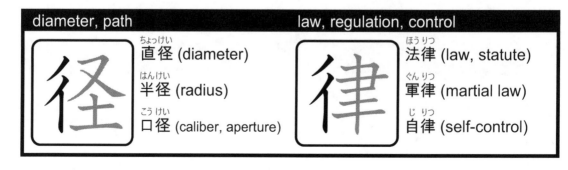

diameter, path

直径 (diameter)
半径 (radius)
口径 (caliber, aperture)

law, regulation, control

法律 (law, statute)
軍律 (martial law)
自律 (self-control)

17 | Words You Can Write かける ことば

通う（かよう）to commute

通	う								

走る（はしる）to run

走	る								

歩く（あるく）to walk

歩	く								

行く（いく）to go

行	く								

来る（くる）to come

来	る								

来年（らいねん）next year

来	年								

帰る（かえる）to return

帰	る								

大通り（おおどおり）broadway, main street

大	通	り					

日帰り（ひがえり）day trip

日	帰	り					

17 | Fill in the Kanji

Fill in the appropriate kanji in the blanks for each sentence.

しゃ　がっ こう　　かよ
1. わたしは でん＿＿で ＿＿ ＿＿に ＿＿ っています。
   I am commuting to school by train.

ゆう　　　　おお どお
2. あしたの ＿＿がた 、 ＿＿ ＿＿りで おまつりが あります。
   Tomorrow evening there is a festival on the main street.

だい がく　　　はし
3. ＿＿ ＿＿ まで ＿＿ りましたが、 ちこくしました。
   I ran to college, but I was late.

やま だ　　　　　にち さん じっ　　　ある
4. ＿＿ ＿＿さんは まい＿＿ ＿＿ ＿＿ぷん、 ＿＿ いてます。
   Yamada san walks 30 minutes every day.

い　　　　　　　　　　　き
5. わたしが＿＿ きましょうか。 それとも、 ＿＿てくれますか。
   Shall I go? Or will you come here?

らい ねん　　あか　　とし
6. ＿＿ ＿＿は、 ＿＿ るい＿＿に なりそうですね。
   It seems next year will be a good (bright) year.

ひ　がえ
7. とうきょうに ＿＿ ＿＿り りょこうしましょう。
   Let's take a day trip to Tokyo.

17 | Kanji meaning

Write the following kanji next to its meaning: 通 帰 広 歩 少 来 親 行 走

1. ____ return

2. ____ spacious

3. ____ go

4. ____ come

5. ____ walk

6. ____ pass

7. ____ few

8. ____ parent

9. ____ run

17 | Kanji matching

Draw a line to connect each kanji with only one of its ON or KUN readings.

帰 •   • き

行 •   • い

楽 •   • ほ

通 •   • そ

歩 •   • き　う
　　　　　　　　　　　　　　　ょ
　　　　　　　　　　　　　　　う

高 •   • と　お
　　　　　　　　　　　　　　　　　う

走 •   • こ　ん

来 •   • し

新 •   • く

強 •   • ら　く

17 | Stroke Order Check

Circle A or B whichever represents the correct stroke order for each kanji.

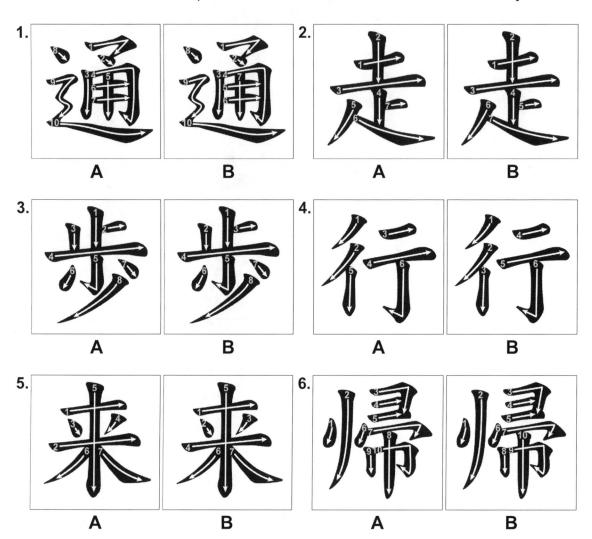

17 Answer Key 答え合わせ

Fill in the kanji (answers)

1. わたしは でん車で学校に通っています。

2. あしたの夕がた、大通りでおまつりが あります。

3. 大学まで走りましたが、ちこくしました。

4. 山田さんはまい日三十ぷん、歩いています。

5. わたしが行きましょうか。それとも、来てくれますか。

6. 来年は、明るい年に なりそうですね。

7. とうきょうに日帰りりょこうしましょう。

Kanji meaning match (answers)

1. 帰 return	2. 広 spacious	3. 行 go
4. 来 come	5. 歩 walk	6. 通 pass
7. 少 few	8. 親 parent	9. 走 run

Kanji matching (answers)

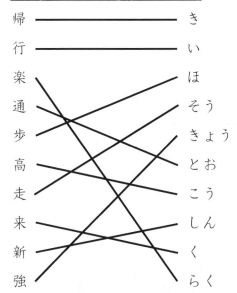

帰 ——— き
行 ——— い
楽 ほ
通 そう
歩 きょう
高 とお
走 こう
来 しん
新 く
強 らく

Stroke order check (answers)

1. A   2. B   3. A   4. B   5. B   6. B

18

Kanji lesson 18:

思教数歌売買

18 | New Kanji あたらしい かんじ

Make sure you learn the correct stroke order. Correct stroke order will mean neater symbols when writing quickly. Also, take time to learn the words listed for each kanji – these will help you memorize the different readings.

105. think, thought, idea — 9画

くんよみ	おも(う)
おんよみ	シ

思

to think	memories	willingness, intention	thought, thinking
おも 思う	おも で 思い出	い し 意思	し こう 思考

106. teach, instruction — 11画

くんよみ	おし(える)、おそ(わる)
おんよみ	キョウ

教

to teach	to be taught	classroom	textbook
おし 教える	おそ 教わる	きょうしつ 教室	きょう か しょ 教科書

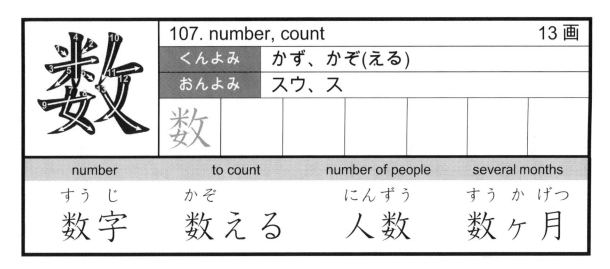

107. number, count   13画

くんよみ	かず、かぞ(える)
おんよみ	スウ、ス

number	to count	number of people	several months
すうじ	かぞ	にんずう	すう か げつ
数字	数える	人数	数ヶ月

108. song   14画

くんよみ	うた(う)
おんよみ	カ

to sing	singing voice	singer	national anthem
うた	うたごえ	か しゅ	こっか
歌う	歌声	歌手	国歌

109. sell   7画

くんよみ	う(る、れる)
おんよみ	バイ

to sell	seller	business, trade	new product or model
う	う て	しょうばい	しんはつばい
売る	売り手	商売	新発売

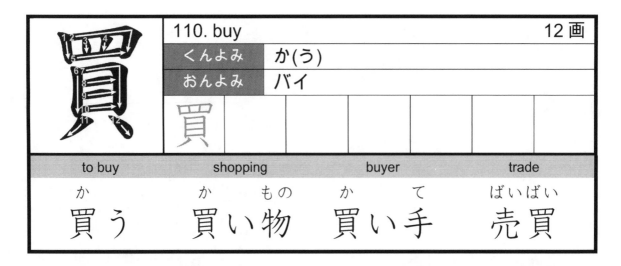

110. buy				12 画
くんよみ	か(う)			
おんよみ	バイ			
買				

to buy	shopping	buyer	trade
か	か　もの	か　て	ばいばい
買う	買い物	買い手	売買

18 | Kanji Usage　かんじの　つかいかた

● 18-1. The religion of kanji (教)

The kanji for religion revolves around the kanji 教 which means "teaching." The word for religion in Japanese is 宗教 (しゅう・きょう) and is made up of the kanji for "sect" and "teach." The word for church is 教会 (きょう・かい) made up of "teach" and "meet / group."

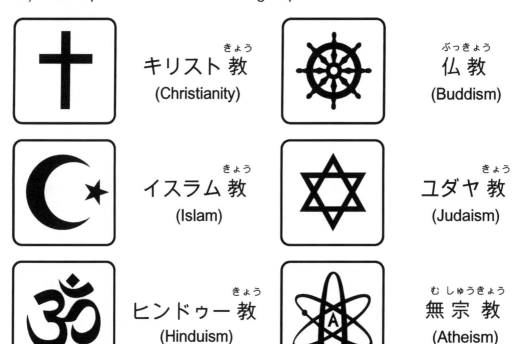

きょう
キリスト 教
(Christianity)

ぶっきょう
仏教
(Buddism)

きょう
イスラム 教
(Islam)

きょう
ユダヤ 教
(Judaism)

きょう
ヒンドゥー 教
(Hinduism)

む　しゅうきょう
無宗教
(Atheism)

18 | **Words You Can Write** かける ことば

思う（おもう）to think

思	う								

数字（すうじ）number

数	字								

歌う（うたう）to sing

歌	う								

歌手（かしゅ）singer

歌	手								

買う（かう）to buy

買	う								

売る（うる）to sell

売	る								

売買（ばいばい）trade

売	買								

教える（おしえる）to teach

教	え	る					

数える（かぞえる）to count

数	え	る					

買い手（かいて）buyer

買	い	手									

売り手（うりて）seller

売	り	手									

18 | Fill in the Kanji

Fill in the appropriate kanji in the blanks for each sentence.

　　　　　　　やす　　　　　　　　　おも　　で
1. このなつ ＿＿＿ みに、たくさんの＿＿＿ い＿＿＿ が できました。
   I made many memories this summer vacation.

　　　せん せい　　　　　　　　　　おし
2. ＿＿＿ ＿＿＿ は どんなきょうかを ＿＿＿ えていますか。
   What subjects are you (teacher) teaching.

　　　た　なか　　　　　うた
3. ＿＿＿ ＿＿＿ さんの ＿＿＿ごえは きれい ですね。
   Tanaka's singing voice is pretty.

　　　　　　　　　　　　　　　　　う　　　　　か
4. コンサートのチケットは ぜんぶ＿＿＿ れて、＿＿＿ えませんでした。
   All of the concert tickets were sold out and I wasn't able to buy them.

　　　こ　　　　　かず　かぞ
5. お＿＿＿ さんは、＿＿＿ を ＿＿＿ えるのが はやい ですね。
   Your children sure are fast at counting numbers.

　　　　　　　　　か　　　て
6. わたしのうちの＿＿＿ い ＿＿＿ が いなくて、こまっています。
   I am troubled because there isn't a buyer for my house.

おん がく　せん せい　　おし　　　　じょう ず
7. ＿＿＿ ＿＿＿の＿＿＿ ＿＿＿は、＿＿＿ えるのが ＿＿＿ ＿＿＿です。
The music teacher is skilled at teaching.

18 | Kanji meaning

Write the following kanji next to its meaning: 思 近 数 多 歌 遠 売 教 買

1.＿＿＿ buy

2. ＿＿＿ number

3. ＿＿＿ many

4. ＿＿＿ sell

5. ＿＿＿ think

6. ＿＿＿ far

7. ＿＿＿ song

8. ＿＿＿ close

9. ＿＿＿ teach

18 | Kanji matching

Draw a line to connect each kanji with only one of its ON or KUN readings.

元 ・　　　　　・ こ
丸 ・　　　　　・ きょう
思 ・　　　　　・ がん
教 ・　　　　　・ うた
数 ・　　　　　・ えん
買 ・　　　　　・ か
古 ・　　　　　・ う
遠 ・　　　　　・ かず
売 ・　　　　　・ おも
歌 ・　　　　　・ まる

18 | Stroke Order Check

Circle A or B whichever represents the correct stroke order for each kanji.

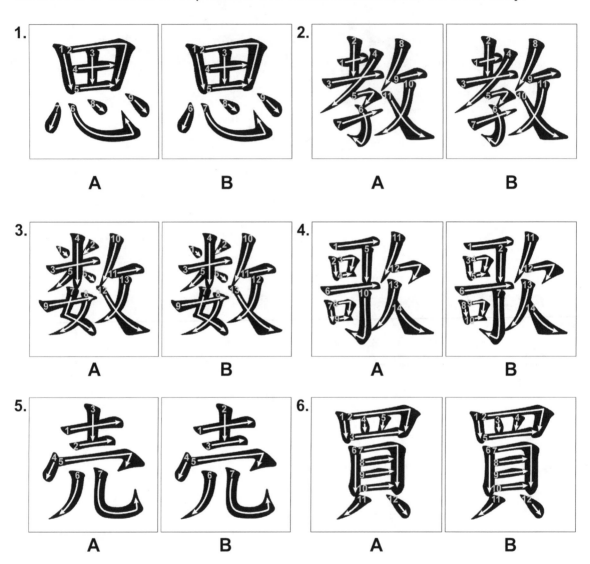

1.   A   B   2.   A   B

3.   A   B   4.   A   B

5.   A   B   6.   A   B

18 | Answer Key 答え合わせ

Fill in the kanji (answers)

1. このなつ休みに、たくさんの思い出が できました。

2. 先生はどんなきょうかを教えていますか。

3. 田中さんの歌ごえはきれい ですね。

4. コンサートのチケットは ぜんぶ売れて、買えませんでした。

5. お子さんは、数を数えるのが はやい ですね。

6. わたしのうちの買い手が いなくて、こまっています。

7. 音楽の先生は、教えるのが上手です。

Kanji meaning match (answers)

1. 買 buy	2. 数 number	3. 多 many
4. 売 sell	5. 思 think	6. 遠 far
7. 歌 song	8. 近 close	9. 教 teach

Kanji matching (answers)

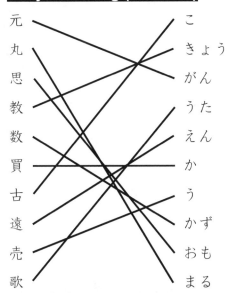

元　　　　こ
丸　　　　きょう
思　　　　がん
教　　　　うた
数　　　　えん
買　　　　か
古　　　　う
遠　　　　かず
売　　　　おも
歌　　　　まる

Stroke order check (answers)
1. B　2. A　3. B　4. A　5. B　6. B

19

Kanji lesson 19:

111-116

聞言読話記計

19 | New Kanji あたらしい かんじ

Make sure you learn the correct stroke order. Correct stroke order will mean neater symbols when writing quickly. Also, take time to learn the words listed for each kanji – these will help you memorize the different readings.

聞	111. hear, listen to, ask			14 画
	くんよみ	き(く、こえる)		
	おんよみ	ブン、モン		
	聞			

to hear, ask	newspaper	listener	unheard-of, unprecedented
き 聞く	しんぶん 新聞	き　て 聞き手	ぜんだい み もん 前代未聞

言	112. say, speak, word			7 画
	くんよみ	い(う)、こと		
	おんよみ	ゲン、ゴン		
	言			

to say	word	language	testament, will
い 言う	こと ば 言葉	げん ご 言語	ゆいごん 遺言

113. read　14 画

くんよみ	よ(む)
おんよみ	ドク、トク、トウ

読

to read	reader	reading	read aloud
よ	どくしゃ	どくしょ	おんどく
読む	読者	読書	音読

114. story, conversation, talk　13 画

くんよみ	はな(す)、はなし
おんよみ	ワ

話

talk, story	to talk	conversation	gossip
はなし	はな	かいわ	うわさばなし
話	話す	会話	噂話

115. chronicle, scribe　10 画

くんよみ	しる(す)
おんよみ	キ

記

to note / mark down	form entry	diary	article, news story
しる	き にゅう	にっき	き じ
記す	記入	日記	記事

計	116. measure, plan, count							9画
	くんよみ	はか(る)						
	おんよみ	ケイ						
	計							

to measure	calculation	plan	clock, watch
はか	けいさん	けいかく	と けい
計る	計算	計画	時計

19 | Kanji Usage かんじの つかいかた

● **19-1. The origin of things (原)**

原 (げん) can mean "source" or "origin" and many big concept words use it.

cause, origin (origin + factor)	principle, theory (origin + logic)
原因	原理
げん・いん	げん・り

primitive man (origin + start + person)	primary color (origin + color)
原始人	原色
げん・し・じん	げん・しょく

native people (origin + living + people)	pure breed (origin + breed)
原住民	原種
げん・じゅう・みん	げん・しゅ

● **19-2. Nuclear kanji (原)**

原 (げん) is used for many words pertaining to "nuclear".

atom (origin + child)	nuclear power plant (origin + emit)
原子	原発
げん・し	げん・ぱつ

atomic bomb (origin + burst open)	nuclear power (origin + child + power)
原爆	原子力
げん・ばく	げん・し・りょく

19 Words You Can Write かける ことば

聞く （きく） to hear, ask

聞	く									

言う （いう） to say

言	う									

読む （よむ） to read

読	む									

話す （はなす） to talk

話	す									

記す（しるす）to mark

記	す								

日記（にっき）diary, journal

日	記								

記入（きにゅう）form entry, input

記	入								

計る（はかる）to measure

計	る								

音読（おんどく）reading aloud

音	読								

手話（しゅわ）sign language

手	話								

先売り（さきうり）advance sale

先	売	り						

聞き上手（ききじょうず）good listener

聞	き	上	手				

読み切る（よみきる）to finish reading

読	み	き	る				

19 | Fill in the Kanji

Fill in the appropriate kanji in the blanks for each sentence.

　　に　ほん　　　　　　　　　　　　　　き
1. ＿＿＿ ＿＿＿ のおこめは おいしいと ＿＿＿ きました。
　　I heard that Japanese rice is delicious.

　　　　　　　　　　　　　き　　じょう　ず
2. わたしのおかあさんは ＿＿＿ き ＿＿＿ ＿＿＿です。
　　My mother is a good listener.

　　　　　　　　い　　　　　　　　　　　　　　い
3. わたしは、＿＿＿いたいことが ぜんぜん＿＿＿えません。
　　I can't say what I want to say at all.

　　　　　　ばなし
4. あねは うわさ ＿＿＿ をするのが すきです。
　　My older sister likes to gossip.

　いち ねん せい　　　　　　おん どく
5. ＿＿＿ ＿＿＿ ＿＿＿のむすめは、＿＿＿ ＿＿＿のしゅくだいが あります。
　　My first grade daughter has out-loud reading homework.

　　　　な　　　　き にゅう　　く だ
6. ここに ＿＿＿ まえを ＿＿＿ ＿＿＿ して＿＿＿さい。
　　Please write (input) your name here.

　　　　　　は か　　　　　　　　はなし
7. タイミングを ＿＿＿ ってから、ちちに ＿＿＿ をします。
　　I will measure (consider) the timing and then talk to my father.

19 | Kanji meaning

Write the following kanji next to its meaning: 買 聞 読 教 言 通 話 記 計

1.____ measure

2. ____ read

3. ____ teach

4. ____ talk

5. ____ buy

6. ____ pass

7. ____ say

8. ____ listen

9. ____ chronicle

19 | Kanji matching

Draw a line to connect each kanji with one of its ON or KUN readings.

帰 •		• どく	
計 •		• ぶん	
話 •		• かえ	
来 •		• く	
読 •		• しる	
細 •		• おもん	
言 •		• げん	
聞 •		• さい	
記 •		• わか	
思 •		• はか	

19 | Stroke Order Check

Circle A or B whichever represents the correct stroke order for each kanji.

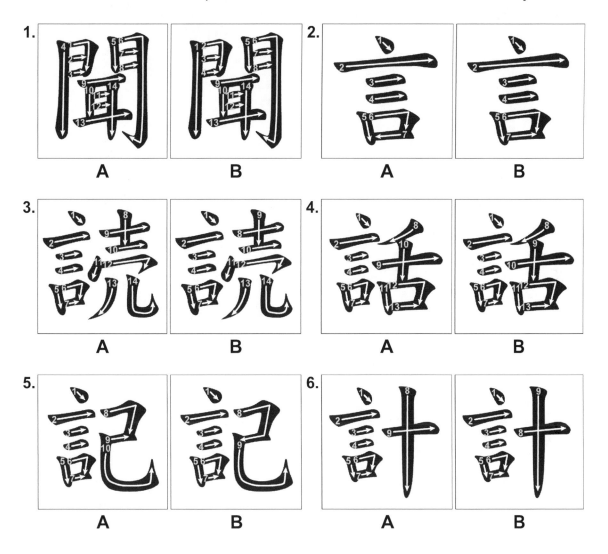

19 | Answer Key 答え合わせ

Fill in the kanji (answers)

1. 日本の おこめは おいしいと 聞きました。

2. わたしの おかあさんは 聞き上手です。

3. わたしは、言いたいことが ぜんぜん 言えません。

4. あねは うわさ話を するのが すきです。

5. 一年生のむすめは、音読の しゅくだいが あります。

6. ここに 名まえを 記入して 下さい。

7. タイミングを 計ってから、ちちに 話をします。

Kanji meaning match (answers)

1. 計 measure   2. 読 read   3. 教 teach
4. 話 talk   5. 買 buy   6. 通 pass
7. 言 say   8. 聞 listen   9. 記 chronicle

Kanji matching (answers)

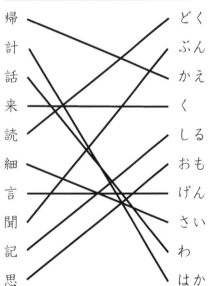

Stroke order check (answers)

1. B   2. B   3. B   4. A   5. A   6. B

20

Kanji lesson 20:

食会考書答鳴

20 | New Kanji あたらしい かんじ

Make sure you learn the correct stroke order. Correct stroke order will mean neater symbols when writing quickly. Also, take time to learn the words listed for each kanji – these will help you memorize the different readings.

食	117. eat					9 画
	くんよみ	た(べる)、く(う)				
	おんよみ	ショク、ジキ				
	食					

to eat	meal	eating out	prey
た	しょく じ	がいしょく	え じき
食べる	食事	外食	餌食

会	118. meet					6 画
	くんよみ	あ(う)				
	おんよみ	カイ、エ				
	会					

to meet	company	conversation	bow, nod
あ	かいしゃ	かい わ	え しゃく
会う	会社	会話	会釈

119. think, consider   6 画

くんよみ	かんが(える)
おんよみ	コウ

考

to think, consider	idea	reference	plan, idea, invention
かんが	かんが	さんこう	こうあん
考える	考え	参考	考案

120. write, book   10 画

くんよみ	か(く)
おんよみ	ショ

書

to write	registered mail	library	bookstore
か	かきとめ	としょかん	しょてん
書く	書留	図書館	書店

121. answer, reply   12 画

くんよみ	こた(え、える)
おんよみ	トウ

答

to answer, reply	back-talk	examination paper	immediate reply
こた	くちごた	とうあん	そくとう
答える	口答え	答案	即答

鳴	122. cry, sing, howl				14 画
	くんよみ	な(く、る、らす)			
	おんよみ	メイ			
	鳴				

to cry (animal)	roar	fearful cries	ringing in the ear
な 鳴く	な　ごえ 鳴き声	ひ めい 悲鳴	みみ な 耳鳴り

20   Kanji Usage かんじの つかいかた

● 20-1. The formality of eating (食)

Politeness levels of Japanese can be changed simply by how a verb is conjugated. For instance, the ます ending for verbs is polite, while the dictionary form (う form) is informal. A good example of politeness based on conjugation is how 食べます is polite and 食べる is informal.

However, sometimes a vulgar version of the verb exists.

standard "eat"	vulgar "eat"
食べる た・べる	食う く・う
Whether in polite or casual form this is a standard way to say "eat."	This vulgar, yet often used verb for "eat" is common among friends.

め　あ
召し上がる is the most polite / formal way to say "eat" and "drink." It's interesting that this word doesn't even include 食 which is often the case with the honorific forms.

● **20-2. The "sun" radical ひへん / にちへん**

The ひへん radical, also called にちへん, is in many words related to time.

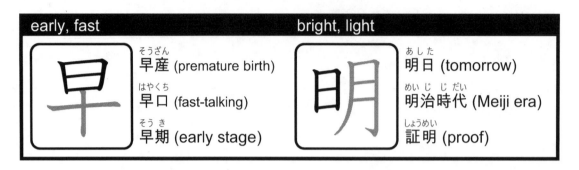

early, fast

早

早産 (premature birth)
そうざん

早口 (fast-talking)
はやくち

早期 (early stage)
そうき

bright, light

明

明日 (tomorrow)
あした

明治時代 (Meiji era)
めいじじだい

証明 (proof)
しょうめい

old times

昔

昔話 (reminiscence)
むかしばなし

昔々 (long ago)
むかしむかし

昔風 (old fashioned)
むかしふう

spring (season)

春

青春 (youth)
せいしゅん

思春期 (puberty)
ししゅんき

春休み (spring break)
はるやす

star

星

星座 (constellation)
せいざ

流れ星 (shooting star)
ながぼし

星空 (starry sky)
ほしぞら

yesterday, previous

昨

昨日 (yesterday)
きのう

昨日 (yesterday) *
さくじつ

昨年 (last year)
さくねん

* 昨日 has two ways to be read. きのう is more commonly used.

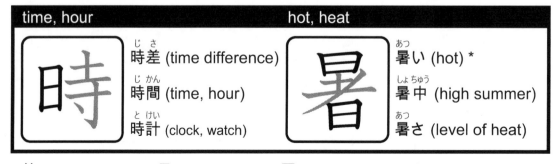

time, hour

時

時差 (time difference)
じさ

時間 (time, hour)
じかん

時計 (clock, watch)
とけい

hot, heat

暑

暑い (hot) *
あつ

暑中 (high summer)
しょちゅう

暑さ (level of heat)
あつ

* 熱い (heat, fever)、暑い (hot, heat)、厚い (thick) are all あつい.

20 Words You Can Write かける ことば

会う（あう）to meet

会	う								

書く（かく）to write

書	く								

読書（どくしょ）reading

読	書								

鳴く（なく）to cry (animal)

鳴	く								

少食（しょうしょく）light eater

少	食								

食べる（たべる）to eat

食	べ	る					

考える（かんがえる）to consider, think

考	え	る					

口答え（くちごたえ）back-talk

口	答	え					

答える（こたえる）to answer, reply

答	え	る					

耳鳴り（みみなり） ringing in the ear

耳	鳴	り									

20 │ Fill in the Kanji

Fill in the appropriate kanji in the blanks for each sentence.

1. ＿＿＿ た べるばしょを きめましたか。

   Have you decided the place to eat?

2. おととい、 ゆうめいな＿＿ か しゅ＿＿ に ＿＿ あ いました。

   The day before yesterday, I met a famous singer.

3. よく ＿＿ かんが えてから、＿＿ こた えを＿＿ か いて＿＿ くだ さい。

   After considering it well, write the answer.

4. わたしのしゅみは ＿＿ どく ＿＿ しょ です。

   My hobby is reading.

5. ＿＿ おや に ＿＿ くち ＿＿ ごた えをするのは、よくないです。

   It's not good to back talk to your parents.

6. ＿＿ きん じょの ＿＿ いぬ の＿＿ な きごえが うるさいです。

   The barking of dogs in our neighborhood is loud.

7. わたしは ＿＿ しょう ＿＿ しょく なので、あまり＿＿ ふと りません。

   Since I'm a light eater I don't gain that much weight.

20 | Kanji meaning

Write the following kanji next to its meaning: 食 鳴 広 会 答 記 考 書 言

1.____ say

2. ____ cry, howl

3. ____ meet

4. ____ eat

5. ____ think

6. ____ answer

7. ____ write

8. ____ spacious

9. ____ note

20 | Kanji matching

Draw a line to connect each kanji with only one of its ON or KUN readings.

考 •   • けい
計 •   • ほ
書 •   • とう
鳴 •   • ちょう
歩 •   • な
会 •   • たき
帰 •   • こう
答 •   • か
食 •   • あ
長 •

20 | Stroke Order Check

Circle A or B whichever represents the correct stroke order for each kanji.

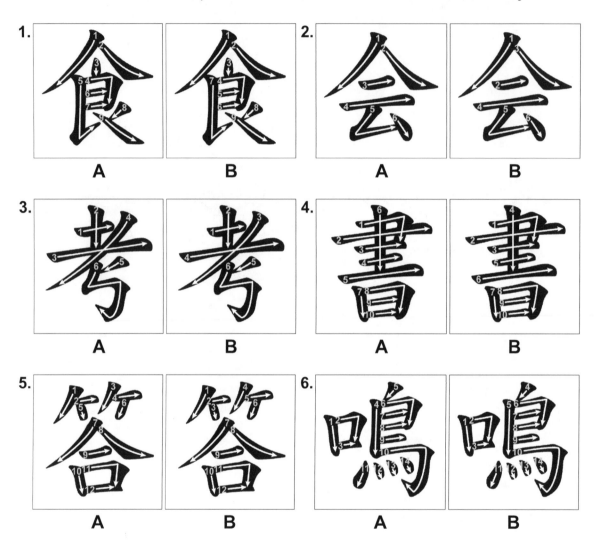

20 | Answer Key 答え合わせ

Fill in the kanji (answers)

1. 食べるばしょを きめましたか。

2. おととい、ゆうめいな 歌手 に 会 いました。

3. よく 考 えてから、答 えを 書 いて 下 さい。

4. わたしのしゅみは 読書 です。

5. 親 に 口答 えをするのは、よくないです。

6. 近 じょの 犬 の 鳴 きごえが うるさいです。

7. わたしは 少食 なので、あまり 太 りません。

Kanji meaning match (answers)

1. 言 say	2. 鳴 cry, howl	3. 会 meet
4. 食 eat	5. 考 think	6. 答 answer
7. 書 write	8. 広 spacious	9. 記 note

Kanji matching (answers)

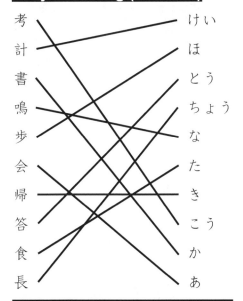

考　　　　けい
計　　　　ほ
書　　　　とう
鳴　　　　ちょう
歩　　　　な
会　　　　た
帰　　　　き
答　　　　こう
食　　　　か
長　　　　あ

Stroke order check (answers)

1. B　　2. A　　3. A　　4. A　　5. B　　6. B

SR | Super Review 4

SR4 | Kanji selection

Select the best kanji to fill in the blank in each sentence.

1. もうじかんないから、いそいで＿＿＿べましょう。
   A. 考   B. 走   C. 食   D. 読

2. よかったら、きょううちに＿＿＿て下さい。
   A. 帰   B. 来   C. 行   D. 会

3. いつもうちから学校へ＿＿＿いて行きます。
   A. 走   B. 通   C. 考   D. 歩

4. わたしのいもうとは元気で、からだが＿＿＿いです。
   A. 細   B. 広   C. 高   D. 多

SR4 | Kanji reading

Select the best reading for the underlined kanji.

1. あした、なんじごろ<u>来</u>られますか。
   A. き   B. こ   C. か   D. く

2. 数学を<u>教</u>えるのは、むずかしいですね。
   A. かんが   B. かぞ   C. おし   D. こた

3. えんぴつは先が<u>細</u>いのが、書きやすいです。
   A. こまか   B. なが   C. ふと   D. ほそ

4. 日よう日は、たいてい<u>読書</u>をしています。
   A. しゃ   B. しょ   C. しゅ   D. じょ

SR4 | Compound kanji word puzzle

Fill in the correct kanji based on the list below the puzzle.

1)		2)	3)
4)		5)	
6)	7)	8)	9)
	10)		11)

Down ↓

1) read aloud

3) popularity

5) New Year's Day

6) light eater

9) form entry

Left to Right →

4) reading

5) energetic

8) diary

10) singer

Right to Left ←

2) numbers

3) number of people

7) more or less

11) taking possession, available

SR4 | Answer Key 答え合わせ

Kanji selection (answers)

1. C – 食_たべましょう

   Because there isn't anymore time, let's hurry up and eat.

2. B – 来_きて下_{くだ}さい。

   If it's okay please come to my house today.

3. D – 歩_{ある}いて

   I always walk to school from my house.

4. A – 細_{ほそ}い

   My younger sister is healthy and her body is thin.

Kanji reading (answers)

1. B – 来_こられますか

   Around what time can you come tomorrow?

2. C – 教_{おし}える

   It's hard to teach math isn't it.

3. D – 細_{ほそ}い

   It's easy to write with pencils that have a sharp (narrow) tip.

4. B – 読書_{どくしょ}

   I usually read on Sunday.

Compound kanji word puzzle (answers)

音	字	数	人
読	書	元	気
少	多	日	記
食	歌	手	入

21

Kanji lesson 21:

作交切引分回

21 | New Kanji あたらしい かんじ

Make sure you learn the correct stroke order. Correct stroke order will mean neater symbols when writing quickly. Also, take time to learn the words listed for each kanji – these will help you memorize the different readings.

作	123. make, production						7 画
	くんよみ	つく(る)					
	おんよみ	サク、サ					
	作						

to make	composition, essay	music composition	work
つく	さくぶん	さっきょく	さ ぎょう
作る	作文	作曲	作業

交	124. exchange, mix, mingle		6 画
	くんよみ	まじ(わる、える) ま(じる、ざる、ぜる) か(う、わす)	
	おんよみ	コウ	
	交		

to exchange	to cross, to mingle	police box	intersection
か	まじ	こうばん	こう さ てん
交わす	交わる	交番	交差点

125. cut — 4 画

くんよみ	き(る、れる)
おんよみ	セツ、サイ

切

to cut	postage stamp	important	not…at all
き	きって	たいせつ	いっさい
切る	切手	大切	一切

126. pull — 4 画

くんよみ	ひ(く)
おんよみ	イン

引

to pull	subtraction	gravity	forceful
ひ	ひ　ざん	いんりょく	ごういん
引く	引き算	引力	強引

127. part, portion, segment — 4 画

くんよみ	わ(ける、かれる、かる、かつ)
おんよみ	ブン、フン、ブ

分

to separate	mood	division	five minutes
わ	き　ぶん	ぶんかつ	ご　ふん
分ける	気分	分割	五分

	128. turn, go around				6 画
回	くんよみ	まわ(る、す)			
	おんよみ	カイ、エ			
	回				

to turn, revolve	once	rotation	detour
まわ	いっかい	かいてん	まわ　みち
回る	一回	回転	回り道

21 | Kanji Usage かんじの つかいかた

● **21-1. Exchanging ideas (交)**

交 is used in many high level words.

negotiation (exchange + crossover)	exchange (exchange + change)
交渉	交換
こう・しょう	こう・かん

friendship (exchange + occasion)	traffic (exchange + pass through)
交際	交通
こう・さい	こう・つう

diplomacy (outside + exchange)	police box (interesect + turn)
外交	交番
がい・こう	こう・ばん

● 21-2. Subtle differences, big changes

Kanji can often look similar. This is one reason it's important to pay attention to the individual parts and radicals. Let's look at some similar looking kanji.

previous, yesterday

昨 — きのう 昨日 yesterday / さくねん 昨年 last year

make, production, build

作 — さくひん 作品 work (book, film) / けっさく 傑作 masterpiece, best work

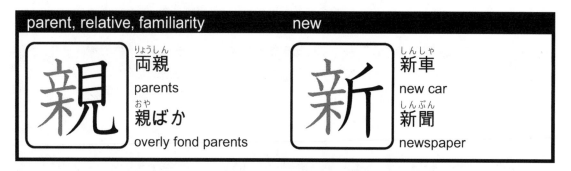

parent, relative, familiarity

親 — りょうしん 両親 parents / おや 親ばか overly fond parents

new

新 — しんしゃ 新車 new car / しんぶん 新聞 newspaper

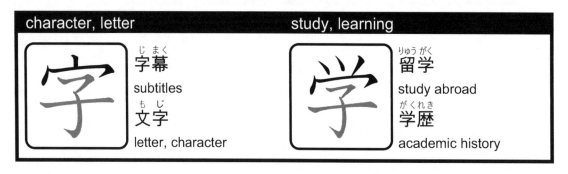

character, letter

字 — じまく 字幕 subtitles / もじ 文字 letter, character

study, learning

学 — りゅうがく 留学 study abroad / がくれき 学歴 academic history

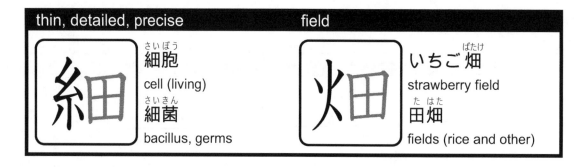

thin, detailed, precise

細 — さいぼう 細胞 cell (living) / さいきん 細菌 bacillus, germs

field

畑 — ばたけ いちご畑 strawberry field / たはた 田畑 fields (rice and other)

● **21-3. Exchanging a variety of things (交)**

Let's look at some phrases that use 交わす (to exchange)

Phrase	English
約束を交わす	to adopt an agreement
契約を交わす	to agree to a contract
意見を交わす	to discuss, to exchange opinions
挨拶を交わす	to exchange bows, to bow to each other
言葉を交わす	to exchange words, to have a conversation
話を交わす	to swap stories
視線を交わす	to exchange glances

21 ｜ Words You Can Write かける ことば

作文（さくぶん）writing, essay, composition

作	文								

交通（こうつう）traffic

交	通								

切る（きる）to cut

切	る								

切手（きって）postage stamp

切	手								

引く（ひく）to pull

引	く								

引力（いんりょく）gravity

引	力									

気分（きぶん）mood

気	分									

水分（すいぶん）moisture

水	分									

回る (まわる) to spin

回	る									

一回（いっかい）one time

一	回									

大切（たいせつ）important

大	切									

十分（じっぷん）10 minutes

十	分									

交わす（かわす）to exchange

交	わ	す						

分ける（わける）to separate

分	け	る						

21 | Fill in the Kanji

Fill in the appropriate kanji in the blanks for each sentence.

く　　　　さく　ぶん

1. ＿＿＿じまでに ＿＿＿ ＿＿＿を かんせい しなければ いけない です。
   I have to complete my essay by 9 o'clock.

ご　ふん　　　　きっ　て　　　ろく

2. ＿＿＿ ＿＿＿まえに ＿＿＿ ＿＿＿を＿＿＿まい、かいました。
   I bought six stamps five minutes ago.

ひ　　　　く だ

3. そのドアを ＿＿＿ いて＿＿＿さい。
   Please pull (open) that door.

こう　　　　み ぎ　　　　　く だ

4. つぎの ＿＿＿ さてんを ＿＿＿ に まがって＿＿＿さい。
   Please turn right at the next intersection.

き　ぶん　　　　　　　　やす

5. ちちは＿＿＿ ＿＿＿がわるくて、かいしゃを＿＿＿んだ。
   My father didn't feel well so he took off from work.

ねん　　　　さん　かい

6. きょ ＿＿＿ 、うみに ＿＿＿ ＿＿＿ いきました。
   Last year, I went to the ocean three times.

さく　ぶん　　か

7. わたしは ＿＿＿ ＿＿＿を＿＿＿ くのが にがてです。
   I am not good at writing essays.

21 | Kanji meaning

Write the following kanji next to its meaning: 作 引 聞 分 回 交 話 切 走

1.＿＿＿ run

2. ＿＿＿ make

3. ＿＿＿ percentage

4. ＿＿＿ talk

5. ＿＿＿ listen

6. ＿＿＿ mix

7. ＿＿＿ spin

8. ＿＿＿ pull

9. ＿＿＿ cut

21 | Kanji matching

Draw a line to connect each kanji with only one of its ON or KUN readings.

回 ・
交 ・
書 ・
切 ・
作 ・
売 ・
分 ・
引 ・
行 ・
帰 ・

・わ
・いん
・かえ
・かい
・まじ
・しょ
・せつ
・ぎょう
・う
・さく

21 | Stroke Order Check

Circle A or B whichever represents the correct stroke order for each kanji.

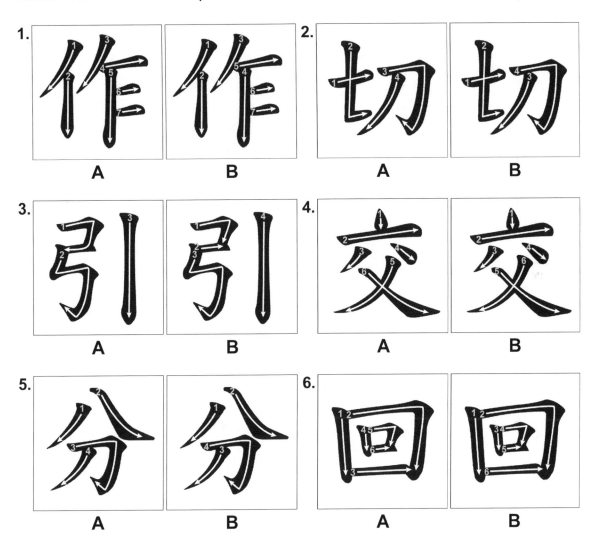

1. A B

2. A B

3. A B

4. A B

5. A B

6. A B

21 | Answer Key 答え合わせ

Fill in the kanji (answers)

1. 九 じまでに 作文 を かんせい しなければ いけない です。

2. 五分 まえに 切手 を 六 まい、かいました。

3. そのドアを 引 いて 下 さい。

4. つぎの 交 さてんを 右 にまがって 下 さい。

5. ちちは 気分 がわるくて、かいしゃを 休 んだ。

6. きょ 年、うみに 三回 いきました。

7. わたしは 作文 を 書 くのがにがてです。

Kanji meaning match (answers)

1. 走 run
2. 作 make
3. 分 percentage
4. 話 talk
5. 聞 listen
6. 交 exchange
7. 回 spin
8. 引 pull
9. 切 cut

Kanji matching (answers)

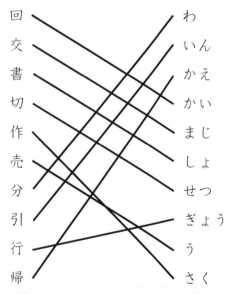

Stroke order check (answers)

1. A   2. A   3. B   4. A   5. A   6. B

22 Kanji lesson 22: 合止用光当活

129-134

22 | New Kanji あたらしい かんじ

Make sure you learn the correct stroke order. Correct stroke order will mean neater symbols when writing quickly. Also, take time to learn the words listed for each kanji – these will help you memorize the different readings.

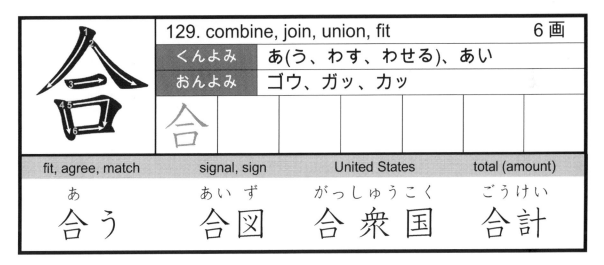

合	129. combine, join, union, fit					6 画
	くんよみ	あ(う、わす、わせる)、あい				
	おんよみ	ゴウ、ガッ、カッ				
	合					

fit, agree, match	signal, sign	United States	total (amount)
あ	あい ず	がっしゅうこく	ごうけい
合う	合図	合衆国	合計

止	130. stop					4 画
	くんよみ	と(まる、める)				
	おんよみ	シ				
	止					

to stop	cancellation	suspension	prohibition
と	ちゅう し	てい し	きん し
止める	中止	停止	禁止

131. business, errand, use   5 画

| くんよみ | もち(いる) |
| おんよみ | ヨウ |

用

to make use of	errands	use	care, precaution
もち	よう じ	し よう	よう じん
用いる	用事	使用	用心

132. light, shine, brilliance   6 画

| くんよみ | ひか(る)、ひかり |
| おんよみ | コウ |

光

to shine	sunlight	sight-seeing	honor
ひか	にっこう	かんこう	こうえい
光る	日光	観光	光栄

133. hit, appropriate, this / that   6 画

| くんよみ | あ(たる、てる) |
| おんよみ | トウ |

当

to hit	allowance	lunch box	on duty
あ	て あ	べんとう	とうばん
当たる	手当て	お弁当	当番

活	134. live, life						9 画
	くんよみ	none					
	おんよみ	カツ					
	活						

living, life	active volcano	eating habits	activity
せいかつ	かっかざん	しょくせいかつ	かつどう
生活	活火山	食生活	活動

22 Kanji Usage かんじの つかいかた

● **22-1. Using (用)**

用 is something you will see any time you purchase something that can be "used" only with certain products.

for iPhone use	for dog use
iPhone 用	犬用
iPhone よう	いぬ・よう

for PC use	official use
PC 用	公用
PC よう	こう・よう

private use / home use	exclusive use
自家用	専用
じ・か・よう	せん・よう

22 | Words You Can Write かける ことば

合う（あう）to fit, match

合	う								

合計（ごうけい）total (amount)

合	計								

中止（ちゅうし）cancellation

中	止								

月光（げっこう）moonlight

月	光								

光る（ひかる）to shine

光	る								

生活（せいかつ）living, life

生	活								

止める（とめる）to stop

止	め	る						

用いる（もちいる）to make use of

用	い	る						

手当て（てあて）allowance

手	当	て						

当たる（あたる）to hit

当	た	る							

食生活（しょくせいかつ）eating habits

食	生	活							

22 | Fill in the Kanji

Fill in the appropriate kanji in the blanks for each sentence.

　　た　なか　　　　　　　き　　あ

1. ＿＿＿ ＿＿＿さんとは、よく＿＿＿ が＿＿＿います。

I match well with Tanaka.

　　　　まち　　い　　ど　　　おお

2. この ＿＿＿ は ＿＿＿き＿＿＿まりが＿＿＿いですね。

There are a lot of dead ends in this town.

　　ど　　び　　　　　よう

3. ＿＿＿ よう ＿＿＿は、ちょっと＿＿＿じが あります。

On Saturday I have some errands to do.

　　　　　　　ひかり　はい

4. このいえには、たくさんの ＿＿＿ が＿＿＿りますね。

A lot of light comes into this house.

　あめ　　　　ちゅう　し

5. ＿＿＿ でゲームが ＿＿＿ ＿＿＿に なりました。

Due to rain, the game was cancelled.

　　　　しょく せい かつ　　　　　おも

6. わたしの ＿＿＿ ＿＿＿ ＿＿＿は よくないと ＿＿＿います。

I don't think my eating habits are good.

あ
7. このあいだ、ボールに＿＿＿ たって、けがを しました。
   The other day, a ball hit me and I got injured.

22 | Kanji meaning

Write the following kanji next to its meaning: 合 活 止 当 考 丸 用 光 売

1.＿＿＿ sell   2. ＿＿＿ live, life,   3. ＿＿＿ round

4. ＿＿＿ combine, join   5. ＿＿＿ errand, use   6. ＿＿＿ hit

7. ＿＿＿ light, shine   8. ＿＿＿ stop   9. ＿＿＿ think

22 | Kanji matching

Draw a line to connect each kanji with only one of its ON or KUN readings.

活 ・	・ よう
光 ・	・ と
回 ・	・ かつ
止 ・	・ らい
合 ・	・ とう
言 ・	・ ひかり
用 ・	・ ごう
当 ・	・ ごい
数 ・	・ かい
来 ・	・ かぞ

22 | Stroke Order Check

Circle A or B whichever represents the correct stroke order for each kanji.

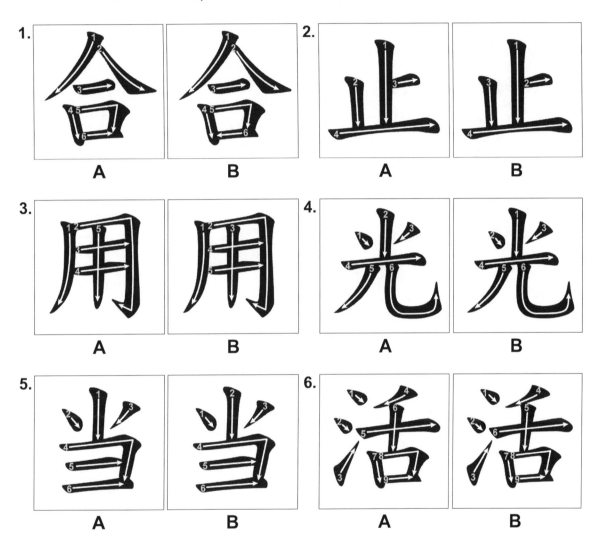

1. A B

2. A B

3. A B

4. A B

5. A B

6. A B

22 | Answer Key 答え合わせ

Fill in the kanji (answers)

1. 田中さんとは、よく気が合います。

2. この町は行き止まりが多い ですね。

3. 土よう日は、ちょっと用じが あります。

4. このいえには、たくさんの光が入りますね。

5. 雨でゲームが中止に なりました。

6. わたしの食生活は よくないと思います。

7. このあいだ、ボールに当たって、けがを しました。

Kanji meaning match (answers)

1. 売 sell
2. 活 live, life
3. 丸 round
4. 合 combine, join
5. 用 errand, use
6. 当 hit
7. 光 light, shine
8. 止 stop
9. 考 think

Kanji matching (answers)

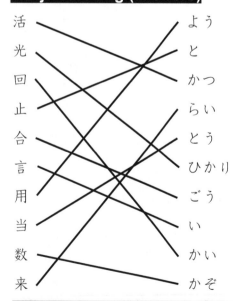

活　　　　　よう
光　　　　　と
回　　　　　かつ
止　　　　　らい
合　　　　　とう
言　　　　　ひかり
用　　　　　ごう
当　　　　　い
数　　　　　かい
来　　　　　かぞ

Stroke order check (answers)

1. A　2. B　3. A　4. B　5. A　6. A

23

Kanji lesson 23:

直晴知友自心声

23 | New Kanji あたらしい かんじ

Make sure you learn the correct stroke order. Correct stroke order will mean neater symbols when writing quickly. Also, take time to learn the words listed for each kanji – these will help you memorize the different readings.

直	135. direct, soon, honestly			8 画
	くんよみ	ただ(ちに)、なお(す、る)		
	おんよみ	チョク、ジキ		
	直			

to repair	immediately	direct	honest
なお	ただ	ちょくせつ	しょうじき
直す	直ちに	直接	正直

晴	136. clear			12 画
	くんよみ	は(れる、らす)		
	おんよみ	セイ		
	晴			

to be clear weather	fine weather	one's best clothes	fine autumn weather
は	せいてん	は　ぎ	あき ば
晴れる	晴天	晴れ着	秋晴れ

137. knowledge　8画

くんよみ	し(る)
おんよみ	チ

知

to know	knowledge	wisdom	news, information
し	ち し き	ち え	し
知る	知識	知恵	お知らせ

138. friend　4画

くんよみ	とも
おんよみ	ユウ

友

friend	close friend	friendship	old friend
ともだち	しんゆう	ゆうじょう	きゅうゆう
友達	親友	友情	旧友

139. oneself　6画

くんよみ	みずか(ら)
おんよみ	ジ、シ

自

myself	freedom	nature	home
じ ぶん	じ ゆう	し ぜん	じ たく
自分	自由	自然	自宅

140. heart, mind　　4 画

くんよみ	こころ
おんよみ	シン

心

heart, mind	feel confident, supportive	heart (medical name)	relief
こころ	こころづよ	しんぞう	あんしん
心	心強い	心臓	安心

141. voice, reputation　　7 画

くんよみ	こえ、こわ
おんよみ	セイ、ショウ

声

voice	singing voice	large voice	cheering
こえ	うたごえ	おおごえ	せいえん
声	歌声	大声	声援

23 | Kanji Usage かんじの つかいかた

● **23-1. Kanji and yourself (自)**

自 is part of a wide variety of commonly used words related to "self" initiated actions. So let's take some time to discover them.

suicide (self + kill)	automatic (self + move)
自殺	自動
じ・さつ	じ・どう

automobile (self + moving + wheel)	self-confidence (self + belief)
自動車	自信
じ・どう・しゃ	じ・しん

bicycle (self + revolve + wheel)	self-reliance (self + stand)
自転車	自立
じ・てん・しゃ	じ・りつ

● 23-2. The heart behind kanji (心)

We only introduced 4 words for 心 which is certainly not enough to show how many words contain 心, which means "heart" and "mind."

center, middle (inside + heart)	determination (decide + heart)
中心	決心
ちゅう・しん	けっ・しん

concern, interest (connection + heart)	ulterior motive (bottom + heart)
関心	下心
かん・しん	した・ごころ

care, precaution (use + heart)	heart (anatomical) (heart + entrails)
用心	心臓
よう・じん	しん・ぞう

woman's heart (woman + mind)	patriotism (love + country + heart)
女心	愛国心
おんな・ごころ	あい・こく・しん

23 | Words You Can Write かける ことば

直す（なおす）to repair

直	す								

正直（しょうじき）honest

正	直								

晴れ（はれ）clear weather

晴	れ								

晴天（せいてん）fine weather

晴	天								

知る（しる）to know

知	る								

友人（ゆうじん）friend

友	人								

自分（じぶん）myself, *sometimes "you" (in Kansai area)

自	分								

自ら（みずから）oneself, for oneself

自	ら								

中心（ちゅうしん）center, middle

中	心								

歌声（うたごえ）singing voice

歌	声									

下心（したごころ）ulterior motive, secret intention

下	心									

大声（おおごえ）large / loud voice

大	声									

通知（つうち）notification, report

通	知									

自白（じはく）confession, acknowledgement

自	白									

女心（おんなごころ）woman's heart

女	心									

音声（おんせい）voice, speech

音	声									

知り合い（しりあい）acquaintance

知	り	合	い				

やり直し（やりなおし）a redo

や	り	直	し			

23 | Fill in the Kanji

Fill in the appropriate kanji in the blanks for each sentence.

くるま　なお

1. こんしゅう、＿＿＿ を＿＿＿ してもらいました。
   This week I had my car fixed.

すう　げつ　　　　は

2. かんさいは ＿＿＿ か＿＿＿ かん、＿＿＿れています。
   The Kansai area has been sunny for several months.

こう ちょう せん せい　　　　　し

3. ＿＿＿ ＿＿＿ ＿＿＿ ＿＿＿からお＿＿＿ らせが あります。
   There is a notification from the principal.

らい ねん　しん ゆう　　　　　　　　　　　き

4. ＿＿＿ ＿＿＿、＿＿＿ ＿＿＿が アメリカから あそびに＿＿＿てくれます。
   Next year my best friend will come from America to play (hang out).

みずか　　ちから

5. かれは ＿＿＿ らの ＿＿＿ で たちあがった。
   He got back up with his own power.

おや　　　　　　こころづよ

6. ＿＿＿がいるから、＿＿＿ ＿＿＿いです。
   Because my parents are around, I am reassured.

み　は　　　　　　　　　ぞら　　み

7. ここは ＿＿＿ ＿＿＿ らしが いいから、ほし＿＿＿がよく＿＿＿える。
   Because the view is good here, you can see the starry sky very well.

か しゅ　たい せつ　　　　うた ごえ

8. ＿＿＿ ＿＿＿ に＿＿＿ ＿＿＿なのは、きれいな＿＿＿ ＿＿＿です。
   For a singer, the (most) important thing is a pretty singing voice.

23 | Kanji matching

Draw a line to connect each kanji with only one of its ON or KUN readings.

声 •   • ち
直 •   • こ う
光 •   • と え
心 •   • こ え
晴 •   • じ は
食 •   • ち ょ く
知 •   • ゆ う ん
友 •   • し ん
自 •   • し ょ く
止 •

23 | Kanji meaning

Write the following kanji next to its meaning: 直 声 用 晴 作 心 知 自 友

1. ____ make

2. ____ heart

3. ____ oneself

4. ____ clear

5. ____ voice

6. ____ knowledge

7. ____ errand, use

8. ____ friend

9. ____ direct, soon

23 | Stroke Order Check

Circle A or B whichever represents the correct stroke order for each kanji.

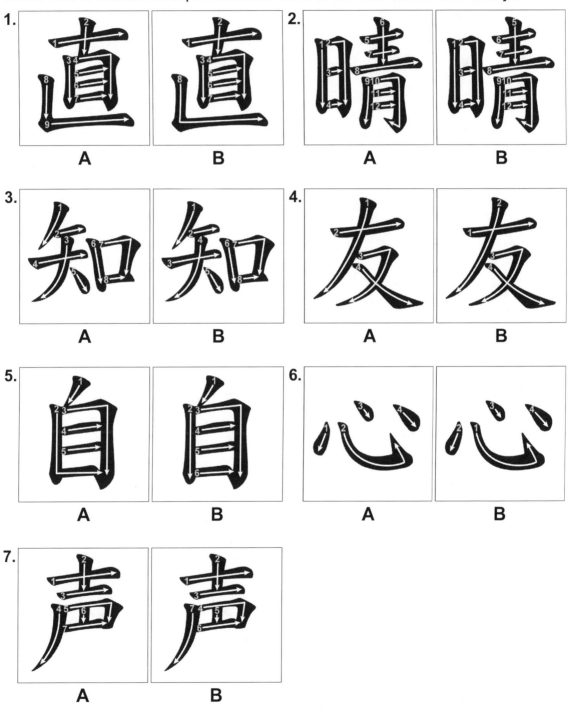

1.

A   B

2.

A   B

3.

A   B

4.

A   B

5.

A   B

6.

A   B

7.

A   B

23 | Answer Key 答え合わせ

Fill in the kanji (answers)

1. こんしゅう、車を直してもらいました。

2. かんさいは数か月かん、晴れています。

3. 校長先生から お知らせが あります。

4. 来年、親友がアメリカから あそびに 来てくれます。

5. かれは自らの力で たちあがった。

6. 親がいるから、心強いです。

7. ここは見晴らしがいいから、ほし空がよく見える。

8. 歌手に大切なのは、きれいな歌声です。

Kanji meaning match (answers)

1. 作 make	2. 心 heart	3. 自 oneself
4. 晴 clear	5. 声 voice	6. 知 knowledge
7. 用 errand, use	8. 友 friend	9. 直 direct, soon

Kanji matching (answers)

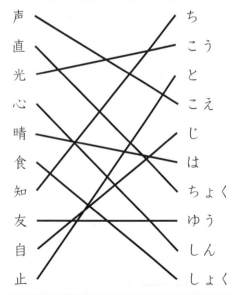

声　　　　　　　ち
直　　　　　　　こう
光　　　　　　　と
心　　　　　　　こえ
晴　　　　　　　じ
食　　　　　　　は
知　　　　　　　ちょく
友　　　　　　　ゆう
自　　　　　　　しん
止　　　　　　　しょく

Stroke order check (answers)

1. B　2. A　3. B　4. B　5. B　6. A　7. B

24 Kanji lesson 24: 父母兄姉弟妹

24 | New Kanji あたらしい かんじ

Make sure you learn the correct stroke order. Correct stroke order will mean neater symbols when writing quickly. Also, take time to learn the words listed for each kanji – these will help you memorize the different readings.

	142. father					4 画
父	くんよみ	ちち				
	おんよみ	フ				
	父					

my father	father	parental guardian	grandfather
ちち	ちちおや	ふ けい	そ ふ
父	父親	父兄	祖父

	143. mother					5 画
母	くんよみ	はは				
	おんよみ	ボ				
	母					

mother	grandparents	native tongue	baby carriage
はは	そ ふ ぼ	ぼ こく ご	う ば ぐるま
母	祖父母	母国語	乳母車

144. elder brother   5画

くんよみ	あに
おんよみ	ケイ、キョウ

兄

one's senior, elder brother	brothers and sisters	buddy, sworn brother	brother-in-law
あに	きょうだい	きょうだいぶん	ぎ　り　　　あに
兄	兄弟	兄弟分	義理の兄

145. elder sister   8画

くんよみ	あね
おんよみ	シ

姉

elder sister	sisters	elder sister	elder sister
あね	しまい	ねえ	あね　き
姉	姉妹	お姉さん	姉貴

146. younger brother   7画

くんよみ	おとうと
おんよみ	テイ、ダイ、デ

弟

younger brother	sibling	disciple	cousin
おとうと	きょうだい	で　し	い　と　こ
弟	兄弟	弟子	従兄弟

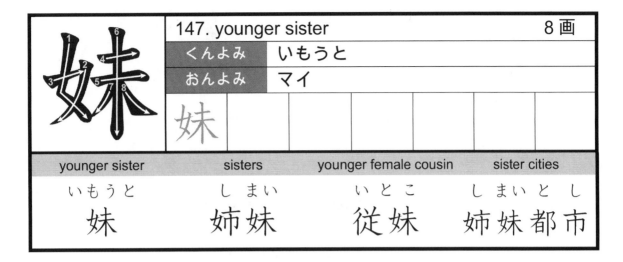

147. younger sister				8 画
くんよみ	いもうと			
おんよみ	マイ			

妹						

younger sister	sisters	younger female cousin	sister cities
いもうと	し　まい	い　と　こ	し　まい　と　し
妹	姉妹	従妹	姉妹都市

---

24 | Kanji Usage かんじの つかいかた

● **24-1. The "woman" radical 女 (おんなへん)**

Women are very important to the human race. After all, they are half of the population! It turns out the "woman" radical is also very important.

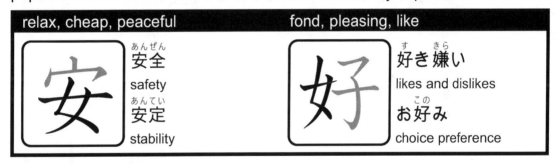

relax, cheap, peaceful	fond, pleasing, like
安 **あんぜん** 安全 safety **あんてい** 安定 stability	好 **す** 好き **きら** 嫌い likes and dislikes **この** お好み choice preference

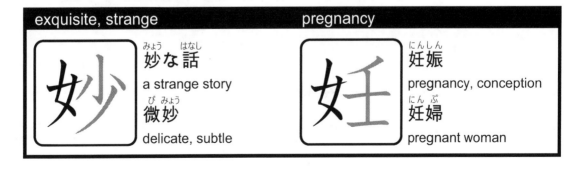

exquisite, strange	pregnancy
妙 **みょう** 妙な **はなし** 話 a strange story **び みょう** 微妙 delicate, subtle	妊 **にんしん** 妊娠 pregnancy, conception **にん ぷ** 妊婦 pregnant woman

toil, diligent		lady, woman, wife, bride	
努	どりょく 努力 effort, exertion どりょくか 努力家 hard worker	婦	ふうふ 夫婦 married couple しゅふ 主婦 housewife, home maker

plan, suggestion		need	
案	ていあん 提案 proposal, suggestion あんない 案内 information, guidance	要	ようきゅう 要求 demand ひつよう 必要 necessary, essential

24 | Words You Can Write かける ことば

父親 (ちちおや) father

父	親										

父兄 (ふけい) parents of children

父	兄										

ぼいん (ぼいん) vowel (sound)

母	音										

母親 (ははおや) mother

母	親										

兄弟 (きょうだい) brothers and sisters

兄	弟										

姉妹 (しまい) sisters

姉	妹										

弟子 (でし) disciple

弟	子										

父母 (ふぼ) father and mother, parents

父	母										

母の日 (ははのひ) Mother's day

母	の	日							

お兄さん (おにいさん) older brother

お	兄	さ	ん						

お姉さん (おねえさん) elder sister

お	姉	さ	ん						

お父さん (おとうさん) father

お	父	さ	ん						

お母さん (おかあさん) mother

お	母	さ	ん				

24 │ Fill in the Kanji

Fill in the appropriate kanji in the blanks for each sentence.

1. お ＿＿ さんは＿＿ ＿＿がわるくて、かいしゃを＿＿んだ。
   とう　　き ぶん　　　　　　　　　　　やす

   My father isn't feeling well so he took time off from the company.

2. わたしのお ＿＿ さんは ＿＿ き ＿＿ ＿＿です。
   か あ　　　　　き　じょう　ず

   My mother is good at listening.

3. わたしは ＿＿ ＿＿が＿＿ ＿＿、います。
   きょう だい　よ にん

   I have four brothers and sisters.

4. ＿＿ は よく＿＿ い ようふくを ＿＿ います。
   あ ね　　　た か　　　　　　か

   My older sister often buys expensive clothing.

5. ＿＿ は＿＿ ＿＿で＿＿ ＿＿にしかられました。
   おとうと　がっ こう　せん せい

   My younger brother got scolded by the teacher at school.

6. まい ＿＿ 、 ＿＿ と＿＿ ＿＿に＿＿きます。
   と し　いもうと　に ほん　い

   Every year, I go to Japan with my younger sister.

7. ＿＿ は ＿＿ ち ＿＿ をするのが すきです。
   は は　た　ば なし

   My mother likes to stand around and talk.

24 | Kanji matching

Draw a line to connect each kanji with only one of its ON or KUN readings.

妹 •　　　• ふん
姉 •　　　• さい
分 •　　　• こう
読 •　　　• よ
父 •　　　• まい
細 •　　　• おとうと
兄 •　　　• ふ
母 •　　　• あに
弟 •　　　• あね
交 •　　　• はは

24 | Kanji meaning

Write the following kanji next to its meaning: 父 兄 弟 妹 合 歩 記 姉 母

1.＿＿＿ younger sister　2. ＿＿＿ mother　　3. ＿＿＿ match

4. ＿＿＿ older brother　5. ＿＿＿ younger brother　6. ＿＿＿ chronicle

7. ＿＿＿ father　　8. ＿＿＿ older sister　9. ＿＿＿ walk

24 | Stroke Order Check

Circle A or B whichever represents the correct stroke order for each kanji.

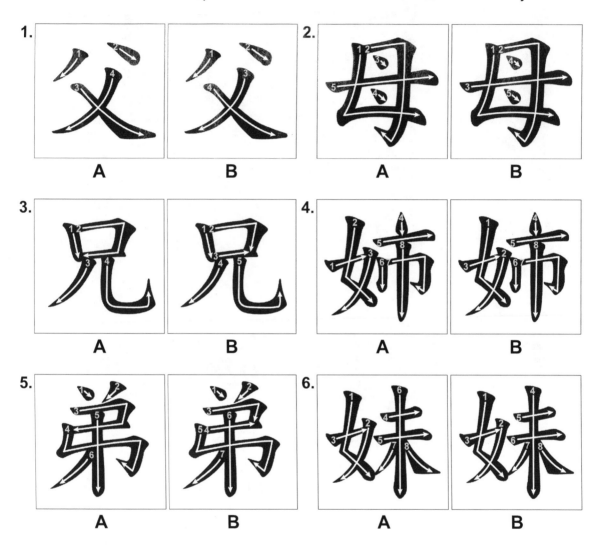

1. A   B
2. A   B
3. A   B
4. A   B
5. A   B
6. A   B

24 | Answer Key 答え合わせ

Fill in the kanji (answers)

1. お父さんは気分がわるくて、かいしゃを休んだ。

2. わたしのお母さんは聞き上手です。

3. わたしは兄弟が四人、います。

4. 姉はよく高いようふくを買います。

5. 弟は学校で先生に しかられました。

6. まい年、妹と日本に行きます。

7. 母は立ち話をするのがすきです。

Kanji meaning match (answers)

1. 妹 younger sister　　2. 母 mother　　3. 合 match

4. 兄 older brother　　5. 弟 younger brother　　6. 記 note

7. 父 father　　8. 姉 older sister　　9. 歩 walk

Kanji matching (answers)

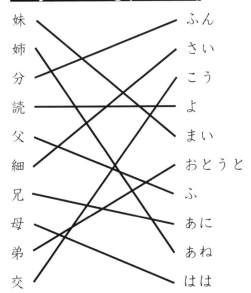

妹	ふん
姉	さい
分	こう
読	よ
父	まい
細	おとうと
兄	ふ
母	あに
弟	あね
交	はは

Stroke order check (answers)

1. B　　2. A　　3. B　　4. B　　5. B　　6. A

25 Kanji lesson 25: 体顔首頭毛肉

25 | New Kanji あたらしい かんじ

Make sure you learn the correct stroke order. Correct stroke order will mean neater symbols when writing quickly. Also, take time to learn the words listed for each kanji – these will help you memorize the different readings.

148. body, style — 7 画

くんよみ	からだ
おんよみ	タイ、テイ

体

body	physical strength	gymnastics	appearance
からだ	たいりょく	たいいく	ていさい
体	体力	体育	体裁

149. face (person) — 18 画

くんよみ	かお
おんよみ	ガン

顔

face	complexion	smiling face	face-washing
かお	かおいろ	えがお	せんがん
顔	顔色	笑顔	洗顔

150. neck, head, first, chief　　　　9画

くんよみ	くび
おんよみ	シュ

首

neck	Prime Minister	ankle	capital city
くび	しゅしょう	あしくび	しゅと
首	首相	足首	首都

151. head　　　　16画

くんよみ	あたま、かしら
おんよみ	トウ、ズ、ト

頭

head	down payment	headache	six (large) animals
あたま	あたまきん	ずつう	ろくとう
頭	頭金	頭痛	六頭

152. hair, fur　　　　4画

くんよみ	け
おんよみ	モウ

毛

hair on the head	fur, skin	knitting wool	blanket
かみ　け	け　がわ	け　いと	もうふ
髪の毛	毛皮	毛糸	毛布

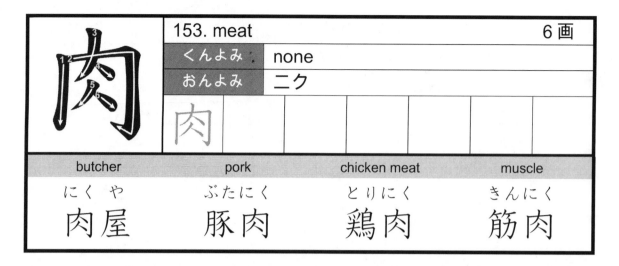

肉	153. meat					6画
	くんよみ	none				
	おんよみ	ニク				

butcher	pork	chicken meat	muscle
にく・や	ぶた・にく	とり・にく	きん・にく
肉屋	豚肉	鶏肉	筋肉

25 | Kanji Usage かんじの つかいかた

● **25-1. A hairy situation! (毛)**

The editors of the book really didn't want to include a section about body hair, but we all have hair… and that hair is on many parts of our body. So we felt it was our duty to add these words.

chest hair	fallen hair
胸毛	抜け毛
むね・げ	ぬけ・げ

eye brows	eye lashes
眉毛	睫毛
まゆ・げ	まつ・げ

nose hair	hair removal
鼻毛	脱毛
はな・げ	だつ・もう

● **25-2. The face of Japanese language (顔)**
Japanese has many phrases related to the face.

顔を潰す　　　　　to make someone lose face

顔を潰される　　　to lose face

顔を立てる　　　　to save face, to make someone look good

顔を合わせる　　　to meet face to face

顔を出す　　　　　to make an appearance

顔を貸す　　　　　to grant a person a moment

顔が広い　　　　　well connected, well known

顔が利く　　　　　to have a lot of influence, to have clout

顔が売れる　　　　to become famous

顔に出る　　　　　to have feelings be known by your face

顔パス　　　　　　to get something for free based on your fame

| **25** | **Words You Can Write かける ことば** |

体力（たいりょく）physical strength

体	力									

丸顔（まるがお）round face

丸	顔									

足首（あしくび）ankle

足	首								

石頭（いしあたま）inflexible, stubborn person

石	頭								

頭金（あたまきん）down payment

頭	金								

毛糸（けいと）knitting wool

毛	糸								

肉体（にくたい）the body, the flesh

肉	体								

新顔（しんがお）new face, newcomer

新	顔								

毛虫（けむし）hairy caterpillar

毛	虫								

ヒレ肉（ひれにく）fillet, tenderloin

ヒ	レ	肉					

頭文字（かしらもじ）initials

頭	文	字					

25 | Fill in the Kanji

Fill in the appropriate kanji in the blanks for each sentence.

　ひろ　た　　　　　　げん　き　　たい りょく

1. ＿＿＿ ＿＿＿ さんは いつも＿＿＿ ＿＿＿で ＿＿＿ ＿＿＿ が あります。
   Hirota san is always cheerful with a lot stamina.

　　　　　　　　かお　　あか

2. おさけをのんで、＿＿＿ が＿＿＿ くなりました。
   My face turned red when I drank alcohol.

　あし くび　　すこ

3. ＿＿＿ ＿＿＿ が ＿＿＿ し いたいです。
   My ankle hurts a little bit.

　　　　　　かしら も　じ　　　か　　　くだ

4. ここに ＿＿＿ ＿＿＿ ＿＿＿を ＿＿＿ いて＿＿＿ さい。
   Please write your initials here.

　　　き いろ　しろ　　け いと　　か　　き　くだ

5. ＿＿＿ ＿＿＿ と＿＿＿の＿＿＿ ＿＿＿を ＿＿＿って＿＿＿て＿＿＿さい。
   Please go and buy yellow, and white yarn.

　　　　　　よう　　　にく

6. すきやき ＿＿＿ の お＿＿＿ は、おいしいですよ。
   Meat for use in Sukiyaki is delicious.

　　　ひと　　　　　　しん がお

7. あの＿＿＿はだれですか。＿＿＿ ＿＿＿ ですね。
   Who is that person over there? He/she is a newcomer.

25 | Kanji meaning

Write the following kanji next to its meaning: 肉 体 母 毛 友 顔 心 首 頭

1.____ friend

2. ____ meat

3. ____ mother

4. ____ face

5. ____ head

6. ____ body

7. ____ hair

8. ____ heart

9. ____ neck

25 | Kanji matching

Draw a line to connect each kanji with only one of its ON or KUN readings.

毛 ・　　　　・ かしら
首 ・　　　　・ しゅ
声 ・　　　　・ もう
肉 ・　　　　・ がん
頭 ・　　　　・ たい
自 ・　　　　・ こ
顔 ・　　　　・ にく
太 ・　　　　・ た
体 ・　　　　・ せい
答 ・　　　　・ みずか

25 | Stroke Order Check

Circle A or B whichever represents the correct stroke order for each kanji.

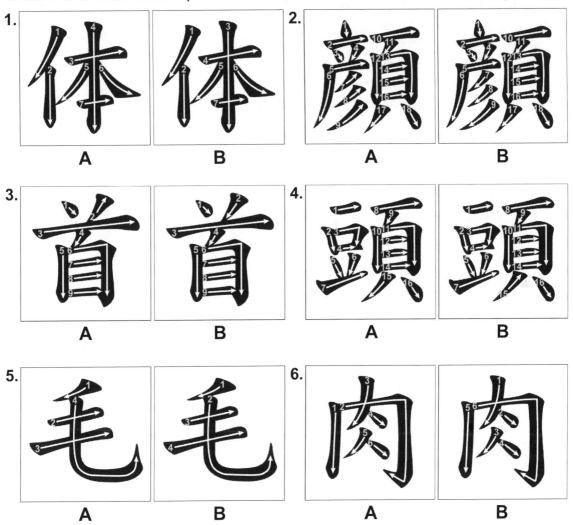

25 | Answer Key 答え合わせ

Fill in the kanji (answers)

1. 広田 さんはいつも 元気 で 体力 が あります。

2. おさけをのんで、顔 が 赤 くなりました。

3. 足首 が 少 し、いたい です。

4. ここに 頭文字 を 書 いて 下 さい。

5. 黄色 と 白 の 毛糸 を 買 って 来 て 下 さい。

6. すきやき 用 のお 肉 は、おいしいですよ。

7. あの 人 はだれですか。新顔 ですね。

Kanji meaning match (answers)

1. 友 friend　　　　2. 肉 meat　　　　3. 母 mother

4. 顔 face　　　　　5. 頭 head　　　　6. 体 body

7. 毛 hair　　　　　8. 心 heart　　　　9. 首 neck

Kanji matching (answers)

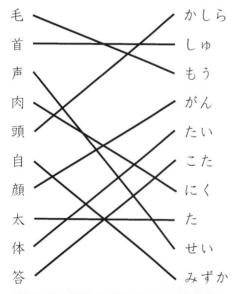

毛　　　　　　かしら
首　　　　　　しゅ
声　　　　　　もう
肉　　　　　　がん
頭　　　　　　たい
自　　　　　　こた
顔　　　　　　にく
太　　　　　　た
体　　　　　　せい
答　　　　　　みずか

Stroke order check (answers)

1. A　　2. B　　3. B　　4. A　　5. A　　6. A

SR | Super Review 5

SR5 | Kanji selection

Select the best kanji to fill in the blank in each sentence.

1. 光が＿＿たって、まぶしい ですね。
   A. 回   B. 交   C. 当   D. 止

2. 兄は＿＿＿文を 書くのが とくいです。
   A. 思   B. 少   C. 作   D. 自

3. わたしは 父と＿＿＿がいて、一人っ子です。
   A. 母   B. 兄   C. 姉   D. 妹

4. わたしは 原さんと とても気が＿＿＿います。
   A. 会   B. 合   C. 思   D. 歌

SR5 | Kanji reading

Select the best reading for the underlined kanji.

1. このケーキを八つに<u>分</u>けて下さい。
   A. き   B. わ   C. ぶん   D. つく

2. この赤ちゃんは、丸<u>顔</u>で かわいいですね。
   A. あたま   B. がお   C. がん   D. かお

3. 母はとても大<u>切</u>な人です。
   A. き   B. へん   C. せつ   D. じ

4. この<u>町</u>には、ぜんぜん知り合いがいません。
   A. し   B. ち   C. い   D. は

SR5 | Compound kanji word puzzle

Fill in the correct kanji based on the list below the puzzle.

1)	2)		3)
	4)	5)	6)
7)			8)
		9)	

Down ↓
1) down payment
3) gaurdians, parents
4) caution
5) disciple
7) cancellation
8) oneself
Left to Right →
7) center
9) five minutes
Right to Left ←
2) inflexible person
3) father
6) siblings
9) five times

SR5 | Answer Key 答え合わせ

Kanji selection (answers)

1. C – 当^あたって

It sure is bright because of the light hitting (shining on) (it / us).

2. C – 作文^{さくぶん}

My older brother is skilled at writing essays.

3. A – 母^{はは}

I have my father and a mother, I am an only child.

4. B – 合^あいます

I get along well with Hara-san.

Kanji reading (answers)

1. B – 分^わけて

Please split this cake into 8 pieces.

2. B – 丸顔^{まるがお}

This baby has a round face and is cute.

3. C – 大切^{たいせつ}

My mother is a very important person.

4. A – 知^しり合^あい

I have no acquaintances at all in this town.

Compound kanji word puzzle (answers)

頭	石	親	父
金	用	弟	兄
中	心	子	自
止	回	五	分

26

Kanji lesson 26:

牛馬魚鳥米麦

---

26 | New Kanji あたらしい かんじ

Make sure you learn the correct stroke order. Correct stroke order will mean neater symbols when writing quickly. Also, take time to learn the words listed for each kanji – these will help you memorize the different readings.

牛

154. cow   4 画

くんよみ	うし
おんよみ	ギュウ

牛						

cow shed	calf	beef	milk
うしごや	こうし	ぎゅうにく	ぎゅうにゅう
牛小屋	子牛	牛肉	牛乳

馬

155. horse   10 画

くんよみ	うま、ま
おんよみ	バ

馬						

horse	stable	horse riding	horsepower
うま	うまごや	じょうば	ばりき
馬	馬小屋	乗馬	馬力

156. fish　　11画

くんよみ	さかな、うお
おんよみ	ギョ

魚						

fish store	fishing	goldfish	mermaid
さかなや	さかなつり	きんぎょ	にんぎょ
魚屋	魚釣り	金魚	人魚

157. bird　　11画

くんよみ	とり
おんよみ	チョウ

鳥						

bird	small bird	goose bumps	turkey
とり	ことり	とりはだ	しちめんちょう
鳥	小鳥	鳥肌	七面鳥

158. rice　　6画

くんよみ	こめ
おんよみ	ベイ、マイ

米						

uncooked rice	Japanese rice	going to U.S.A.	brown rice
こめ	にほんまい	とべい	げんまい
お米	日本米	渡米	玄米

159. wheat, barley						7 画
くんよみ	むぎ					
おんよみ	バク					
麦						

wheat, barley	barley tea	wheat flour	malt
むぎ	むぎちゃ	こ むぎ こ	ばく が
麦	麦茶	小麦粉	麦芽

26 | Kanji Usage かんじの つかいかた

● **26-1. Thank you for all the fish – literally (魚)**
Some fish related words might surprise you when you see them. You could probably guess their meaning just by looking at them.

goldfish (gold + fish)	mermaid (human + fish)
金魚	人魚
きん・ぎょ	にん・ぎょ

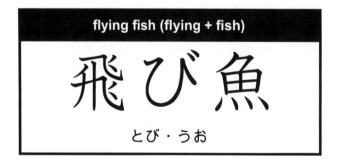

flying fish (flying + fish)
飛び魚
とび・うお

● **26-2. Thanks for all the fish and the fish radical (魚)**

Not surprisingly the kanji for fish 魚 is a really common radical in the kanji for types of fish.

まぐろ tuna	さけ salmon	くじら whale
鮪	鮭	鯨
fish / existence	fish / angle, rough	fish / capital

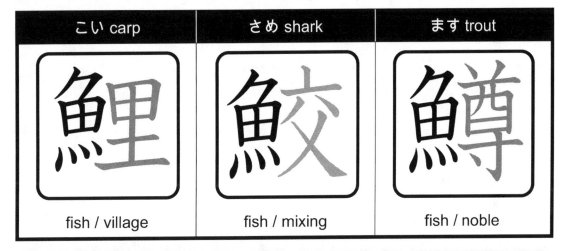

こい carp	さめ shark	ます trout
鯉	鮫	鱒
fish / village	fish / mixing	fish / noble

ひらめ flounder	さば mackerel	いわし sardines
鮃	鯖	鰯
fish / flat	fish / blue, green	fish / weak

● **26-3. Fish that aren't actually fish!**
Okay, these words are fun because they don't have much to do with fish.

torpedo (fish + thunder)	corn (on one's foot)
魚雷	魚の目
ぎょ・らい	うお・の・め

snapdragon flower (gold + fish + grass)
金魚草
きん・ぎょ・そう

26 | Words You Can Write かける ことば

子牛 （こうし） calf

子	牛								

牛肉 （ぎゅうにく） beef

牛	肉								

馬力 （ばりき） horsepower, a lot of energy

馬	力								

馬車 （ばしゃ） carriage, coach

馬	車								

金魚（きんぎょ）goldfish

金	魚								

人魚（にんぎょ）mermaid

人	魚								

小鳥（ことり）small bird

小	鳥								

麦茶（むぎちゃ）barley tea

麦	茶								

日米（にちべい）Japan-America

日	米								

大麦（おおむぎ）barley

大	麦								

鳥肉（とりにく）chicken meat

鳥	肉								

日本米（にほんまい）Japanese rice

日	本	米						

一石二鳥（いっせきにちょう）killing two birds with one stone

一	石	二	鳥				

26 | Fill in the Kanji

Fill in the appropriate kanji in the blanks for each sentence.

ぎゅうにく　　た

1. ＿＿＿ ＿＿＿を ＿＿＿べて、おなかいっぱいです。
   I am full from eating beef.

た　なか　　　からだ　おお　　　　ば　りき

2. ＿＿＿＿＿＿ さんは ＿＿＿ が＿＿＿きくて、＿＿＿ ＿＿＿ が あります。
   Because Tanaka's body is big he has a lot of power.

さかな　　　　　よん　　　か　　くだ

3. ＿＿＿ やで まぐろを＿＿＿ ひき、＿＿＿って＿＿＿さい。
   Please buy 4 tuna at the fish shop.

こ　とり　ご　　きんぎょ　さん

4. いえに＿＿＿ ＿＿＿が＿＿＿わと ＿＿＿ ＿＿＿が＿＿＿びき、います。
   I have 5 small birds, and 3 goldfish at my house.

に　ほん　まい　たか　　き

5. ＿＿＿ ＿＿＿ ＿＿＿は ＿＿＿いと ＿＿＿いたことが あります。
   I have heard that Japanese rice is expensive.

にち　むぎ　ちゃ

6. なつは、まい＿＿＿ ＿＿＿ ＿＿＿を のんでいます。
   In summer I drink barley tea every day.

こ　　　　　　　たけ　うま

7. ＿＿＿どものときは、よく＿＿＿ ＿＿＿で あそんでいました。
   When I was a child I often played with stilts.

26 | Kanji meaning

Write the following kanji next to its meaning: 麦 牛 首 米 顔 馬 妹 魚 鳥

1. ____ bird

2. ____ younger sister

3. ____ cow

4. ____ wheat, barley

5. ____ face

6. ____ neck

7. ____ fish

8. ____ uncooked rice

9. ____ horse

26 | Kanji matching

Draw a line to connect each kanji with only one of its ON or KUN readings.

米　・　　　　　・べ　い
直　・　　　　　・ゆ　う
魚　・　　　　　・あ
友　・　　　　　・ち　よ　く
牛　・　　　　　・ぎ　ゅ　う
麦　・　　　　　・な　ぎ
会　・　　　　　・ぎ　よ
馬　・　　　　　・う　ま
鳥　・　　　　　・ち　よ　う
鳴　・　　　　　・む　ぎ

26 | Stroke Order Check

Circle A or B whichever represents the correct stroke order for each kanji.

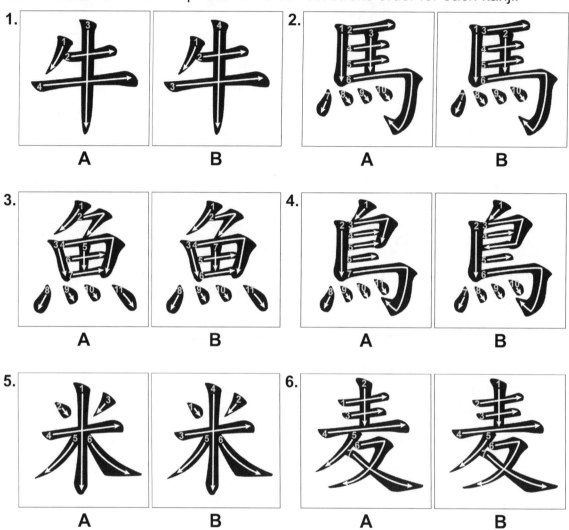

26 | Answer Key 答え合わせ

Fill in the kanji (answers)

1. 牛肉 を 食 べて、おなかいっぱいです。

2. 田中 さんは 体 が 大 きくて、馬力 が あります。

3. 魚 やでまぐろを 四 ひき、買 って 下 さい。

4. いえに 小鳥 が 五 わと 金魚 が 三 びき、います。

5. 日本米 は 高 いと 聞 いたことが あります。

6. なつは、まい 日 麦茶 を のんでいます。

7. 子 どものときは、よく 竹馬 で あそんでいました。

Kanji meaning match (answers)

1. 鳥 bird　　　　　2. 妹 younger sister　　3. 牛 cow
4. 麦 wheat, barley　5. 顔 face　　　　　　6. 首 neck
7. 魚 fish　　　　　8. 米 uncooked rice　　9. 馬 horse

Kanji matching (answers)

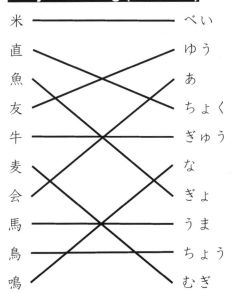

米	べい
直	ゆう
魚	あ
友	ちょく
牛	ぎゅう
麦	な
会	ぎょ
馬	うま
鳥	ちょう
鳴	むぎ

Stroke order check (answers)

1. B　2. A　3. A　4. A　5. B　6. A

27 Kanji lesson 27: 台組画番点語

160-165

27 | New Kanji あたらしい かんじ

Make sure you learn the correct stroke order. Correct stroke order will mean neater symbols when writing quickly. Also, take time to learn the words listed for each kanji – these will help you memorize the different readings.

160. stand, basis   5画

くんよみ	none
おんよみ	ダイ、タイ

two (machinery)	kitchen	script	typhoon
に だい 二台	だいどころ 台所	だいほん 台本	たいふう 台風

161. group, team   11画

くんよみ	く(む)、くみ
おんよみ	ソ

group	program (e.g. TV)	association, union	organization
くみ 組	ばんぐみ 番組	くみあい 組合	そ しき 組織

162. stroke, picture, painting　8画

くんよみ	none
おんよみ	カク、ガ

画

movie	plan	painter, artist	image
えいが	けいかく	がか	がぞう
映画	計画	画家	画像

163. number, turn, watch, guard　12画

くんよみ	none
おんよみ	バン

番

first, number one	program	number (phone etc.)	watchdog
いちばん	ばんぐみ	ばんごう	ばんけん
一番	番組	番号	番犬

164. dot, mark, points　9画

くんよみ	none
おんよみ	テン

点

100 points	score	flaw, weak point, defect	perfect score
ひゃくてん	てんすう	けってん	まんてん
百点	点数	欠点	満点

語	165. speak, word, language						14 画
	くんよみ	かた(る、らう)					
	おんよみ	ゴ					
	語						

to talk about, to narrate	language study	English	story
かた	ご がく	えい ご	ものがたり
語る	語学	英語	物語

---

27 | Kanji Usage かんじの つかいかた

● **27-1. Speaking in kanji (語)**

Most languages are made by adding 語 (ご) after the country name.

スペイン語 (Spanish)　　　ドイツ語 (German)

ちゅうごく ご
中国語 (Chinese)　　　に ほん ご
日本語 (Japanese)

えい ご
英語 (English)　　　かんこく ご
韓国語 (Korean)

フランス語 (French)　　　ロシア語 (Russian)

● **27-2. Get to the point (点)**

Here are some other じゅくご (compound words) that contain 点 (てん).

weak point	advantage, point in favor
弱点	利点
じゃく・てん	り・てん

the dot in decimal numbers	the dot in ip addresses
2.5	10.2.2.2
2 <u>てん</u> 5	10 てん 2 てん 2 てん 2

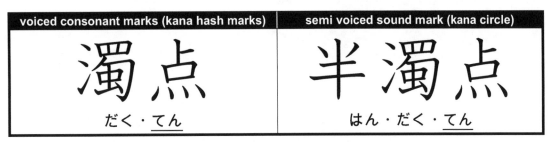

voiced consonant marks (kana hash marks)	semi voiced sound mark (kana circle)
濁点	半濁点
だく・<u>てん</u>	はん・だく・<u>てん</u>

the casual name for kana hash marks
点々
<u>てん</u>・てん

● **27-3. Time to learn more about (番)**

番 is used in a variety of words. Many of them are work related.

house number (number + ground)	order of things (order + number)
番地	順番
ばん・ち	じゅん・ばん

being on duty (hit + turn)	store tending (store + guard)
当番	店番
とう・ばん	みせ・ばん

early shift (early + turn)	late shift (late + turn)
早番	遅番
はや・ばん	おそ・ばん

27 | Words You Can Write かける ことば

台本 （だいほん） script (for movie etc)

台	本								

四台 （よんだい） four (machinery)

四	台								

組合 （くみあい） association, guild, union

組	合								

点火 （てんか） ignition, set fire to

点	火								

三組 （さんくみ） three groups

三	組								

画家 （がか） painter, artist

画	家								

三画 （さんかく） three strokes

三	画								

言語（げんご）language

言	語									

一番（いちばん）first, number one

一	番									

番組（ばんぐみ）program

番	組									

百点（ひゃくてん）100 points

百	点									

点数（てんすう）score

点	数									

語る（かたる）talk, recite

語	る									

語学（ごがく）language study

語	学									

当番（とうばん）being on duty, duty

当	番									

日本語（にほんご）Japanese language

日	本	語						

27 | Fill in the Kanji

Fill in the appropriate kanji in the blanks for each sentence.

は　つ　か　　　　だい ほん　　よ

1. ____ ____ ____ までに____ ____ を____まなければなりません。
   I have to read a script by the 20th.

く　　あ　　　　　　た の

2. パズルを ____ み____わせるのは ____しいですね。
   Putting together a puzzle sure is fun.

も り　　　　　　　　じ　じゅう　に　かく

3. 「____」というかん ____ は ____ ____ ____ですよね。
   The MORI kanji has 12 strokes right?

がっ こう　　　　　　とう ばん

4. あしたは ____ ____ で そうじ____ ____です。
   Tomorrow I am on cleaning duty at school.

てん すう　　　　　　　　　　　や す　　　　きょう

5. ____ ____ がわるかったので、ふゆ ____みにべん ____ します。
   Because my score was bad, I will study on (during) winter break.

に　ほん　ご　　うた　　うた

6. ____ ____ ____で ____ を ____いました。
   I sang a song in Japanese.

ばん ぐみ

7. おもしろい テレビ____ ____ を すすめてください。
   Please recommend an interesting TV show.

27 | Kanji meaning

Write the following kanji next to its meaning: 台 語 体 画 組 点 毛 番 弟

1._____ turn, number   2. _____ speak, word   3. _____ hair

4. _____ dot, points   5. _____ stand, basis   6. _____ younger brother

7. _____ stroke, picture 8. _____ body   9. _____ group, team

27 | Kanji matching

Draw a line to connect each kanji with one of its ON or KUN readings.

語 ・   ・ ばん
番 ・   ・ てん
頭 ・   ・ ご
組 ・   ・ く み
顔 ・   ・ こ う
台 ・   ・ か お
画 ・   ・ か く
考 ・   ・ と う
点 ・   ・ だ い
声 ・   ・ こ え

27 | Stroke Order Check

Circle A or B whichever represents the correct stroke order for each kanji.

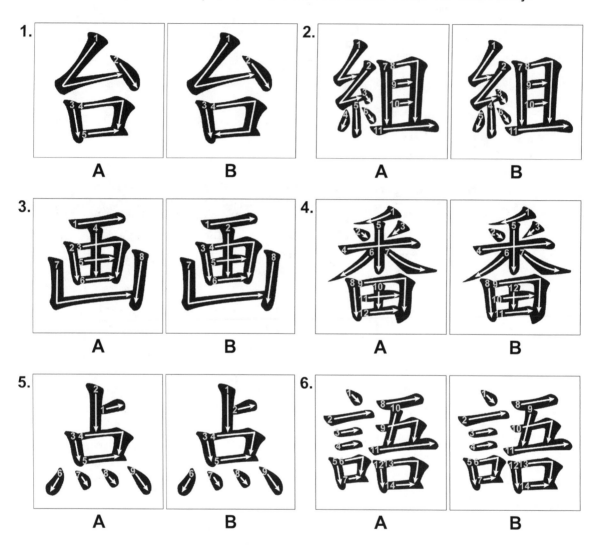

1. A B

2. A B

3. A B

4. A B

5. A B

6. A B

27 | Answer Key 答え合わせ

Fill in the kanji (answers)

1. 二十日までに台本を読まなければなりません。

2. パズルを組み合わせるのは楽しいですね。

3. 「森」というかん字は十二画ですよね。

4. あしたは学校でそうじ当番です。

5. テストの点数がわるかったので、ふゆ休みにべん強します。

6. 日本語で歌を歌いました。

7. おもしろいテレビ番組を すすめてください。

Kanji meaning match (answers)

1. 番 turn, number   2. 語 speak, word   3. 毛 hair

4. 点 dot, points   5. 台 stand, basis   6. 弟 younger brother

7. 画 stroke, picture   8. 体 body   9. 組 group, team

Kanji matching (answers)

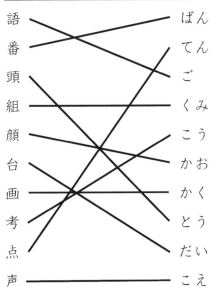

語　　　　　　　ばん
番　　　　　　　てん
頭　　　　　　　ご
組　　　　　　　くみ
顔　　　　　　　こう
台　　　　　　　かお
画　　　　　　　かく
考　　　　　　　とう
点　　　　　　　だい
声　　　　　　　こえ

Stroke order check (answers)

1. A   2. B   3. A   4. A   5. B   6. B

28 Kanji lesson 28: 羽週曜才毎半

28 | New Kanji あたらしい かんじ

Make sure you learn the correct stroke order. Correct stroke order will mean neater symbols when writing quickly. Also, take time to learn the words listed for each kanji – these will help you memorize the different readings.

---

166. feather, wing   6画

くんよみ	は、はね
おんよみ	ウ

羽

wing, feather	one bird	down feather	Haori (Japanese overgarment)
はね	いちわ	うもう	はおり
羽	一羽	羽毛	羽織

---

167. week   11画

くんよみ	none
おんよみ	シュウ

週

every week	weekend	one week	this week
まいしゅう	しゅうまつ	いっしゅうかん	こんしゅう
毎週	週末	一週間	今週

168. day of the week　　18 画

くんよみ	none
おんよみ	ヨウ

曜

Sunday	Monday	Tuesday	Wednesday
にちよう び	げつよう び	か ようび	すいよう び
日曜日	月曜日	火曜日	水曜日

169. wit, talent, ability　　3 画

くんよみ	none
おんよみ	サイ

才

one year old	ability	genius	comic backchat
いっさい	さいのう	てんさい	まんざい
一才	才能	天才	漫才

170. every, each　　6 画

くんよみ	none
おんよみ	マイ

毎

every day	every month	every year	every time
まいにち	まいつき	まいとし	まいかい
毎日	毎月	毎年	毎回

半	171. half, middle			5画
	くんよみ	なか(ば)		
	おんよみ	ハン		

half	half price	2:30	middle
はんぶん	はんがく	に　じ　はん	なか
半分	半額	二時半	半ば

28 | Kanji Usage　かんじの　つかいかた

● 28-1. The genius behind (才)

才 (さい) means "talent" or "wit" but it's commonly used as a substitute for the 歳 (さい) kanji that means "years old" despite the fact that it doesn't actually mean "years old." It's used instead of 歳 mainly because 才 shares the same sound as 歳 and it's much quicker to write.

Japanese children learn 才 in elementary school, but don't learn 歳 until junior high. Therefore younger children will always use 才 instead of 歳. Typically younger ages, up to 20 years old, are written using 才 and ages above that tend to be written using 歳. Luckily there isn't any official rule, so you can use whichever you like.

Beyond this ONE usage, 歳 and 才 can not be interchanged. Here are some other words using 才.

multi-talented (many + talent)	literary talent (sentence + talent)
多才	文才
た・さい	ぶん・さい

● **28-2. Birds and rabbits (羽)**

The counter for birds is 羽 (わ), which really makes sense since birds have feathers. It certainly seems weird that rabbits are also counted using the same counter despite having no feathers. You would think that rabbits would be counted with 匹 (ひき) counter the same way that dogs, cats, and pigs are counted since they are similar.

One theory as to why rabbits are counted the same as birds, is that monks were not allow to eat animals with fur. To make an exception to this rule they considered the long ears of rabbits to be feathers. It also helped to consider that rabbits can stand on two legs like a bird.

one rabbit / bird	how many rabbits / birds
一羽	何羽
いち・わ	なん・わ

two animals	how many animals
二匹	何匹
に・ひき	なん・ひき

28 Words You Can Write かける ことば

羽毛 （うもう） feather (down)

羽	毛								

二羽 （にわ） two birds (or rabbits)

二	羽								

毎週 （まいしゅう） every week

毎	週								

先週 (せんしゅう) last week

先 週

五才 (ごさい) five years old

五 才

天才 (てんさい) genius

天 才

毎日 (まいにち) every day

毎 日

半分 (はんぶん) half

半 分

半日 (はんにち) a half day

半 日

月曜日 (げつようび) Monday

月 曜 日

水曜日 (すいようび) Wednesday

水 曜 日

金曜日 (きんようび) Friday

金 曜 日

28 | Fill in the Kanji

Fill in the appropriate kanji in the blanks for each sentence.

う　もう　　　　よん　まん　えん

1. この ＿＿ ＿＿ ぶとんは、＿＿ ＿＿ ＿＿ しました。
This feather (down) quilt cost 40,000 yen.

せん　しゅう　くるま　なお

2. ＿＿ ＿＿ 、＿＿ を＿＿ してもらいました。
I had my car fixed last week.

ど　よう　び　よう　　　　　きん　よう　び

3. ＿＿ ＿＿ ＿＿は＿＿ じが あるから、＿＿ ＿＿ ＿＿は どう？
Since I have things to do on Saturday how about Friday?

に　じゅう　ろく　さい

4. わたしは、＿＿ ＿＿ ＿＿ ＿＿に なりました。
I turned 26 years old.

く　がつ　なか　　あ

5. じゃあ、こんどは＿＿ ＿＿ ＿＿ばに＿＿ いましょう。
Ok then, let's meet next time in the middle of September.

まい　とし　いもうと　　　　　に　ほん　かえ

6. ＿＿ ＿＿ 、＿＿ といっしょに ＿＿ ＿＿に ＿＿ ります。
Every year I return to Japan (together) with my younger sister.

まい　しゅう　にち　よう　び　さかな　　　い

7. ＿＿ ＿＿ ＿＿ ＿＿ ＿＿に ＿＿ つりに ＿＿ きます。
Every Sunday I go fishing.

28 | Kanji meaning

Write the following kanji next to its meaning: 羽 毎 鳥 半 週 妹 曜 才 肉

1. ____ meat

2. ____ feather, wing

3. ____ half, middle

4. ____ day of the week

5. ____ bird

6. ____ younger sister

7. ____ week

8. ____ every, each

9. ____ wit, talent

28 | Kanji matching

Draw a line to connect each kanji with only one of its ON or KUN readings.

半 ・	・ べい
才 ・	・ てん
週 ・	・ まい
点 ・	・ さい
羽 ・	・ はね
曜 ・	・ しゅう
毎 ・	・ しん
米 ・	・ はん
毛 ・	・ け
心 ・	・ よう

28 | Stroke Order Check

Circle A or B whichever represents the correct stroke order for each kanji.

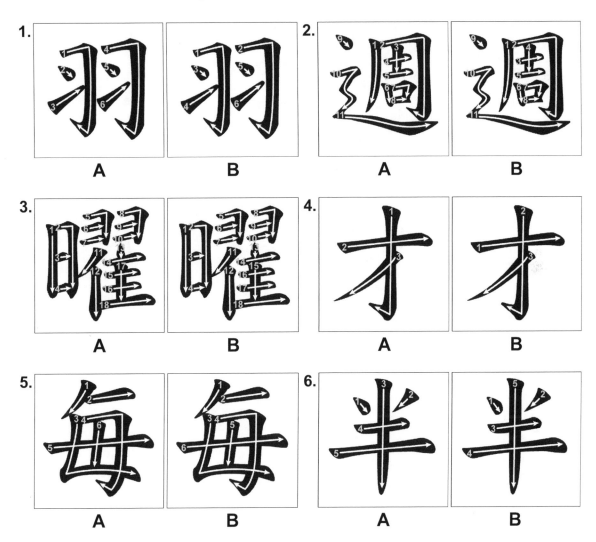

28 | Answer Key 答え合わせ

Fill in the kanji (answers)

1. この 羽毛 ぶとんは、四万円 しました。

2. 先週、車 を 直 してもらいました。

3. 土曜日 は 用 じがあるから、金曜日 は どう？

4. わたしは、二十六才 に なりました。

5. じゃあ、こんどは 九月半 ばに 会 いましょう。

6. 毎年、妹 といっしょに 日本 に 帰 ります。

7. 毎週日曜日 に 魚 つりに 行 きます。

Kanji meaning match (answers)

1. 肉 meat
2. 羽 feather, wing
3. 半 half, middle
4. 曜 day of the week
5. 鳥 bird
6. 妹 younger sister
7. 週 week
8. 毎 every, each
9. 才 wit, talent

Kanji matching (answers)

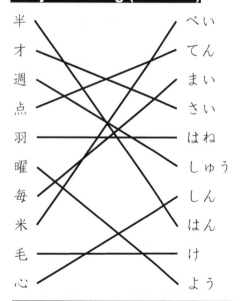

半　　　べい
才　　　てん
週　　　まい
点　　　さい
羽　　　はね
曜　　　しゅう
毎　　　しん
米　　　はん
毛　　　け
心　　　よう

Stroke order check (answers)

1. A　2. B　3. B　4. B　5. B　6. B

29

Kanji lesson 29:

東西南北方角

29 New Kanji あたらしい かんじ

Make sure you learn the correct stroke order. Correct stroke order will mean neater symbols when writing quickly. Also, take time to learn the words listed for each kanji – these will help you memorize the different readings.

172. east			8 画
くんよみ	ひがし		
おんよみ	トウ		

east	Tokyo	orient	Middle East
ひがし	とうきょう	とうよう	ちゅうとう
東	東京	東洋	中東

173. west			6 画
くんよみ	にし		
おんよみ	セイ、サイ		

west	the setting sun	west coast	the Kansai region
にし	にしび	にしかいがん	かんさい
西	西日	西海岸	関西

174. south   9画

| くんよみ | みなみ |
| おんよみ | ナン、ナ |

南

south	South pole	north and south	southern country
みなみ	なんきょく	なんぼく	なんごく
南	南極	南北	南国

175. north   5画

| くんよみ | きた |
| おんよみ | ホク、ボク |

北

north	north wind	Northern Europe	defeat
きた	きたかぜ	ほくおう	はいぼく
北	北風	北欧	敗北

176. direction, side   4画

| くんよみ | かた |
| おんよみ | ホウ、ポウ |

方

direction	method	how to make	dialect
ほうこう	ほうほう	つく かた	ほうげん
方向	方法	作り方	方言

角	177. angle, corner				7 画
	くんよみ	かど、つの			
	おんよみ	カク			
	角				

corner	street corner	triangle	angle
かど	まちかど	さんかく	かく　ど
角	街角	三角	角度

29 | Kanji Usage かんじの つかいかた

● **29-1. Train station exit strategy (南北東西)**

American cities are often designed around intersections; prime real estate is normally on 'X' and 'Y' road. However, in Japan, it's *much* more important to be near a train station, so businesses fight to be just minutes from a station.

In Japan's metropolitan areas, huge sprawling train stations are common. The exits for the stations are named based on the direction they face.

north exit	south exit
北口	南口
きた・ぐち	みなみ・ぐち

west exit	east exit
西口	東口
にし・ぐち	ひがし・ぐち

● 29-2. Regions in Japan (南北東西)

The word for "region" is 地方 (ちほう). Japan is split up into 9 major regions including the southern islands of Okinawa prefecture.

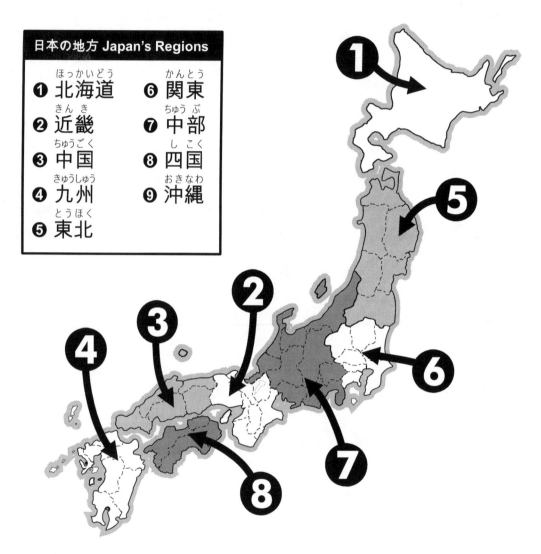

日本の地方 Japan's Regions

❶	ほっかいどう 北海道	❻	かんとう 関東
❷	きんき 近畿	❼	ちゅうぶ 中部
❸	ちゅうごく 中国	❽	しこく 四国
❹	きゅうしゅう 九州	❾	おきなわ 沖縄
❺	とうほく 東北		

Okinawa is not shown, but it is below the main islands of Japan in the Pacific Ocean. Okinawa is famous for its beaches and is considered the "Hawaii" of Japan. Okinawan people speak standard Japanese, however there is a dialect unique to Okinawa called *Uchinaaguchi* that is not understood by the mainlanders.

After Japan lost World War II, Okinawa became a territory of the United States until it was returned to Japan in 1972.

● **29-3. Other direction words (南北東西)**

Directions are a big part of life. Here are some words that you will encounter for sure when speaking Japanese that contain direction kanji.

U.S. Civil War	Tokyo (east capital)
南北戦争	東京
なん・ぼく・せん・そう	とう・きょう

South pole	North pole
南極	北極
なん・きょく	ほっ・きょく

westerner	asian person, oriental person
西洋人	東洋人
せい・よう・じん	とう・よう・じん

west coast	east coast
西海岸	東海岸
にし・かい・がん	ひがし・かい・がん

29 | Words You Can Write かける ことば

中東 （ちゅうとう） Middle East

中	東								

西日 （にしび） west sun, setting sun

西	日								

南口 （みなみぐち） south exit

南	口								

北口 （きたぐち） north exit

北	口								

南北 （なんぼく） north and south

南	北								

北西 （ほくせい） northwest

北	西								

方言 （ほうげん） dialect

方	言								

四角 （しかく） square

四	角								

方角 （ほうがく） direction

方	角								

行き方（いきかた）directions

行	き	方								

東西南北（とうざいなんぼく）north, south, east and west

東	西	南	北							

29 | Fill in the Kanji

Fill in the appropriate kanji in the blanks for each sentence.

　　ひがし　ほう　　　　　　やま

1. ＿＿＿ の ＿＿＿ にきれいな＿＿＿ が ありますよ。

   In the direction of the east, there is a pretty mountain.

　　　　さい　すう　げつ　　　　は　　ひ　おお

2. かん＿＿＿ は ＿＿＿ か＿＿＿ かん、＿＿＿れの＿＿＿が ＿＿＿かった。

   For several months, the Kansai area has had many sunny days.

　　　あ　し た　　　　　きたぐち　あ

3. ＿＿＿＿＿＿、えきの＿＿＿＿＿＿で＿＿＿いましょう。

   Let's meet at the north exit of the station tomorrow.

　　　に　ほん　　おお　　ほうげん

4. ＿＿＿＿＿＿には＿＿＿くの＿＿＿＿＿＿が あります。

   Japanese has many dialects.

　　　　かど　みぎ　　　　　くだ

5. あの ＿＿＿ を＿＿＿ に まがって＿＿＿ さい。

   Please turn right at that corner over there.

　　がっこう　みなみ　ほう　がく

6. ＿＿＿＿＿＿は ＿＿＿ の＿＿＿＿＿＿に ありますよ。

   School is in the southern direction.

なん ぼく　はし

7. このどうろは、＿＿＿ ＿＿＿ に＿＿＿っています。
This road runs north to south.

---

29 | Kanji meaning

Write the following kanji next to its meaning: 角 北 西 羽 画 東 南 方 麦

1.＿＿＿ wheat, barley   2. ＿＿＿ west   3. ＿＿＿ feather, wing

4. ＿＿＿ south   5. ＿＿＿ angle, corner 6. ＿＿＿ east

7. ＿＿＿ stroke, picture 8. ＿＿＿ north   9. ＿＿＿ direction, side

---

29 | Kanji matching

Draw a line to connect each kanji with one of its ON or KUN readings.

東 ・	・ ほう
南 ・	・ なん
週 ・	・ ひがし
角 ・	・ かく
方 ・	・ にし
台 ・	・ しゅう
西 ・	・ うま
北 ・	・ ほく
馬 ・	・ だい
友 ・	・ ゆう

29 | Stroke Order Check

Circle A or B whichever represents the correct stroke order for each kanji.

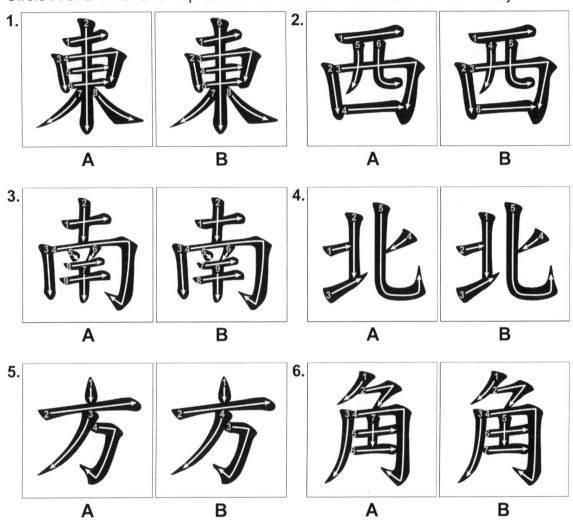

1.

A　B

2.

A　B

3.

A　B

4.

A　B

5.

A　B

6.

A　B

29 | Answer Key 答え合わせ

Fill in the kanji (answers)

1. 東 の 方 にきれいな 山 が ありますよ。

2. かん 西 は 数 か 月 かん、晴れの 日 が 多 かった。

3. 明日、えきの 北口 で 会 いましょう。

4. 日本 には 多 くの 方言 が あります。

5. あの 角 を 右 にまがって 下 さい。

6. 学校 は 南 の 方角 に ありますよ。

7. このどうろは、南北 に 走 っています。

Kanji meaning match (answers)

1. 麦 wheat, barley   2. 西 west   3. 羽 feather, wing

4. 南 south   5. 角 angle, corner   6. 東 east

7. 画 stroke, picture   8. 北 north   9. 方 direction, side

Kanji matching (answers)

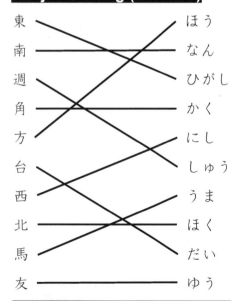

東　　　　ほう
南　　　　なん
週　　　　ひがし
角　　　　かく
方　　　　にし
台　　　　しゅう
西　　　　うま
北　　　　ほく
馬　　　　だい
友　　　　ゆう

Stroke order check (answers)

1. B　2. B　3. B　4. A　5. B　6. B

30 Kanji lesson 30: 風雪雲星海谷岩

30 New Kanji あたらしい かんじ

Make sure you learn the correct stroke order. Correct stroke order will mean neater symbols when writing quickly. Also, take time to learn the words listed for each kanji – these will help you memorize the different readings.

風	178. wind, breeze			9 画
	くんよみ	かぜ、かざ		
	おんよみ	フウ、フ		
	風			

wind	gust of wind	balloon	appearance
かぜ	とっぷう	ふうせん	ふ ぜい
風	突風	風船	風情

雪	179. snow			11 画
	くんよみ	ゆき		
	おんよみ	セツ		
	雪			

snow	snow country	first snow	accumulation of snow
ゆき	ゆきぐに	はつゆき	せきせつ
雪	雪国	初雪	積雪

180. cloud — 12 画

くんよみ	くも
おんよみ	ウン

雲

cloud	a rain cloud	a bank of clouds, cumulonimbus cloud	a sea of clouds
くも	あまぐも	にゅうどうぐも	うんかい
雲	雨雲	入道雲	雲海

181. star — 9 画

くんよみ	ほし
おんよみ	セイ

星

starry sky	shooting star	Mars	constellation
ほしぞら	ながれぼし	かせい	せいざ
星空	流れ星	火星	星座

182. ocean — 9 画

くんよみ	うみ
おんよみ	カイ

海

beach side	abroad, overseas	navy	sea water
うみべ	かいがい	かいぐん	かいすい
海辺	海外	海軍	海水

	183. valley		7 画
谷	くんよみ	たに	
	おんよみ	コク	
	谷		

valley	bottom of the valley	canyon	ravine
たに	たにそこ	けいこく	たに ま
谷	谷底	渓谷	谷間

	184. rock		8 画
岩	くんよみ	いわ	
	おんよみ	ガン	
	岩		

rock	cliff	rock	lava
いわ	いわ ば	がんせき	ようがん
岩	岩場	岩石	溶岩

30 Kanji Usage かんじの つかいかた

● 30-1. The water radical さんずい

さんずい is a radical that lets you know there is a chance that the kanji is related to water. Remember, sometimes the parts don't make sense.

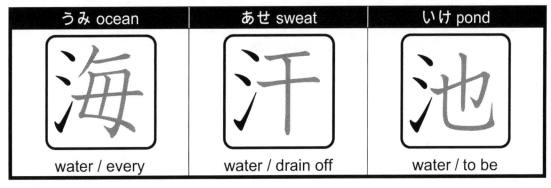

うみ ocean	あせ sweat	いけ pond
海	汗	池
water / every	water / drain off	water / to be

き vapor, steam	なみ wave	なみだ tears
汽	波	涙
water / spirit	water / skin	water / to return

あら(う) to wash	えき liquid	どろ mud
洗	液	泥
water / prior	water / night	water / nun

● **30-2. Any way the wind blows (風)**

As you probably already know, sometimes 漢字 is used in unexpected ways. Here are some interesting words using 風 (かぜ).

Japanese style	Western style
和風	洋風
わ・ふう	よう・ふう

Italian style	headwind
イタリア風	向かい風
イタリア・ふう	むかい・かぜ

windmill, pinwheel	typhoon
風車	台風
かざ・ぐるま	たい・ふう

northern wind	hot wind
北風	熱風
きた・かぜ	ねっ・ぷう

old fashioned	feng shui
昔風	風水
むかし・ふう	ふう・すい

30 | Words You Can Write かける ことば

風力（ふうりょく）wind power

風	力								

風車（ふうしゃ）windmill

風	車								

台風（たいふう）typhoon

台	風								

大雪（おおゆき）heavy snow

大	雪									

雨雲（あまぐも）a rain cloud

雨	雲									

星空（ほしぞら）starry sky

星	空									

火星（かせい）Mars

火	星									

海水（かいすい）sea water

海	水									

谷川（たにがわ）valley river

谷	川									

岩石（がんせき）rock

岩	石									

日本風（にほんふう）Japanese style

日	本	風						

日本海（にほんかい）Sea of Japan

日	本	海						

30 | Fill in the Kanji

Fill in the appropriate kanji in the blanks for each sentence.

　　かぜ　つよ

1. ＿＿＿ が＿＿＿ いから、そとで あそぶのは やめましょう。
Let's stop playing outside because the wind is strong.

　　ちい　　　　　　ゆき

2. ＿＿＿ さいときは よく＿＿＿ がっせんを しました。
When I was small (young) I often had snow fights.

　　　　おお　　あまぐも　み

3. あの ＿＿＿ きい＿＿＿ ＿＿＿が ＿＿＿えますか。
Can you see that big rain cloud?

　　　　　み　は　　　　　　　ほしぞら　　　み

4. ここは ＿＿＿ ＿＿＿らしが いいから、＿＿＿ ＿＿＿がよく＿＿＿える。
Because the view is good here, you can see the starry sky very well.

　　　　ねん　うみ　さん かい

5. きょ ＿＿＿ 、＿＿＿に ＿＿＿ ＿＿＿ いきました。
Last year, I went to the ocean three times.

　　　　ちちおや　　　　やま　たに　い

6. むかしは ＿＿＿ ＿＿＿と、よく＿＿＿や＿＿＿ に＿＿＿きました。
Long ago, I would often go to the mountain and valley with my father.

　　ど　よ　び　　いわ

7. ＿＿＿ ＿＿＿ ＿＿＿に ＿＿＿ のぼりを しました。
I went rock climbing on Saturday.

30 | Kanji meaning

Write the following kanji next to its meaning: 風 岩 角 雪 谷 東 雲 海 星

1.____ star

2. ____ rock

3. ____ valley

4. ____ wind

5. ____ corner, angle

6. ____ east

7. ____ ocean

8. ____ snow

9. ____ cloud

30 | Kanji matching

Draw a line to connect each kanji with only one of its ON or KUN readings.

谷 •
星 •
雪 •
頭 •
岩 •
海 •
雲 •
風 •
声 •
魚 •

• たに
• とう
• ふう
• こえ
• がん
• ほし
• ゆき
• うん
• かい
• ぎょ

30 | Stroke Order Check

Circle A or B whichever represents the correct stroke order for each kanji.

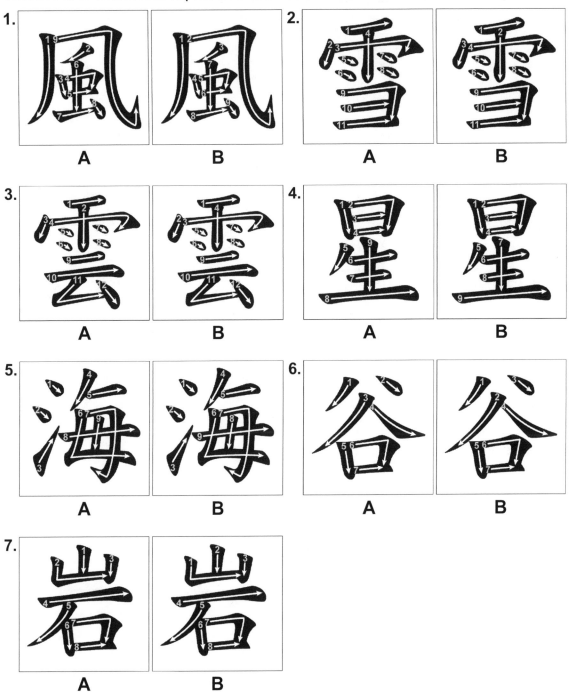

30 | Answer Key 答え合わせ

Fill in the kanji (answers)

1. 風が強いから、そとであそぶのは やめましょう。

2. 小さいときはよく雪がっせんを しました。

3. あの大きい雨雲が見えますか。

4. ここは見晴らしがいいから、星空がよく見える。

5. きょ年、海に三回 いきました。

6. むかしは父親と、よく山や谷に行きました。

7. 土曜日に岩のぼりをしました。

Kanji meaning match (answers)

1. 星 star
2. 岩 rock
3. 谷 valley
4. 風 wind
5. 角 corner, angle
6. 東 east
7. 海 ocean
8. 雪 snow
9. 雲 cloud

Kanji matching (answers)

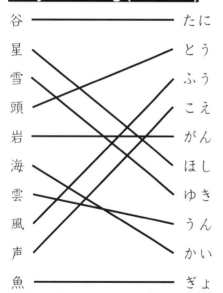

谷 ——————— たに
星 　　　　　　 とう
雪 　　　　　　 ふう
頭 　　　　　　 こえ
岩 ——————— がん
海 　　　　　　 ほし
雲 　　　　　　 ゆき
風 　　　　　　 うん
声 　　　　　　 かい
魚 ——————— ぎょ

Stroke order check (answers)

1. B   2. A   3. B   4. B   5. B   6. A   7. A

SR Super Review 6

SR6 | Kanji selection

Select the best kanji to fill in the blank in each sentence.

1. テストで百____をとって、すごくうれしかったです。
   A. 点   B. 画   C. 番   D. 台

2. あの木に鳥が三____、いますよ。
   A. 組   B. 才   C. 羽   D. 人

3. 今日は天気がよかったから、____が よく見えますね。
   A. 海   B. 星   C. 雪   D. 谷

4. わたしは____アメリカに すんでいます。
   A. 東   B. 西   C. 米   D. 北

SR6 | Kanji reading

Select the best reading for the underlined kanji.

1. 日本海でふねに のりました。
   A. うみ   B. うん   C. かい   D. がい

2. 八月半ばに、日本に 帰ることに しました。
   A. はん   B. なん   C. なか   D. ばん

3. このでん車は、東西に 走っていますよ。
   A. にし   B. とう   C. さい   D. ざい

4. 大人になってから、牛肉が 食べられなくなりました。
   A. とり   B. うま   C. うし   D. ぎゅう

SR6 | **Compound kanji word puzzle**

Fill in the correct kanji based on the list below the puzzle.

1)	2)	3)	4)
5)		6)	
	7)		8)
		9)	

Down ↓
1) every day
3) ocean water
4) horse power
5) Japanese language
6) Mercury
7) typhoon
8) goldfish
Left to Right →
2) sea of clouds
6) hydraulic power
9) mermaid
Right to Left ←
6) Wednesday
7) script
8) Venus

SR6 | Answer Key 答え合わせ

Kanji selection (answers)

1. A – 百点
   <ruby>ひゃくてん</ruby>

   I was so happy I got 100 points on the test.

2. C – 三羽
   <ruby>さんわ</ruby>

   There are three birds in that tree.

3. B – 星
   <ruby>ほし</ruby>

   Since the weather was good today you can see the stars really well.

4. D – 北アメリカ
   <ruby>きた</ruby>

   I live in North America.

Kanji reading (answers)

1. C – 日本海
   <ruby>にほんかい</ruby>

   I rode on a boat in the Japan sea.

2. C – 半ば
   <ruby>なか</ruby>

   I decided to return to Japan in the middle of August.

3. D – 東西
   <ruby>とうざい</ruby>

   This train runs east to west.

4. D – 牛肉
   <ruby>ぎゅうにく</ruby>

   Now that I'm an adult, I can't eat beef.

Compound kanji word puzzle (answers)

毎	雲	海	馬
日	曜	水	力
本	台	星	金
語	風	人	魚

<table>
<tr><td>**31**</td><td>Kanji lesson 31:</td><td>185-190</td></tr>
</table>

家寺門店園場

<table>
<tr><td>**31**</td><td>**New Kanji** あたらしい かんじ</td></tr>
</table>

Make sure you learn the correct stroke order. Correct stroke order will mean neater symbols when writing quickly. Also, take time to learn the words listed for each kanji – these will help you memorize the different readings.

家	**185. house**					10 画
	くんよみ	いえ、や、うち				
	おんよみ	カ、ケ				
	家					

house	rent	family	servant
いえ、うち	や ちん	か ぞく	け らい
家	家賃	家族	家来

寺	**186. temple**					6 画
	くんよみ	てら				
	おんよみ	ジ				
	寺					

temple	mountain temple	zen temple	visiting / entering a temple
てら	やまでら	ぜんでら	にゅうじ
お寺	山寺	禅寺	入寺

門	187. gate			8 画
	くんよみ	かど		
	おんよみ	モン		
	門			

gate	school gate	main gate	New Year's pine decoration
もん	こうもん	せいもん	かどまつ
門	校門	正門	門松

店	188. store, a shop			8 画
	くんよみ	みせ		
	おんよみ	テン		
	店			

store, a shop	clerk	shop manager	branch store
みせ	てんいん	てんちょう	してん
お店	店員	店長	支店

園	189. garden			13 画
	くんよみ	その		
	おんよみ	エン		
	園			

park	gardening	kindergarten pupil	flower garden
こうえん	えんげい	えんじ	はなぞの
公園	園芸	園児	花園

場	190. place			12 画
	くんよみ	ば		
	おんよみ	ジョウ		
	場			

place	factory	assembly hall	scene, setting
ば しょ	こう じょう	かい じょう	ば めん
場所	工場	会場	場面

---

31 | Kanji Usage かんじの つかいかた

● 31-1. Professions using 家

In English we often add **–er** or **–ist** to a word to turn that into a profession. For example: *photograph* + *er* = photographer, *and art* + *ist* = artist. Japanese does the same thing using 家 (か).

のう か
農家 (farmer)

しょうせつ か
小説家 (novelist)

せんもん か
専門家 (expert, specialist)

まんが か
漫画家 (manga artist)

はつめい か
発明家 (inventor)

せいじ か
政治家 (politician)

さっ か
作家 (writer)

しゃしん か
写真家 (photographer)

However, other words ending in 家 do not do the same thing to the word, but simply mean "house."

じっ か
実家 (parent's home)

あ や
空き家 (vacant home)

しゃく や
借家 (house for rent)

いっけん や
一軒家 (detached house)

● **31-2. The roof radical うかんむり**

Kanji radicals often give a hint as to what the overall meaning is of the character. Sometimes it's *very* clear as to why a certain radical is used. Unfortunately, this isn't always the case and sometimes you might be left very confused as to why a kanji is made up with certain parts.

While it is true that kanji is often "pictographic", at times it has been estimated that 80% of Chinese characters are made up based on the sound of the individual radicals rather than the individual meanings

house	**parts:** roof / pig radical

Having a roof over a pig means it becomes a house. A pig under a roof would mean that it was domesticated. In ancient China, people lived with pigs in their house. This only makes sense if you know the underlying history.

letter, character	**parts:** roof / child

Perhaps a child inside the house is learning how to write? Even if this logic doesn't make sense, it just might be enough for you to remember how to write, or at a minimum, recognize this kanji when you see it.

treasure	**parts:** roof / ball

If you are a sports fan, having a ball inside your house would be a treasure. Or maybe playing ball in an indoor stadium is a "treasured" experience when compared to playing under the hot sun. Either way, without history this doesn't make much sense.

protect	**parts:** roof / measurement, a little

This is a good example of the parts not being any help in knowing the meaning. This is also another reason why we aren't a fan of the pictogram method, because often, the picture is harder to remember than the kanji itself.

injury, harm	**parts:** roof / lie / mouth

The "lie" and "mouth" portions of this kanji are no longer used in Japanese. The original Chinese *hanzi* makes sense since lying about things in a house is harmful. If you have time to study Chinese, all the power to you. Chinese From Zero! anyone?

● 31-3. Japanese New Year's decoration (門松)

Japanese New Year's, お正月 (おしょうがつ) is the largest, most important holiday in Japan. Families gather for large meals and homes are garnished with 門松 (かどまつ) and other traditional decorations. 門松 are made with bamboo, pine, and ornamental kale flowers.

門松 are placed outside on both sides of the main entrance of a house. Prices for 門松 can range from a few hundred U.S. dollars, to over $2,000, depending on how fancy they are.

Another popular decoration, しめかざり (straw decoration) are hung on the door like Christmas wreaths. Some people even attach しめかざり to the front of cars and trucks.

かがみもち (stacked rice cakes) are also displayed inside homes.

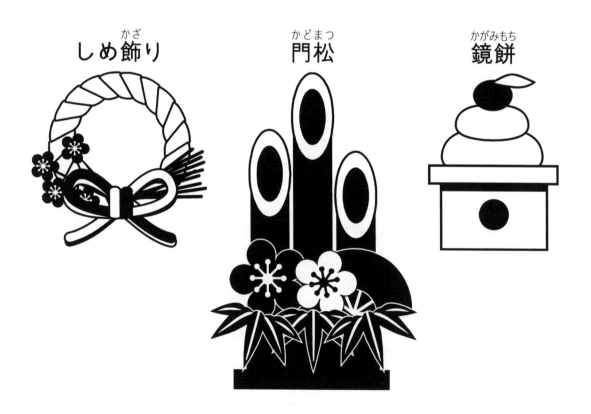

しめ飾り　　　　門松　　　　鏡餅

31 | Words You Can Write かける ことば

大家（おおや）landlord

大	家								

画家（がか）painter, artist

画	家								

山寺（やまでら）mountain temple

山	寺								

校門（こうもん）school gate

校	門								

正門（せいもん）main gate

正	門								

お店（おみせ）store, a shop

お	店								

店長（てんちょう）shop manager

店	長								

花園（はなぞの）flower garden

花	園								

田園（でんえん）rural districts

田	園								

会場（かいじょう）assembly hall, meeting place

会	場								

場合（ばあい）case, situation

場	合								

お正月（おしょうがつ）New Year's

お	正	月							

31 | Fill in the Kanji

Fill in the appropriate kanji in the blanks for each sentence.

せん げつ　おお や　　　　や

1. ＿＿ ＿＿、＿＿ ＿＿さんに ＿＿ちんを はらいました。
Last month, I paid the owner the rent.

しょう がつ　　てら

2. お ＿＿ ＿＿ に お＿＿ に いきました。
I went to a temple on New Year's Day.

はは　こう もん　　　　あ

3. ＿＿と＿＿ ＿＿のまえで＿＿うことに なっています。
It's decided that I'm meeting my mother in front of the school gate.

おとうと　　みせ　　　　　　か

4. ＿＿ は、お＿＿ で おもちゃを ＿＿いました。
My little brother bought toys at the store.

えん　ほん　よ

5. こう ＿＿ で ＿＿を ＿＿むのが すきです。
I like reading books at the park.

しち　が つ よっ　か　　　　かい じょう

6. ＿＿＿ ＿＿＿ ＿＿＿ ＿＿＿ に、あの＿＿＿ ＿＿＿ でコンサートが ある。
On July 4th, there is a concert at that meeting hall.

うち　　　ちか　　　てら　　　　あ る　　じっ ぷん

7. ＿＿＿ から ＿＿＿ くのお＿＿＿ までは、＿＿＿ いて＿＿＿ ＿＿＿です。
It's 10 minutes by foot to the nearby temple from our house.

31 | Kanji meaning

Write the following kanji next to its meaning: 家 場 北 寺 園 組 門 店 牛

1.＿＿＿ store, shop　　2. ＿＿＿ place　　3. ＿＿＿ garden

4. ＿＿＿ group　　5. ＿＿＿ house, home　　6. ＿＿＿ gate

7. ＿＿＿ temple　　8. ＿＿＿ north　　9. ＿＿＿ cow

31 | Kanji matching

Draw a line to connect each kanji with only one of its ON or KUN readings.

場 •	• もう
店 •	• えん
寺 •	• じ
園 •	• じょう
門 •	• もん
番 •	• や
麦 •	• むぎ
家 •	• てん
毛 •	• ばん
母 •	• ぼ

31 | Stroke Order Check

Circle A or B whichever represents the correct stroke order for each kanji.

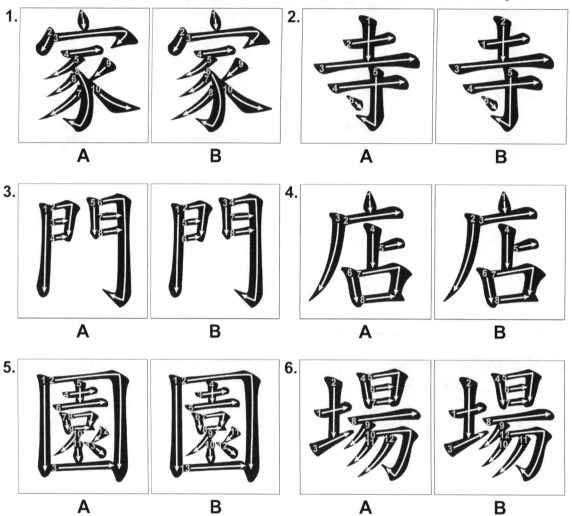

1.   A   B   2.   A   B

3.   A   B   4.   A   B

5.   A   B   6.   A   B

31 | Answer Key 答え合わせ

Fill in the kanji (answers)

1. 先月、大家さんに家ちんを はらいました。

2. お正月にお寺に いきました。

3. 母と校門のまえで会うことに なっています。

4. 弟は、お店でおもちゃを買いました。

5. こう園で本を読むのが すきです。

6. 七月四日に、あの会場でコンサートが ある。

7. 家から近くのお寺までは、歩いて十分です。

Kanji meaning match (answers)

1. 店 store, shop
2. 場 place
3. 園 garden
4. 組 group
5. 家 house, home
6. 門 gate
7. 寺 temple
8. 北 north
9. 牛 cow

Kanji matching (answers)

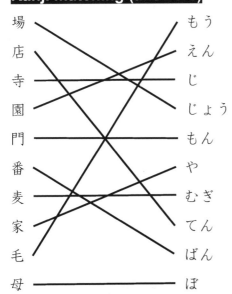

Stroke order check (answers)

1. B 2. B 3. A 4. A 5. B 6. A

32

原里野道地池

32 | New Kanji あたらしい かんじ

Make sure you learn the correct stroke order. Correct stroke order will mean neater symbols when writing quickly. Also, take time to learn the words listed for each kanji – these will help you memorize the different readings.

191. field, source, origin | 10 画

くんよみ	はら
おんよみ	ゲン

原

field	cause, reason	raw materials	plaintiff, prosecutor
の はら	げんいん	げんざいりょう	げんこく
野原	原因	原材料	原告

192. village, hometown | 7 画

くんよみ	さと
おんよみ	リ

里

visiting one's parents	foster parents	home town	nautical mile
さとがえ	さとおや	きょう り	かい り
里帰り	里親	郷里	海里

193. field, plains　　11画

くんよみ	の
おんよみ	ヤ

野

field	vegetable	stray cat	baseball
の はら	や さい	の ら ねこ	や きゅう
野原	野菜	野良猫	野球

194. road, street, way　　12画

くんよみ	みち
おんよみ	ドウ、トウ

道

way, street	shortcut	road	implement
みち	ちかみち	どう ろ	どう ぐ
道	近道	道路	道具

195. ground, soil, land　　6画

くんよみ	none
おんよみ	チ、ジ

地

underground	earth	ground	map
ちか	ち きゅう	じ めん	ち ず
地下	地球	地面	地図

池	196. pond					6画
	くんよみ	いけ				
	おんよみ	チ				
	池					

pond	battery	mud pond	reservoir
いけ	でん・ち	どろ・いけ	ちょ・すい・ち
池	電池	泥池	貯水池

32 | Kanji Usage かんじの つかいかた

● **32-1. The way 道**

Martial arts 武道 (ぶ・どう) are "ways of life" and therefore some of them contain 道 in them.

JUDO (soft + way)	KENDO (sword + way)
柔道	剣道
じゅう・どう	けん・どう
Judo is an unarmed martial art using leverage to unbalance the opponent.	Kendo is Japan's form of fencing using two-handed bamboo swords.

KYUDO (arrow + way)	AIKIDO (fit + spirit + way)
弓道	合気道
きゅう・どう	あい・き・どう
Kyudo is the Japanese martial art of archery. It is even taught in high school.	Aikido is a martial art where redirection of an opponent's force is important.

● 32-2. The soil radical (つちへん)

Kanji containing つちへん tend to be land related. Of course, just because つちへん is part of the kanji doesn't mean this will always be the case.

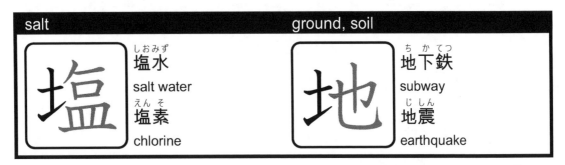

salt	ground, soil
塩	地

salt

塩水 (しおみず)
salt water

塩素 (えんそ)
chlorine

ground, soil

地下鉄 (ちかてつ)
subway

地震 (じしん)
earthquake

slope, hill

坂道 (さかみち)
sloped road

下り坂 (くだざか)
downhill

level, wide

平坦 (へいたん)
flat, level

坦坦 (たんたん)
level, peaceful

location, place

場所 (ばしょ)
place, location, spot

職場 (しょくば)
work place

range, region

地域 (ちいき)
area, region

区域 (くいき)
limits, boundary

ditch, moat, canal

掘り返す (ほかえす)
to dig up

堀江 (ほりえ)
canal

boy, priest

赤ん坊 (あかぼう)
baby, infant

お坊さん (ぼう)
Buddhist priest, monk

32 | Words You Can Write かける ことば

草原（そうげん）grasslands, meadow

草	原								

野原（のはら）field

野	原								

里親（さとおや）foster parents

里	親								

分野（ぶんや）area

分	野								

近道（ちかみち）shortcut

近	道								

地下（ちか）underground

地	下								

地元（じもと）local

地	元								

里帰り（さとがえり）visiting one's parents

里	帰	り						

池田さん（いけださん）Mr. (Ms.) Ikeda

池	田	さ	ん				

32 | Fill in the Kanji

Fill in the appropriate kanji in the blanks for each sentence.

いぬ　そうげん　はし　まわ

1. ＿＿＿ は ＿＿＿ ＿＿＿ を ＿＿＿ り ＿＿＿ りました。
   The dog ran around the meadow.

さと　がえ　　　たの　　　き　くだ

2. ＿＿＿ ＿＿＿ りを ＿＿＿ しんで ＿＿＿ て ＿＿＿ さい。
   Enjoy the visit to your parents.

や　　　た　　　　からだ

3. ＿＿＿ さいを ＿＿＿ べないと、 ＿＿＿ に よくないですよ。
   If you don't eat vegetables, it isn't good for your body.

みち　くるま　おお

4. この ＿＿＿ は ＿＿＿ が ＿＿＿ いから やめましょう。
   Let's quit (get off) this road since there are many cars.

に　ほん　　　　ち　か　　　　　た

5. ＿＿＿ ＿＿＿ のデパートの ＿＿＿ ＿＿＿ には、いろんな ＿＿＿ べものが

あります。
   In the bottom (underground) of Japanese department stores there
   are a variety of foods.

おお　　　いけ　　　さかな

6. あの ＿＿＿ きい ＿＿＿ には、 ＿＿＿ が いますよ。
   There are fish in that big pond over there.

の　はら　とも　　　　や

7. むかしはよく、 ＿＿＿ ＿＿＿ で ＿＿＿ だちと ＿＿＿ きゅうを しました。
   A long time ago I often played baseball with my friends in the field.

32 | Kanji meaning

Write the following kanji next to its meaning: 池 地 原 寺 里 場 野 道 門

1. ____ gate

2. ____ ground, soil

3. ____ hometown

4. ____ pond

5. ____ place

6. ____ temple

7. ____ street, road

8. ____ origin

9. ____ field, opposition

32 | Kanji matching

Draw a line to connect each kanji with only one of its ON or KUN readings.

原 ·　　　· げん
池 ·　　　· ち
羽 ·　　　· わ
里 ·　　　· の
地 ·　　　· みち
雲 ·　　　· か
道 ·　　　· いけ
近 ·　　　· きん
野 ·　　　· さと
角 ·　　　· うん

32 | Stroke Order Check

Circle A or B whichever represents the correct stroke order for each kanji.

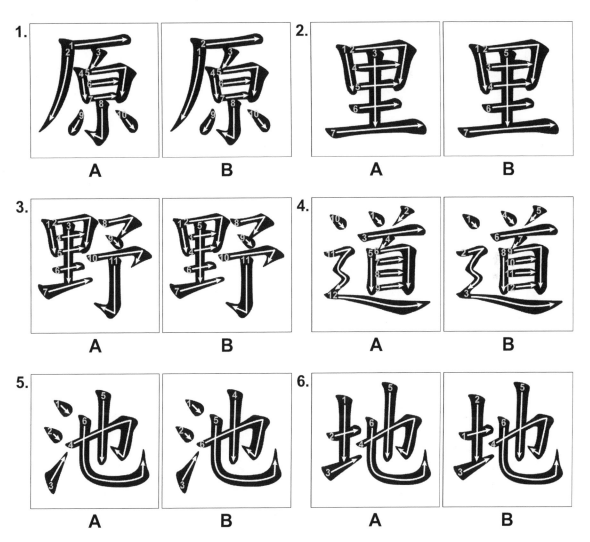

32 | Answer Key 答え合わせ

Fill in the kanji (answers)

1. 犬は草原を走り回りました。

2. 里帰りを楽しんで来て下さい。

3. 野さいを食べないと、体に よくないですよ。

4. この道は車が多いから、やめましょう。

5. 日本のデパートの地下には、いろんな食べものが あります。

6. あの大きい池には、魚が いますよ。

7. むかしはよく、野原で友だちと野きゅうを しました。

Kanji meaning match (answers)

1. 門 gate
2. 地 ground, soil
3. 里 hometown
4. 池 pond
5. 場 place
6. 寺 temple
7. 道 street, road
8. 原 origin
9. 野 field, the opposition

Kanji matching (answers)

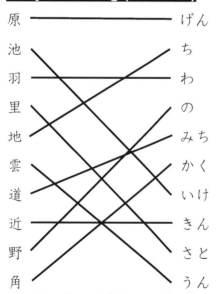

原 ——————— げん
池   ち
羽   わ
里   の
地   みち
雲   かく
道   いけ
近   きん
野   さと
角   うん

Stroke order check (answers)

1. A 2. B 3. B 4. A 5. A 6. B

33

Kanji lesson 33:

国市京公内外

33 | New Kanji あたらしい かんじ

Make sure you learn the correct stroke order. Correct stroke order will mean neater symbols when writing quickly. Also, take time to learn the words listed for each kanji – these will help you memorize the different readings.

国	197. country, nation			8 画
	くんよみ	くに		
	おんよみ	コク		
	国			

country	international	snow country	return to country
くに	こくさい	ゆきぐに	きこく
国	国際	雪国	帰国

市	198. market, city, municipal			5 画
	くんよみ	いち		
	おんよみ	シ		
	市			

citizen	morning market	city hall	marketplace
しみん	あさいち	しやくしょ	しじょう
市民	朝市	市役所	市場

199. capital, ten quadrillion — 8 画

くんよみ	none
おんよみ	キョウ、ケイ

京

Tokyo	Kyoto	proceeding to the capital	Keihan (Kyoto-Osaka area)
とうきょう	きょうと	じょうきょう	けいはん
東京	京都	上京	京阪

200. public, official, governmental — 4 画

くんよみ	おおやけ
おんよみ	コウ

公

official, public	park	fairness	community center
おおやけ	こうえん	こうへい	こうみんかん
公	公園	公平	公民館

201. inside, within — 4 画

くんよみ	うち
おんよみ	ナイ、ダイ

内

inside	own wife	within	within the company
うちがわ	かない	いない	しゃない
内側	家内	以内	社内

外	202. outside					5画
	くんよみ	そと、ほか、はず(す)				
	おんよみ	ゲ、ガイ				
	外					

outside	to remove	outward appearance	foreign currency
そと	はず	がいけん	がい か
外	外す	外見	外貨

| **33** | **Kanji Usage かんじの つかいかた** |

● **33-1. Other ways to go**

As you become more advanced you will begin to move away from textbook sentence patterns. Knowledge of various kanji and kanji words will allow you to form sentences that sound more natural to a native speaker.

Common sentence	Other sentence
とう きょう　　い 東京に行きます。 I'm going to go to Tokyo.	じょう きょう 上京します。 I'll be heading up to Tokyo.
に ほん　　　き 日本に来ます。 (He, she) is coming to Japan.	らい にち 来日します。 (He, she) is coming to Japan.

In English we say "going up or down to (place)", but 上京する, despite having 上 (up) in the word, has nothing to do with the location of Tokyo in relation to the speaker. 上京する can be used by ANYONE outside of 東京 (とうきょう). "Up" is part of 上京 because the capital city is where the emperor lives. The surrounding regions are considered lower in status.

However, people living in 京都 (きょうと) do NOT use 上京する because the emperor once resided in 京都 when it was the capital.

● **33-2. Commentary: Foreigners 外人**

It isn't customary for westerners to refer to someone as a "foreigner" and it can be quite rude. However the term is much more commonly used in Japan. There are typically three levels of the word used.

<ruby>外国人<rt>がいこくじん</rt></ruby> / <ruby>外国<rt>がいこく</rt></ruby>の<ruby>人<rt>ひと</rt></ruby> (foreign national)

外国人 is the official and probably most common way Japanese people refer to people not born in Japan. However, during your time in Japan you might notice that Chinese people are more commonly referred to simply as 中国人 (ちゅうごくじん) and Koreans as 韓国人 (かんこくじん) while people with European ancestry, or caucasian in appearance, tend to be exclusively called 外国人. This is not hard to understand since Caucasian people stand out more than a Chinese or Korean person who are often similar in appearance to Japanese people.

<ruby>外人<rt>がいじん</rt></ruby> (foreigner)

This is the shortest way to say "foreigner." Some Japanese people avoid this word as some people consider it rude. As an American, I was never offended by this word and never considered its usage rude. I personally only learned of people considering 外人 rude while watching a Japanese TV program with a panel of foreigner's debating whether it was rude or not. It was a 50/50 split decision. I am not offended and don't believe 外人 is racist at all.

I have never been in an argument with a Japanese person and been called 外人 out of anger. I have been called ばか (stupid) many more times than 外人. Also, it's important to note that Japanese language is well known for it's shortening of words. 外国人 being shortened to 外人 is not out of character for the Japanese language.

In western countries, like America, we commonly interact with people from a variety of ethnic backgrounds and have even had a black president. So calling someone a "foreigner" in America is generally considered rude. This might make it easy for non-Japanese to consider being called a foreigner, in any form, rude.

Japan, on the other hand, has been a single race country for its entire existence and, despite the common appearance of foreigners in Japanese media, it's still not a common experience for Japanese people to interact with foreigners. In a country where everyone has black hair and brown eyes, a person with different colored hair and different facial features will stand out. For this reason it's easy for Japanese people to separate Japanese people from "outsiders" and call them 外人 or 外国人.

In the end, it's important to remember that all people have opinions based on their personal experience. For example, I have heard American teenagers say "Jap" as short for "Japanese" not knowing that it's a racist term. It might be interesting to ask your Japanese friends if 外人 is rude to them in order to get a variety of opinions on this topic.

外国の方 (person of a foreign country)

外国の方 is the most polite way to say "foreigner" but is certainly not as commonly used as 外国人. This is typically used by a person who wants to make absolutely sure they aren't being offensive. 方 (かた) is a very polite way of saying "person" in Japanese.

33 | Words You Can Write かける ことば

帰国 （きこく） to return to one's own country

帰	国								

雪国 （ゆきぐに） snow country

雪	国								

市場 （いちば） market, marketplace

市	場								

上京 （じょうきょう） proceeding to the capital

上	京								

東京（とうきょう）Tokyo

東	京								

公園（こうえん）park

公	園								

公立（こうりつ）institution

公	立								

家内（かない）speaker's wife

家	内								

内心（ないしん）back of one's mind, real intention

内	心								

外す（はずす）to remove

外	す								

外見（がいけん）outward appearance

外	見								

33 | Fill in the Kanji

Fill in the appropriate kanji in the blanks for each sentence.

に　ほん　　き　こく

1. きのう、＿＿＿ ＿＿＿に ＿＿＿ ＿＿＿しました。
   Yesterday, I returned to Japan.

いち ば　　さかな　　か

2. わたしは よく ＿＿＿ ＿＿＿ で ＿＿＿ を ＿＿＿います。
I often buy fish at the marketplace.

とうきょう　　　ひ がえ

3. ＿＿＿ ＿＿＿ に ＿＿＿ ＿＿＿り りょこうを しましょう。
Let's take a day trip to Tokyo.

ちち　 こう りつ　しょう がっこう　　おし

4. ＿＿＿ は ＿＿＿ ＿＿＿ の ＿＿＿ ＿＿＿ ＿＿＿ で ＿＿＿えています。
My father teaches at a public elementary school.

とも　　　　　　　　 こころぼそ

5. ＿＿＿ だちが いないと、＿＿＿ ＿＿＿ いです。
If you don't have friends, it's lonely.

ひと　 がい けん

6. ＿＿＿ は ＿＿＿ ＿＿＿だけでは、はんだんできません。
You can't decide on a human just by outer appearance.

はら　　　 ない しん　　　　　　い

7. ＿＿＿ さんは＿＿＿ ＿＿＿、みんなと＿＿＿きたかったんですよ。
Hara-san's real intention was to go with everyone.

33 | Kanji meaning

Write the following kanji next to its meaning: 国 外 店 市 公 門 京 内 場

1.＿＿＿ place   2. ＿＿＿ outside   3. ＿＿＿ store, shop

4. ＿＿＿ country   5. ＿＿＿ capital   6. ＿＿＿ market, city

7. ＿＿＿ inside   8. ＿＿＿ gate   9. ＿＿＿ the public

33 | Kanji matching

Draw a line to connect each kanji with only one of its ON or KUN readings.

外 •　　　• がい
内 •　　　• し り
国 •　　　• り
道 •　　　• おおやけ
里 •　　　• こく
市 •　　　• ない
京 •　　　• きょう
地 •　　　• みち
公 •　　　• ち
寺 •　　　• てら

33 | Stroke Order Check

Circle A or B whichever represents the correct stroke order for each kanji.

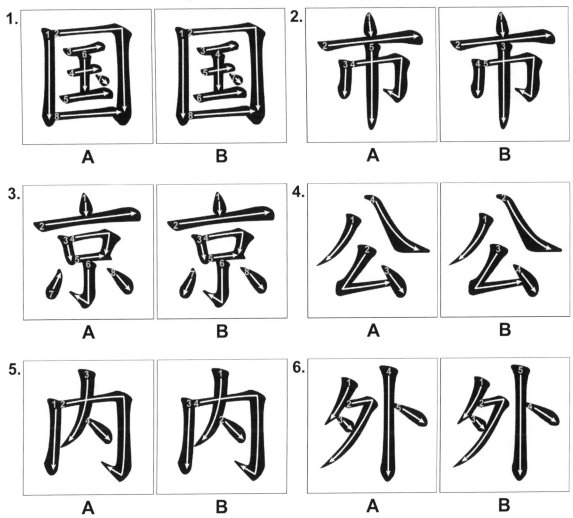

1.
A   B

2.
A   B

3.
A   B

4.
A   B

5.
A   B

6.
A   B

33 | Answer Key 答え合わせ

Fill in the kanji (answers)

1. きのう、日本に帰国しました。

2. わたしはよく市場で魚を買います。

3. 東京に日帰りりょこうをしましょう。

4. 父は公立の小学校で教えています。

5. 友だちがいないと、心細いです。

6. 人は外見だけでは、はんだんできません。

7. 原さんは内心、みんなと行きたかったんですよ。

Kanji meaning match (answers)

1. 場 place
2. 外 outside
3. 店 store, shop
4. 国 country
5. 京 capital
6. 市 market, city
7. 内 inside
8. 門 gate
9. 公 the public

Kanji matching (answers)

外 ——————— がい
内 ——————— し
国 ——————— り
道 ——————— おおやけ
里 ——————— こく
市 ——————— ない
京 ——————— きょう
地 ——————— みち
公 ——————— ち
寺 ——————— てら

Stroke order check (answers)

1. B   2. A   3. B   4. B   5. A   6. A

34

Kanji lesson 34:

色黄黒茶紙絵線

34 | New Kanji あたらしい かんじ

Make sure you learn the correct stroke order. Correct stroke order will mean neater symbols when writing quickly. Also, take time to learn the words listed for each kanji – these will help you memorize the different readings.

色	203. color						6 画
	くんよみ	いろ					
	おんよみ	ショク、シキ					
	色						

various	complexion	three-color	cardboard placard
いろいろ	かおいろ	さんしょく	しきし
色々	顔色	三色	色紙

黄	204. yellow						11 画
	くんよみ	き(いろ)、こ					
	おんよみ	コウ、オウ					
	黄						

yellow	gold	yolk	Yellow River
き いろ	おうごん	き み	こう が
黄色	黄金	黄身	黄河

205. black — 11画

くんよみ	くろ(い)
おんよみ	コク

黒

black	black hair	blackboard	pitch black
くろ	くろかみ	こくばん	ま　くろ
黒い	黒髪	黒板	真っ黒

206. tea — 9画

くんよみ	none
おんよみ	チャ、サ

茶

tea	brown	tea ceremony	coffee lounge
ちゃ	ちゃいろ	さどう	きっさてん
お茶	茶色	茶道	喫茶店

207. paper — 10画

くんよみ	かみ
おんよみ	シ

紙

paper	letter	origami	paper money
かみ	てがみ	お　がみ	し　へい
紙	手紙	折り紙	紙幣

絵	208. picture			12 画
	くんよみ	none		
	おんよみ	カイ、エ		
	絵			

picture book	paints	picture diary	picture, painting
え ほん	え　　ぐ	え にっ き	かい　が
絵本	絵の具	絵日記	絵画

線	209. line			15 画
	くんよみ	none		
	おんよみ	セン		
	線			

line	straight line	railway track	bullet train
せん	ちょくせん	せん ろ	しんかんせん
線	直線	線路	新幹線

34 | Kanji Usage かんじの つかいかた

● **34-1. Colorful people**

In western culture we commonly refer to people as black or white and even have phrases like "yellow fever" to describe a person who favors Asian women or men. In some cultures it can be considered racist to describe people by a color, especially Asians as "yellow." However, Japanese has じゅくご (compound words) using color to describe different enthnicities which are not considered racist.

There is no official word for "brown" people however, they are covered with the word 有色人種.

white + people	black + people
白人	黒人
はく・じん	こく・じん

yellow + color + people + type	having + color + people + type
黄色人種	有色人種
おう・しょく・じん・しゅ	ゆう・しょく・じん・しゅ

● **34-2. The many tea types (茶)**

Tea is an important part of Japanese culture.

Japanese tea	barley tea
日本茶	麦茶
にほん・ちゃ	むぎ・ちゃ

black tea	oolong tea
紅茶	ウーロン茶
こう・ちゃ	ウーロン・ちゃ

green tea	green tea powder
緑茶	抹茶
りょく・ちゃ	まっ・ちゃ

● **34-3. Same kanji, different reading, Japanese is hard?**

Japanese isn't known for being easy (no matter how easy *you* find it to be). Of course many books and online courses like to claim that you can easily learn Japanese in just 30 days or something impossible like that. However, at this point in the book you know how much work is involved. Good job!!! You are going above and beyond what 99% of other people would do.

I promise you it's worth the effort. *Now* are you feeling good? Because this next thing might make you go crazy.

There are times when the *exact* same kanji can mean different things. The only way to know the difference is by the surrounding context.

the eye of a fish	a corn (on foot etc)
魚 の 目	魚 の 目
さかな・の・め	うお・の・め
うおのめ is sometimes written in hiragana or just as うおの目 to avoid this easily mixed up reading.	

colored paper	autograph board
色 紙	色 紙
いろ・がみ	しき・し
しきし are commonly used by fans of entertainers to get autographs. Some places of business will have the autographs of famous people on their wall and they will always be on しきし. They are white colored squares, 25 by 25 cm hard cardboard placards with gold edges. They are also commonly used by friends at school graduations or goodbye parties to have everyone sign as a keepsake.	

34 | Words You Can Write かける ことば

三色 （さんしょく） three-color

三	色									

黄色 （きいろ） yellow

黄	色									

黄金 （おうごん） gold

黄	金									

白黒 （しろくろ） black and white

白	黒									

黒い （くろい） black

黒	い									

お茶 （おちゃ） tea

お	茶									

茶色 （ちゃいろ） brown

茶	色									

手紙 （てがみ） letter

手	紙									

絵本（えほん）picture book

絵	本								

黒人（こくじん）black person

黒	人								

絵画（かいが）picture, painting

絵	画								

下線（かせん）underline, underscore

下	線								

直線（ちょくせん）straight line

直	線								

色紙（いろがみ）colored papered

色	紙								

中国人（ちゅうごくじん）Chinese person

中	国	人							

絵日記（えにっき）picture diary

絵	日	記							

外国人（がいこくじん）foreigner

外	国	人							

34 | Fill in the Kanji

Fill in the appropriate kanji in the blanks for each sentence.

いろ　　あか　しろ

1. わたしのすきな＿＿＿ は ＿＿＿と＿＿＿です。
   My favorite colors are red and white.

あお　　　　　　　き いろ

2. ＿＿＿ がすきだけど、＿＿＿ ＿＿＿は すきじゃないです。
   I like blue, but I don't like yellow.

くろ　くるま　　　　　う

3. さいきん、＿＿＿ い ＿＿＿ を ２だい ＿＿＿ りました。
   Recently, I sold two black cars.

やす　　　　さ てん　ちゃ

4. ひる ＿＿＿ みに きっ＿＿＿ ＿＿＿でお＿＿＿をしませんか。
   At the lunch break, won't you have tea (with me) at the coffee shop?

きょう　　　　て がみ　か

5. ＿＿＿ しつで ＿＿＿ ＿＿＿を ＿＿＿きました。
   I wrote a letter in the classroom.

かい　が　　み

6. ヨーロッパで ＿＿＿ ＿＿＿ が ＿＿＿ たいです。
   I want to see paintings in Europe.

か ない　しん　せん

7. ＿＿＿ ＿＿＿ は、＿＿＿かん＿＿＿ に のるのが すきです。
   My wife likes riding the bullet train.

34 | Kanji meaning

Write the following kanji next to its meaning: 線 絵 紙 野 色 黄 池 黒 茶

1.＿＿＿ picture

2. ＿＿＿ black

3. ＿＿＿ color

4. ＿＿＿ field

5. ＿＿＿ line

6. ＿＿＿ pond

7. ＿＿＿ yellow

8. ＿＿＿ paper

9. ＿＿＿ tea

34 | Kanji matching

Draw a line to connect each kanji with only one of its ON or KUN readings.

紙 ・　　　・ せん
黒 ・　　　・ えん
線 ・　　　・ し
色 ・　　　・ おう
園 ・　　　・ こく
黄 ・　　　・ しょく
茶 ・　　　・ かい
家 ・　　　・ け
絵 ・　　　・ ちゃ
星 ・　　　・ せい

34 | Stroke Order Check

Circle A or B whichever represents the correct stroke order for each kanji.

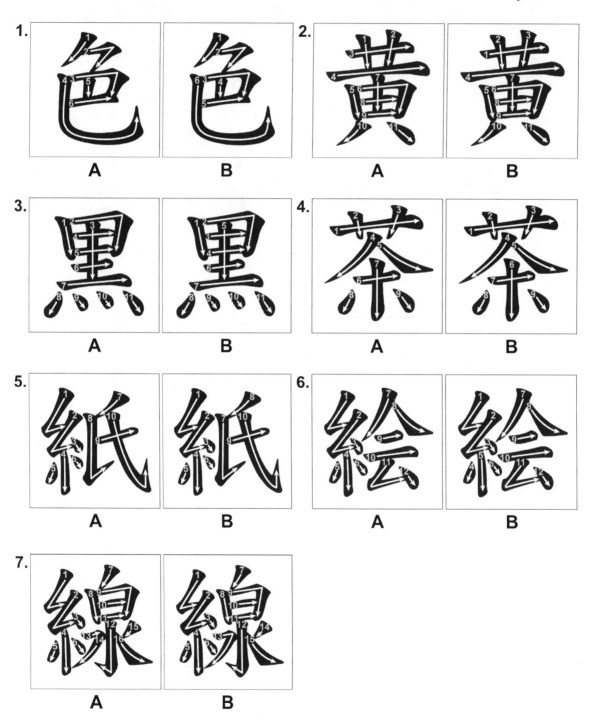

34 Answer Key 答え合わせ

Fill in the kanji (answers)

1. わたしのすきな色は赤と白です。

2. 青がすきだけど、黄色は すきじゃないです。

3. さいきん、黒い車を2だい売りました。

4. ひる休みにきっ茶店でお茶を しませんか。

5. 教しつで手紙を書きました。

6. ヨーロッパで絵画が見たいです。

7. 家内は、新かん線にのるのが すきです。

Kanji meaning match (answers)

1. 絵 picture
2. 黒 black
3. 色 color
4. 野 field
5. 線 line
6. 池 pond
7. 黄 yellow
8. 紙 paper
9. 茶 tea

Kanji matching (answers)

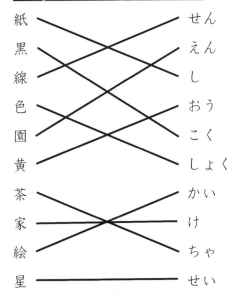

紙	せん
黒	えん
線	し
色	おう
園	こく
黄	しょく
茶	かい
家	け
絵	ちゃ
星	せい

Stroke order check (answers)

1. B 2. B 3. B 4. A 5. A 6. A 7. B

35

Kanji lesson 35:

春夏秋冬時間

35 New Kanji あたらしい かんじ

Make sure you learn the correct stroke order. Correct stroke order will mean neater symbols when writing quickly. Also, take time to learn the words listed for each kanji – these will help you memorize the different readings.

210. spring								9画
くんよみ	はる							
おんよみ	シュン							
春								

a spring day	first storm of spring	youth	puberty
はる　　ひ	はるいちばん	せいしゅん	し　しゅん　き
春の日	春一番	青春	思春期

211. summer							10画
くんよみ	なつ						
おんよみ	カ、ゲ						
夏							

summer vacation	mid-summer	summer solstice	early summer
なつやす	ま　なつ	げ　し	しょ　か
夏休み	真夏	夏至	初夏

212. fall, autumn　9画

| くんよみ | あき |
| おんよみ | シュウ |

秋

fall, autumn	fine autumn day	autumnal equinox	first day of autumn
あき	あきば	しゅうぶん	りっしゅう
秋	秋晴れ	秋分	立秋

213. winter　5画

| くんよみ | ふゆ |
| おんよみ | トウ |

冬

winter	winter vacation	hibernation	mid winter
ふゆ	ふゆやす	とうみん	まふゆ
冬	冬休み	冬眠	真冬

214. time, hour, occasion　10画

| くんよみ | とき |
| おんよみ | ジ |

時

time	sometimes	watch, clock	time difference
じかん	ときどき	とけい	じさ
時間	時々	時計	時差

間	215. space, interval		12画
	くんよみ	あいだ、ま	
	おんよみ	カン、ケン	
	間		

between	time, hour	during the day	human being
あいだ	じかん	ひるま	にんげん
間	時間	昼間	人間

35 | Kanji Usage かんじの つかいかた

● **35-1. Seasonal phrases (春夏秋冬)**

Ready to stretch your Japanese? The following phrases are explained in Japanese. Cover up the English and see how much you understand.

春眠 暁 を覚えず
しゅん みん あかつき　おぼ

A spring sleep that knows no dawn.

春の夜は心地よいので、朝になったことにも気づかず眠り込んでしまうということ。
はる よる ここち　　　　　　　　あさ　　　　　　　　　　　ねむ こ

A spring night is comfortable, so you don't realize that it's become morning and you continue to sleep deeply.

冬来りなば春遠からじ
ふゆ きた　　　　　はる とお

If winter comes, can spring be far behind?

今は不幸な状況であっても、じっと耐えていれば、いずれ幸せがくるというたとえ。
いま ふ こう じょうきょう　　　　　　　　た　　　　　　　　しあわ

This metaphor shows that even if you are in an unhappy situation, if you continue to bear it, eventually you will become happy.

とんで ひ い なつ むし
飛んで火に入る夏の虫
Summer bugs fly and enter into the fire.

じぶん すす きけん と こ
自分から進んで危険なところに飛び込むことのたとえ。

A metaphor of progressing forward to a dangerous place on your own and jumping in. Similar to "Drawn like a moth to the flame."

おんなごころ あき そら
女心 と秋の空
A woman's heart and the autumn sky.

か あき そら じょせい きも うつ ぎ
変わりやすい秋の空のように、女性の気持ちは移り気だということ。

This means that just like the easily changing sky of autumn, a woman's mood is fickle.

● **35-2. It's about time (時)**

Time doesn't stop for anyone! Take some time though to learn these words that contain time.

era, period, epoch	point in time, occasion
時代	時点
じ・だい	じ・てん

hourly wage	temporary, special
時給	臨時
じ・きゅう	りん・じ

at the time	moment, instant
当時	瞬時
とう・じ	しゅん・じ

nowadays, these days	speed (per hour)
今 時	時 速
いま・どき	じ・そく

35 Words You Can Write かける ことば

青春 （せいしゅん） youth

青	春							

立秋 （りっしゅう） the first day of autumn

立	秋							

今時 （いまどき） nowadays, present day

今	時							

秋分 （しゅうぶん） autumnal equinox

秋	分							

時間 （じかん） time

時	間							

時計 （とけい） watch, clock

時	計							

人間（にんげん）human being

人 間

冬毛（ふゆげ）winter fur

冬 毛

時点（じてん）point in time

時 点

春休み（はるやすみ）spring vacation

春 休 み

秋晴れ（あきばれ）fine autumn day

秋 晴 れ

この間（このあいだ）the other day

こ の 間

夏休み（なつやすみ）summer vacation

夏 休 み

冬休み（ふゆやすみ）winter vacation

冬 休 み

春夏秋冬（しゅんかしゅうとう）the four seasons

春 夏 秋 冬

35 | Fill in the Kanji

Fill in the appropriate kanji in the blanks for each sentence.

はる やす　　さく ぶん　　か

1. ＿＿ ＿＿ みに ＿＿ ＿＿ を ＿＿きました。
   I wrote an essay on spring vacation.

なつ やす　　　に ほん　さと がえ

2. ＿＿ ＿＿ みに ＿＿ ＿＿ に ＿＿ ＿＿ り しました。
   Over summer vacation I went to Japan to visit my parents.

あき　　　　　　えん　うみ　い

3. ＿＿には、こう ＿＿や＿＿ に ＿＿きたいです。
   In Autumn, I want to go to the park and to the ocean.

ふゆ やす　　ちゅうごく　　　きょう

4. ＿＿ ＿＿みに ＿＿ ＿＿にべん ＿＿ しに いきます。
   Over winter vacation I am going to China to study.

じ かん　　　とき　　　　　　た

5. ＿＿ ＿＿ がない＿＿は、ごはんを＿＿べるのを わすれます。
   When I don't have time I forget to eat dinner.

あいだ はは　あたら　　と けい　か

6. この ＿＿ 、＿＿が ＿＿しい ＿＿ ＿＿を＿＿ってくれた。
   The other day, my mother bought me a new watch.

しゅん か しゅう とう　　　　ご

7. ＿＿ ＿＿ ＿＿ ＿＿とはえい＿＿で 「four seasons」と いいます。
   In English, ShunKaShuuTou is "four seasons."

35 | Kanji meaning

Write the following kanji next to its meaning: 間 冬 夏 黒 春 紙 秋 時 色

1.____ time, hour
2. ____ summer
3. ____ color

4. ____ paper
5. ____ black
6. ____ fall

7. ____ winter
8. ____ spring
9. ____ space, interval

35 | Kanji matching

Draw a line to connect each kanji with only one of its ON or KUN readings.

冬 •
夏 •
線 •
春 •
間 •
池 •
時 •
原 •
秋 •
店 •

• しゅん
• か
• しゅう
• じ
• あいだ
• とう
• てん
• いけ
• せん
• げん

35 | Stroke Order Check

Circle A or B whichever represents the correct stroke order for each kanji.

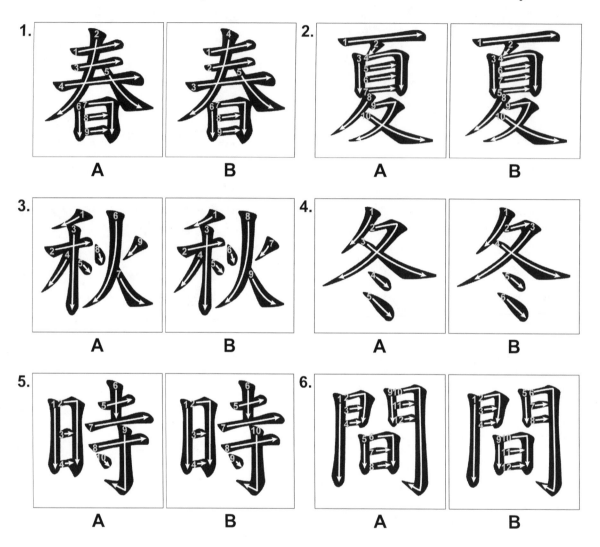

1. A   B   2. A   B

3. A   B   4. A   B

5. A   B   6. A   B

35 | Answer Key 答え合わせ

Fill in the kanji (answers)

1. 春休みに作文を書きました。

2. 夏休みに日本に里帰り しました。

3. 秋には、こう園や海に行きたいです。

4. 冬休みに中国にべん強しに いきます。

5. 時間がない時は、ごはんを食べるのをわすれます。

6. この間、母が新しい時計を買ってくれた。

7. 春夏秋冬は えい語で、「four seasons」といいます。

Kanji meaning match (answers)

1. 時 time, hour
2. 夏 summer
3. 色 color
4. 紙 paper
5. 黒 black
6. 秋 fall
7. 冬 winter
8. 春 spring
9. 間 space, interval

Kanji matching (answers)

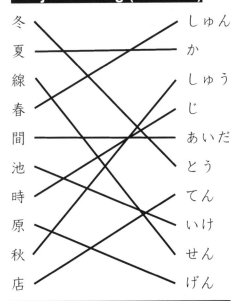

冬	しゅん
夏	か
線	しゅう
春	じ
間	あいだ
池	とう
時	てん
原	いけ
秋	せん
店	げん

Stroke order check (answers)

1. B   2. A   3. B   4. A   5. A   6. B

SR Super Review 7

SR7 | Kanji selection

Select the best kanji to fill in the blank in each sentence.

1. 八時四十五分に、学校の＿＿＿がしまります。
   A. 寺   B. 店   C. 門   D. 園

2. 日本のしんごうの色は、青と＿＿＿色と赤です。
   A. 茶   B. 水   C. 黒   D. 黄

3. そとが明るい時間が一番みじかいきせつは、＿＿＿です。
   A. 冬   B. 夏   C. 秋   D. 春

4. 雨と＿＿＿が強くて、ぬれてしまいました。
   A. 雪   B. 風   C. 雲   D. 海

SR7 | Kanji reading

Select the best reading for the underlined kanji.

1. こんど、海外に 行くので 楽しみです。
   A. うみ   B. かい   C. がい   D. う

2. 家内とわたしは、よくえい画を見に行きます。
   A. け   B. か   C. いえ   D. うち

3. 姉は毎週土曜日に、茶道をならっています。
   A. ちゃ   B. か   C. さ   D. しょ

4. 高校のさいごの日に、友だちに色紙に名前を書いてもらいました。
   A. いろ   B. しょく   C. しき   D. じき

SR7 | Compound kanji word puzzle

Fill in the correct kanji based on the list below the puzzle.

1)		2)	3)
	4)		5)
6)	7)	8)	9)
	10)	11)	

Down ↓
1) brown
3) a rain cloud
5) a sea of clouds
6) best friend
8) foreign country

Left to Right →
1) tea ceremony
4) gold
10) snow country
11) within the country

Right to Left ←
2) shortcut
4) yellow
7) foster parent
9) overseas

SR7 | Answer Key 答え合わせ

Kanji selection (answers)

1. C – 門
   <ruby>門<rt>もん</rt></ruby>

   At 8:45, the school gate closes.

2. D – 黄色
   <ruby>黄<rt>き</rt>色<rt>いろ</rt></ruby>

   The colors of Japanese stop lights are blue, yellow, and red.

3. D – 冬
   <ruby>冬<rt>ふゆ</rt></ruby>

   The season that has the shortest amount of time that's bright outside is winter.

4. B – 風
   <ruby>風<rt>かぜ</rt></ruby>

   I got wet because the rain and the wind were strong.

Kanji reading (answers)

1. B – 海外
   <ruby>海<rt>かい</rt>外<rt>がい</rt></ruby>

   Since I'm going abroad this time, I am looking forward to it.

2. B – 家内
   <ruby>家<rt>か</rt>内<rt>ない</rt></ruby>

   My wife and I often go to watch movies.

3. C – 茶道
   <ruby>茶<rt>さ</rt>道<rt>どう</rt></ruby>

   My older sister is learning tea ceremony (the way of tea) every Saturday.

4. C – 色紙
   <ruby>色<rt>しき</rt>紙<rt>し</rt></ruby>

   On the last day of high school I had my friends sign an autograph board.

Compound kanji word puzzle (answers)

茶	道	近	雨
色	黄	金	雲
親	里	外	海
友	雪	国	内

36

Kanji lesson 36:

朝昼夜前後午今

36 | New Kanji あたらしい かんじ

Make sure you learn the correct stroke order. Correct stroke order will mean neater symbols when writing quickly. Also, take time to learn the words listed for each kanji – these will help you memorize the different readings.

朝

216. morning　　**12 画**

くんよみ	あさ
おんよみ	チョウ

朝						

every morning	morning sun	breakfast	early morning
まいあさ	あさ ひ	ちょう しょく	そう ちょう
毎朝	朝日	朝食	早朝

昼

217. daytime, lunch　　**9 画**

くんよみ	ひる
おんよみ	チュウ

昼						

daytime	lunch	nap	lunch break
ひる ま	ちゅう しょく	ひる ね	ひる やす
昼間	昼食	昼寝	昼休み

218. night　　　8画

くんよみ	よ、よる
おんよみ	ヤ

夜

night	midnight, dead of night	night shift	night view
よる	よなか	やきん	やけい
夜	夜中	夜勤	夜景

219. front, before　　　9画

くんよみ	まえ
おんよみ	ゼン

前

in front	name	in front of station	last time
まえ	なまえ	えきまえ	ぜんかい
前	名前	駅前	前回

220. after, behind, later　　　9画

くんよみ	のち、うし(ろ)、あと、おく(れる)
おんよみ	ゴ、コウ

後

behind	later on, afterwards	to postpone	last
うし	のち	あとまわ	さいご
後ろ	後ほど	後回し	最後

午	221. noon		4 画
	くんよみ	none	
	おんよみ	ゴ	
	午		

morning, A.M.	afternoon, P.M.	noon	person who stays out all night
ご　ぜん	ご　ご	しょう　ご	ご　ぜん　さま
午前	午後	正午	午前様

今	222. now, immediately		4 画
	くんよみ	いま	
	おんよみ	コン、キン	
	今		

now	this time	this morning	today
いま	こんかい	け　さ	きょう
今	今回	今朝	今日

36 | Kanji Usage かんじの つかいかた

● **36-1. Party all night long (夜)**

From "night owl" to "late night train", 夜 has a lot of useful words to offer.

tonight, this evening	dead of night (middle of night)
今夜	真夜中
こん・や	ま・よ・なか

dawn, daybreak	late-night snack
夜明け	夜食
よ・あけ	や・しょく

late night train, overnight train	nocturnal, "night owl"
夜行列車	夜型
や・こう・れっ・しゃ	よる・がた

● 36-2. Before we talk too much... (前)

Here are some words using 前 (before).

appetizer	in front of your eyes (under your nose)
前菜	目の前
ぜん・さい	め・の・まえ

advance sale	in advance, previously
前売り	前もって
まえ・うり	まえ・もって

the previous day	pre-payment
前日	前払い
ぜん・じつ	まえ・ばらい

● 36-3. After all is said and done... (後)

And now here are some words using 後 (after).

after dinner	underling (opposite of senpai)
食後	後輩
しょく・ご	こう・はい

before and after	the day after tomorrow
前後	明後日
ぜん・ご	あさって

putting off, postponing	regret, remorse
後回し	後悔
あと・まわし	こう・かい

36 Words You Can Write かける ことば

朝日（あさひ）morning sun

朝	日									

早朝（そうちょう）early morning

早	朝									

昼間（ひるま）daytime

昼	間									

昼食（ちゅうしょく）lunch

昼	食									

夜中（よなか）midnight

夜	中									

夜間（やかん）night time

夜 間

前後 (ぜんご) before and after

前 後

前回（ぜんかい）last time

前 回

後ろ（うしろ）behind, back

後 ろ

正午（しょうご）noon

正 午

午後（ごご）afternoon, PM

午 後

今年（ことし）this year

今 年

今日（きょう）today

今 日

昼休み（ひるやすみ）lunch break

昼 休 み

36 | Fill in the Kanji

Fill in the appropriate kanji in the blanks for each sentence.

はは　　け　さ　　　みせ　　と　けい　　か

1. ＿＿は ＿＿＿ ＿＿＿、お＿＿ で ＿＿＿ ＿＿＿を ＿＿いました。
My mother bought a watch at the store this morning.

ひる やす　　　　　てん　　ちゃ

2. ＿＿＿ ＿＿＿ みに きっさ＿＿で お＿＿を しませんか。
Won't you have tea at the coffee shop with me during the lunch break?

よ　なか　おお　　おと

3. ＿＿＿ ＿＿＿ に ＿＿きな＿＿がして、びっくりしました。
In the middle of the night I was surprised by a big (loud) sound.

ご ぜん　　ご　ご

4. ＿＿＿ ＿＿＿ と＿＿＿ ＿＿＿と どっちが いいですか。
Which is better, morning or afternoon?

うし　　せん せい

5. ＿＿＿ ろに ＿＿＿ ＿＿＿が いますよ。
The teacher is behind you.

きょ　う　　　ひる まえ　　あ

6. ＿＿＿ ＿＿＿、お＿＿ ＿＿＿に ＿＿＿ いましょう。
Let's meet today before noon.

こと　し　　に じゅうろく さい

7. わたしは ＿＿＿ ＿＿＿、＿＿＿ ＿＿＿ ＿＿＿ ＿＿＿に なります。
I will turn 26 years old this year.

36 | Kanji meaning

Write the following kanji next to its meaning: 今 朝 午 後 昼 秋 夜 京 前

1.＿＿＿ front, before　　2. ＿＿＿ after, behind　　3. ＿＿＿ capital

4. ＿＿＿ night　　5. ＿＿＿ now　　6. ＿＿＿ morning

7. ＿＿＿ noon　　8. ＿＿＿ fall　　9. ＿＿＿ daytime, lunch

36 | Kanji matching

Draw a line to connect each kanji with only one of its ON or KUN readings.

午 ・	・ あ と
牛 ・	・ ぎ ゅ う
前 ・	・ か
後 ・	・ ひ る
今 ・	・ ご
夜 ・	・ か ん
昼 ・	・ ぜ ん
朝 ・	・ ち ょ う
夏 ・	・ よ
間 ・	・ い ま

36 | Stroke Order Check

Circle A or B whichever represents the correct stroke order for each kanji.

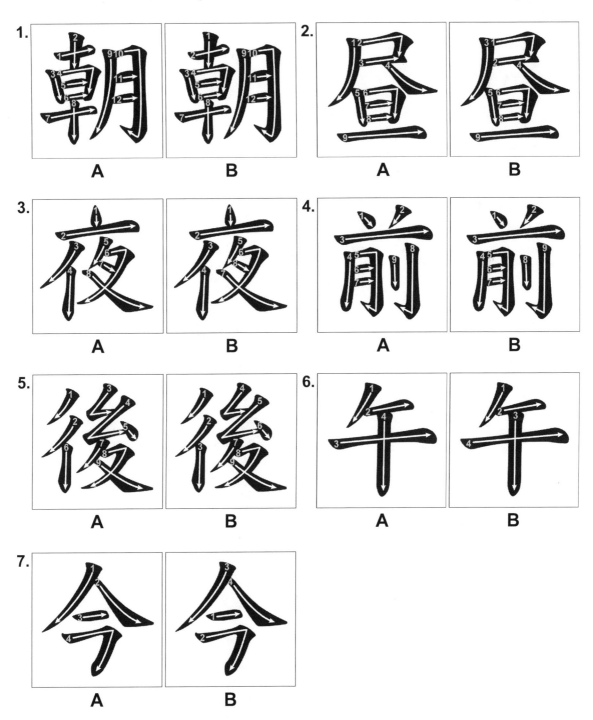

1. A   B
2. A   B
3. A   B
4. A   B
5. A   B
6. A   B
7. A   B

36 | Answer Key 答え合わせ

Fill in the kanji (answers)

1. 母は今朝、お店で時計を買いました。

2. 昼休みにきっさ店でお茶を しませんか。

3. 夜中に大きな音がして、びっくりしました。

4. 午前と午後とどっちが いいですか。

5. 後ろに先生が いますよ。

6. 今日、お昼前に会いましょう。

7. わたしは今年、二十六才に なります。

Kanji meaning match (answers)

1. 前 front, before
2. 後 after, behind
3. 京 capital
4. 夜 night
5. 今 now
6. 朝 morning
7. 午 noon
8. 秋 fall
9. 昼 daytime, lunch

Kanji matching (answers)

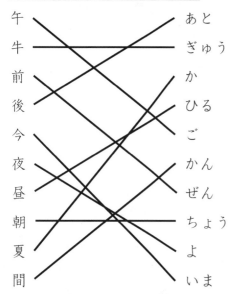

午　　　　　あと
牛　　　　　ぎゅう
前　　　　　か
後　　　　　ひる
今　　　　　ご
夜　　　　　かん
昼　　　　　ぜん
朝　　　　　ちょう
夏　　　　　よ
間　　　　　いま

Stroke order check (answers)
1. A　2. B　3. A　4. B　5. B　6. A　7. A

37 Kanji lesson 37: 工理算図社科

37 New Kanji あたらしい かんじ

Make sure you learn the correct stroke order. Correct stroke order will mean neater symbols when writing quickly. Also, take time to learn the words listed for each kanji – these will help you memorize the different readings.

223. artisan, work, craft			3 画
くんよみ	none		
おんよみ	コウ、ク		

handicraft	factory	scheme, device	carpenter
こうさく	こうじょう	く ふう	だい く
工作	工場	工夫	大工

224. reason, justice			11 画
くんよみ	none		
おんよみ	リ		

reason, cause	science	repair	geography
り ゆう	り か	しゅう り	ち り
理由	理科	修理	地理

225. count, calculation — 14 画

くんよみ	none
おんよみ	サン

算						

arithmetic	calculation	budget, estimate	balance sheet
さんすう	けいさん	よさん	けっさん
算数	計算	予算	決算

226. figure, drawing — 7 画

くんよみ	はか(る)
おんよみ	ズ、ト

図						

arts and crafts	intention, purpose	map	book certificate
ずこう	いと	ちず	としょけん
図工	意図	地図	図書券

227. shrine, company, society — 7 画

くんよみ	やしろ
おんよみ	シャ

社						

society	company	company employee	Shinto shrine
しゃかい	かいしゃ	しゃいん	じんじゃ
社会	会社	社員	神社

科	228. subject				9画
	くんよみ	none			
	おんよみ	カ			
	科				

school subject	science	internal medicine	brain surgery
か　も　く	か　が　く	ない　か	のう　げ　か
科目	科学	内科	脳外科

37 Kanji Usage かんじの つかいかた

● **37-1. Subjects (科) and (学)**

科 is used to create words that are "categories of science." Many of our examples are medical but 科 is used for any family of science or study.

English literature	science	social studies	home economics
えい　ぶん　か	り　か	しゃ　かい　か	か　てい　か
英文科	理科	社会科	家庭科
★ gynecology	★ obstetrics	★ surgery	★ psychiatry
ふ　じん　か	さん　か	げ　か	せい　しん　か
婦人科	産科	外科	精神科
★ dentistry	★ pediatrics	★ neurology	★ ear, nose, throat
し　か	しょう　に　か	しん　けい　か	じ　び　か
歯科	小児科	神経科	耳鼻科

★ For any of the medical science professions you can add 医 (い) to say "doctor of" the particular science. In English, we can have "doctors" of non-medical sciences, but in Japanese 医 is limited to medical doctors. Here are a few examples using 医:

さん　か　い
産科医　　　　obstetrician

し　か　い
歯科医　　　　dentist

ふ　じん　か　い
婦人科医　　　gynecologist

しん　けい　か　い
神経科医　　　neurologist

Words with 学 are used to explain certain fields of study. For example these can be the names of classes you are taking or your major in college.

science	chemistry	mathematics	literature
か が く 科学	か が く 化学	すう がく 数学	ぶん がく 文学

physics	theology	philosophy	engineering
ぶ つ り が く 物理学	しん がく 神学	て つ がく 哲学	こう がく 工学

linguistics	law	geology	social science
げん ご がく 言語学	ほう がく 法学	ち がく 地学	しゃ かい か が く 社会科学

biology	astronomy	psychology	anthropology
せい ぶつがく 生物学	てん もん がく 天文学	しん り がく 心理学	じん るい がく 人類学

To describe your profession for or a person who does these things you add 者 (しゃ) to make "scholar" 学者 (がくしゃ). It's like adding **–ist** or **–er**.

か がくしゃ 科学者	scientist	か がくしゃ 科学者	chemist
すうがくしゃ 数学者	mathematician	ぶんがくしゃ 文学者	scholar of literature
ぶ つ り がくしゃ 物理学者	physicist	しんがくしゃ 神学者	theologist
て つ がくしゃ 哲学者	philosopher	こうがくしゃ 工学者	engineer
ご がくしゃ 語学者	linguist	ほうがくしゃ 法学者	jurist, studier of law
ち がくしゃ 地学者	geologist	しゃかい か がくしゃ 社会科学者	sociologist
せいぶつがくしゃ 生物学者	biologist	てんもんがくしゃ 天文学者	astronomer
しん り がくしゃ 心理学者	psychologist	じんるいがくしゃ 人類学者	anthropologist

● 37-2. In good company (社)

社 (しゃ) is used in many business related words involving companies. Here is a small sampling of some of the big ones.

corporation	limited corporation
株式会社	有限会社
かぶ・しき・がい・しゃ	ゆう・げん・がい・しゃ

trading company	newspaper company
商社	新聞社
しょう・しゃ	しん・ぶん・しゃ

publishing company	branch office
出版社	支社
しゅっ・ぱん・しゃ	し・しゃ

airline company	subsidiary
航空会社	子会社
こう・くう・がい・しゃ	こ・がい・しゃ

our company	your company
弊社	御社
へい・しゃ	おん・しゃ

37 | Words You Can Write かける ことば

大工（だいく）carpenter

大	工								

工作（こうさく）handicraft

工	作								

地理（ちり）geography

地	理								

理科（りか）science

理	科								

計算（けいさん）calculation

計	算								

算数（さんすう）arithmetic, math

算	数								

図る（はかる）to plan

図	る								

合図（あいず）sign, signal

合	図								

地図（ちず）map

地	図								

会社（かいしゃ）company

会	社								

社会（しゃかい）society

社	会								

科学（かがく）science

科	学								

科目（かもく）subject

科	目								

37 | Fill in the Kanji

Fill in the appropriate kanji in the blanks for each sentence.

　　だい く　　あめ　ひ

1. ＿＿ ＿＿ は ＿＿ の＿＿に しごとが できません。
   Carpenters can't work on rainy days.

　　　　　　　　か もく　　り か　しゃ かい か

2. わたしがすきな ＿＿ ＿＿ は＿＿ ＿＿と＿＿ ＿＿ ＿＿です。
   My favorite subjects are science and social studies.

　　けい さん　　さく ぶん

3. ＿＿ ＿＿ より＿＿ ＿＿のほうが かんたんです。
   Essays are easier than calculations.

　　はや　　しゃ かい　　で

4. ＿＿ く、＿＿ ＿＿に ＿＿たほうが いいですよ。
   You should enter society soon.

あい　ず　　　　　　　　　　　　く　だ

5. わたしが ＿＿ ＿＿ をするまで、まって＿＿ さい。
Please wait until I make a signal.

しょう がく せい　とき　　ず　こう

6. ＿＿ ＿＿ ＿＿の＿＿ は、＿＿ ＿＿ が すきでした。
When I was an elementary school student, I liked arts and crafts.

ゆう じん　　こう じょう

7. ＿＿ ＿＿は ＿＿ ＿＿ で はたらいています。
My friend works at a factory.

37 | Kanji matching

Draw a line to connect each kanji with only one of its ON or KUN readings.

```
工 ・        ・とう
科 ・        ・か
理 ・        ・さん
夜 ・        ・こしゃ
社 ・        ・よ
図 ・        ・ずり
算 ・        ・こう
今 ・
冬 ・        ・どう
道 ・
```

37 Kanji meaning

Write the following kanji next to its meaning: 科 図 理 前 工 算 朝 社 線

1._____ shrine, company   2. _____ morning   3. _____ before, front

4. _____ subject   5. _____ figure, drawing   6. _____ reason, justice

7. _____ line   8. _____ count, calculation   9. _____ work, craft

37 Stroke Order Check

Circle A or B whichever represents the correct stroke order for each kanji.

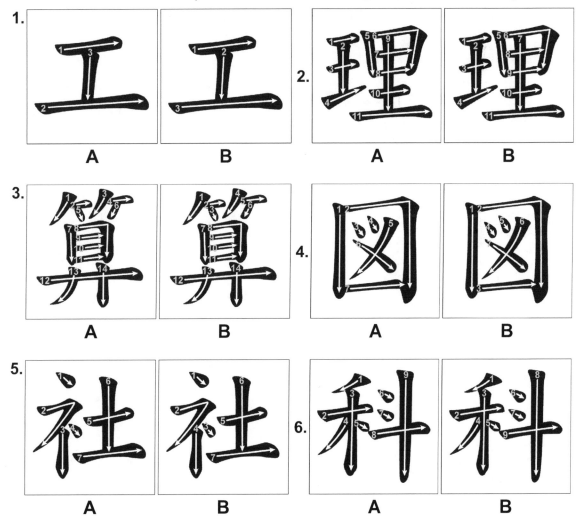

1.　A　B   2.　A　B

3.　A　B   4.　A　B

5.　A　B   6.　A　B

37 | Answer Key 答え合わせ

Fill in the kanji (answers)

1. 大工は雨の日にしごとが できません。

2. わたしがすきな科目は理科と社会科です。

3. 計算より作文のほうが かんたんです。

4. 早く、社会に出たほうが いいですよ。

5. わたしが合図をするまで、まって下さい。

6. 小学生の時は、図工が すきでした。

7. 友人は工場で はたらいています。

Kanji meaning match (answers)

1. 社 shrine, company   2. 朝 morning   3. 前 before, front
4. 科 subject   5. 図 figure, drawing 6. 理 reason, justice
7. 線 line   8. 算 count, calculation 9. 工 work, craft

Kanji matching (answers)

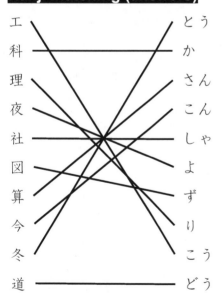

Stroke order check (answers)

1. B   2. A   3. B   4. A   5. A   6. A

38

電船汽弓矢形

38 | New Kanji あたらしい かんじ

Make sure you learn the correct stroke order. Correct stroke order will mean neater symbols when writing quickly. Also, take time to learn the words listed for each kanji – these will help you memorize the different readings.

229. electricity, lightning			13 画
くんよみ	none		
おんよみ	デン		
電			

electricity	electric train	telephone	power outage, blackout
でんき	でんしゃ	でんわ	ていでん
電気	電車	電話	停電

230. ship, boat			11 画
くんよみ	ふね、ふな		
おんよみ	セン		
船			

ship, boat	trip by boat	fishing boat	captain
ふね	ふなたび	ぎょせん	せんちょう
船	船旅	漁船	船長

231. steam, vapor — 7画

くんよみ	none
おんよみ	キ

汽

train (steam)	steamboat	steam whistle	train fare
き しゃ	き せん	き てき	き しゃちん
汽車	汽船	汽笛	汽車賃

232. bow, bow-shaped — 3画

くんよみ	ゆみ
おんよみ	キュウ

弓

bow	Japanese archery	bow and arrow	archery equipment
ゆみ	きゅうどう	ゆみ や	きゅう ぐ
弓	弓道	弓矢	弓具

233. arrow — 5画

くんよみ	や
おんよみ	シ

矢

arrow	arrow (symbol)	arrowhead, moment	dart
や	や じるし	や さき	な や
矢	矢印	矢先	投げ矢

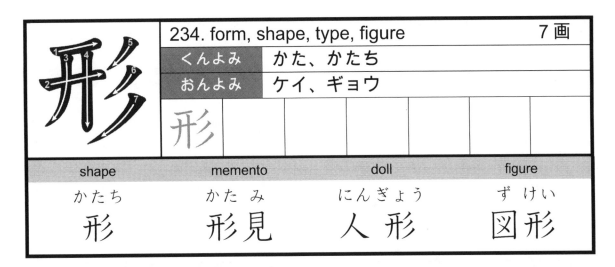

234. form, shape, type, figure	7 画

くんよみ	かた、かたち
おんよみ	ケイ、ギョウ

shape	memento	doll	figure
かたち	かたみ	にんぎょう	ずけい
形	形見	人形	図形

38 | Kanji Usage かんじの つかいかた

● 38-1. Are う serious?

An extra う at the end of a reading will change the Japanese word. An extra or missing う might prevent the kanji you are trying to type from showing up.

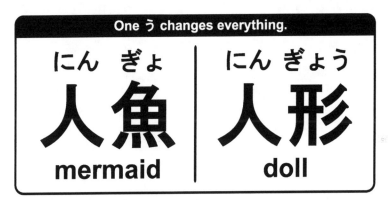

One う changes everything.

にん ぎょ
人魚
mermaid

にん ぎょう
人形
doll

● 38-2. Electric culture (電)

Some phrases involving electricity might not immediately make sense since the context of the phrase changes the meaning of the word.

Phrase	Meaning
でん き 電気をつける	turn on power, turn on the lights
でん き け 電気を消す	turn off power, turn off the lights
でん き き 電気が切れる	power turns off, light bulb burned out

● **38-3. Shapes 角 (かく) and 角形 (かっけい)**
Japanese shapes are made based on how many corners they have.

triangle (three + corners)	square (four + corners)
三角	四角
さん・かく	し・かく

pentagon (five + corner + shape)	hexagon (six + corner + shape)
五角形	六角形
ご・かっ・けい	ろっ・かっ・けい

Shapes with 5 corners and above are (number + 角形 (かっけい). If you leave off 形 (けい) you might not be understood. For example 六角 (ろっかく) is the common name for what we call and "allen wrench" in the USA.

● **38-4. An electrifying situation (電)**
Here are some more words that use 電.

nuclear power plant	power consumption
原子力発電	消費電力
げん・し・りょく・はつ・でん	しょう・ひ・でん・りょく

black out, loss of power	static electricity
停電	静電気
てい・でん	せい・でん・き

convervation of energy	consumer electronics
節電	家電
せつ・でん	か・でん

38 | Words You Can Write かける ことば

電気（でんき）electricity

電	気							

電車（でんしゃ）electric train

電	車							

船長（せんちょう）captain

船	長							

汽車（きしゃ）steam train

汽	車							

汽水（きすい）brackish water

汽	水							

弓矢（ゆみや）bow and arrow

弓	矢							

弓道（きゅうどう）Japanese archery

弓	道							

矢先（やさき）arrowhead, moment

矢	先							

形見（かたみ）memento

形	見							

人形（にんぎょう）doll

人 形 　 　 　 　 　 　 　 　

38 Fill in the Kanji

Fill in the appropriate kanji in the blanks for each sentence.

でん しゃ　　がっ こう　　かよ

1. わたしは ____ ____で ____ ____に ____ っています。
   I commute to (go to and from) school by train.

うみ　　　　　　なつ やす　　ふね　　　こう

2. ____ がすきだから、____ ____みには____でりょ____します。
   Because I like the ocean, I will take a trip by boat on summer break.

き しゃ　　おお　　　　ふる

3. あの ____ ____ は ____きくて、____いです。
   That steam train (over there) is big and old.

とも　　　ゆみ や　　　　じょう ず

4. わたしの____だちは ____ ____をつかうのが ____ ____です。
   My friend is skilled at using a bow and arrow.

いま　　　　　　　かた み　　も

5. ____ でも、おじいさんの____ ____を____っています。
   Even now, I have mementos of my grandfather.

こう こう　とき　　きゅう どう

6. ____ ____の____は、　____ ____をしていました。
   When I was in high school I did Japanese archery.

でん き　　き　　　　か　　い

7. ____ ____が ____れたから、____いに____きましょう。
   Because the light bulb burned out let's go buy one.

38 | Kanji meaning

Write the following kanji next to its meaning: 形 弓 船 図 電 理 汽 矢 社

1. ____ electricity

2. ____ bow

3. ____ form, shape

4. ____ ship, boat

5. ____ arrow

6. ____ reason

7. ____ steam, vapor

8. ____ figure, drawing

9. ____ shrine

38 | Kanji matching

Draw a line to connect each kanji with only one of its ON or KUN readings.

矢 •	• ちゅう
汽 •	• き
電 •	• でん
昼 •	• や
船 •	• か
夜 •	• よる
形 •	• せん
弓 •	• けい
前 •	• まえ
科 •	• きゅう

38 | Stroke Order Check

Circle A or B whichever represents the correct stroke order for each kanji.

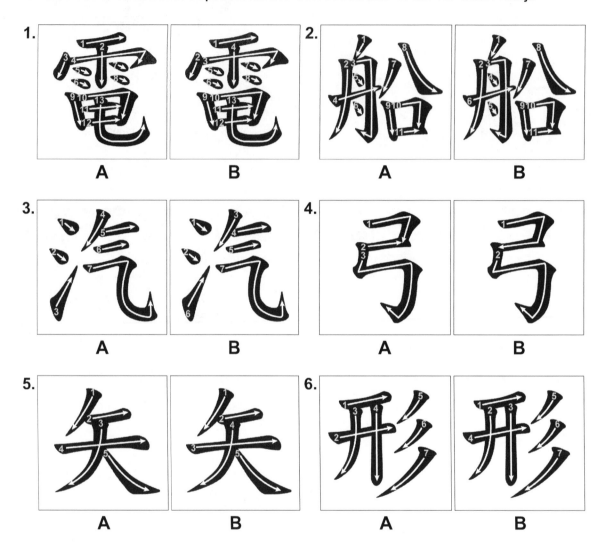

38 | Answer Key 答え合わせ

Fill in the kanji (answers)

1. わたしは 電車 で 学校 に 通 っています。

2. 海 がすきだから、 夏休 みには 船 でりょ 行 します。

3. あの 汽車 は 大 きくて、 古 いです。

4. わたしの 友 だちは 弓矢 をつかうのが 上手 です。

5. 今 でも、おじいさんの 形見 を 持 っています。

6. 高校 の 時 は、 弓道 を していました。

7. 電気 が 切 れたから、 買 いに 行 きましょう。

Kanji meaning match (answers)

1. 電 electricity
2. 弓 bow
3. 形 form, shape
4. 船 ship, boat
5. 矢 arrow
6. 理 reason
7. 汽 steam, vapor
8. 図 figure, drawing
9. 社 shrine

Kanji matching (answers)

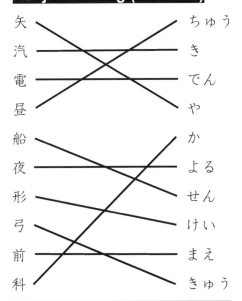

矢　　　　　ちゅう
汽　　　　　き
電　　　　　でん
昼　　　　　や
船　　　　　か
夜　　　　　よる
形　　　　　せん
弓　　　　　けい
前　　　　　まえ
科　　　　　きゅう

Stroke order check (answers)

1. B　2. B　3. A　4. A　5. B　6. A

39 Kanji lesson 39:
235-240
万戸室刀何同

39 | New Kanji あたらしい かんじ

Make sure you learn the correct stroke order. Correct stroke order will mean neater symbols when writing quickly. Also, take time to learn the words listed for each kanji – these will help you memorize the different readings.

万	235. ten thousand, myriad		3 画
	くんよみ	none	
	おんよみ	マン、バン	

10,000 yen	hundred thousand	all-purpose	thorough, flawless
いちまんえん	じゅうまん	ばんのう	ばんぜん
一万円	十万	万能	万全

戸	236. door		4 画
	くんよみ	と	
	おんよみ	コ	

door	cupboard	sliding door	official family registry
とぐち	とだな	ひ　ど	こせき
戸口	戸棚	引き戸	戸籍

237. room　　9画

くんよみ	むろ
おんよみ	シツ

室

inside the room	classroom	basement	room temperature
しつない	きょうしつ	ちかしつ	しつおん
室内	教室	地下室	室温

238. sword, blade, knife　　2画

くんよみ	かたな
おんよみ	トウ

刀

sword	small knife	Japanese sword	wooden sword
かたな	こがたな	にほんとう	ぼくとう
刀	小刀	日本刀	木刀

239. what?　　7画

くんよみ	なに、なん
おんよみ	カ

何

something	what time?	what day?	what color?
なに	なんじ	なんにち	なにいろ
何か	何時	何日	何色

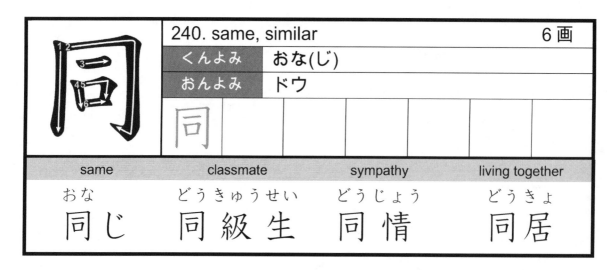

	240. same, similar			6 画
くんよみ	おな(じ)			
おんよみ	ドウ			

same	classmate	sympathy	living together
おな 同じ	どうきゅうせい 同級生	どうじょう 同情	どうきょ 同居

---

39 │ Kanji Usage かんじの つかいかた

● 39-1. 10,000 more cool things (万)

Let's look at some interesting words using 万.

The Great Wall in China	"hooray"
ばん り　　　ちょうじょう 万里の長城	ばん ざい 万歳
The literal translation of the "great wall" is "the 10,000 mile long wall."	The Japanese version of "hooray" is made with 10,000 and years old.

shoplifting	just in case, in the worst case
まん び 万引き	まん　いち 万が一
This was originally 間引き (まびき), "to thin out" but over time 万 replaced 間.	"10,000 is 1" means that sometimes the unexpected could happen.

The "pinky swear" song
ゆび きり げん まん 指切拳万
ゆび　　　　　　　　うそ　　　　　はりせんぼん　の 指きりげんまん嘘ついたら針千本飲ます。 Cut off the finger, 10,000 fists, if you lie, will be made to swallow 1000 needles. **Similar to:** Cross my heart and hope to die, stick a needle in my eye.

● 39-2. More small changes big differences

We did this way back in lesson 9! Do you even remember that far back?
Let's look at some characters that look similar but are different.

sword	power, strength
刀	力
かたな	ちから

interval, space	gate
間	門
あいだ	もん

spirit, mind	vapor, steam
気	汽
き	き

39 | Words You Can Write かける ことば

十万（じゅうまん）hundred thousand

十	万										

戸口（とぐち）door, doorway

戸	口										

教室（きょうしつ）classroom

教	室										

小刀（こがたな）small knife

小	刀									

竹刀（しない）bamboo sword (not common reading)

竹	刀									

何月（なんがつ）what month?

何	月									

何日（なんにち）what day of the month?

何	日									

同じ（おなじ）same

同	じ									

合同（ごうどう）joint, combination

合	同									

引き戸（ひきど）sliding door

引	き	戸							

地下室（ちかしつ）basement

地	下	室							

日本刀（にほんとう）Japanese sword

日	本	刀							

39 | Fill in the Kanji

Fill in the appropriate kanji in the blanks for each sentence.

まん　いち　　　　でん　わ　ばん　　　い

1. ＿＿＿が＿＿＿のために、＿＿＿＿＿＿＿＿＿ごうを＿＿＿いますね。
   Just in case, I will tell you my phone number.

ひ　　　ど　　ふる

2. この ＿＿＿ き ＿＿＿は ＿＿＿ いですか。
   Is this sliding door old?

きょう しつ　　て　が み　　か

3. ＿＿＿ ＿＿＿で ＿＿＿ ＿＿＿を ＿＿＿きました。
   I wrote a letter in the classroom.

なん　がつ　なん　にち

4. きょうは ＿＿＿ ＿＿＿ ＿＿＿ ＿＿＿ですか。
   What is the date (what month what day) today?

おな　　みせ　　た

5. いつも＿＿＿ じ＿＿＿で ＿＿＿べるのは、あきました。
   I am sick of always eating at the same place (store).

あいだ　　に　ほん　とう　　か

6. この ＿＿＿ 、＿＿＿ ＿＿＿ ＿＿＿を＿＿＿いました。
   The other day I bought a Japanese sword.

なん　じ　　　と　しょ しつ　あ

7. ＿＿＿ ＿＿＿に、＿＿＿ ＿＿＿ ＿＿＿ で＿＿＿いましょうか。
   At what time shall me meet in the library room?

39 | Kanji meaning

Write the following kanji next to its meaning: 戸 刀 矢 万 同 何 船 室 今

1. ____ ten thousand   2. ____ room   3. ____ what?

4. ____ now   5. ____ ship, boat   6. ____ arrow

7. ____ door   8. ____ sword, knife 9. ____ same

39 | Kanji matching

Draw a line to connect each kanji with only one of its ON or KUN readings.

万 ・	・ なん
同 ・	・ と
算 ・	・ まん
戸 ・	・ かたな
何 ・	・ しゅん
工 ・	・ どう
室 ・	・ しつ
刀 ・	・ さん
社 ・	・ しゃ
春 ・	・ こう

39 | Stroke Order Check

Circle A or B whichever represents the correct stroke order for each kanji.

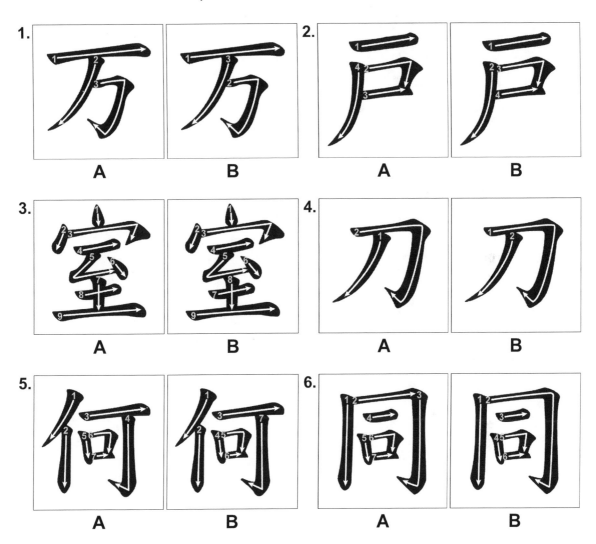

39 | Answer Key 答え合わせ

Fill in the kanji (answers)

1. 万が一のために、電話番ごうを言いますね。

2. この引き戸は古いですか。

3. 教室で手紙を書きました。

4. きょうは何月何日ですか。

5. いつも同じ店で食べるのは、あきました。

6. この間、日本刀を買いました。

7. 何時に、図書室で会いましょうか。

Kanji meaning match (answers)

1. 万 ten thousand   2. 室 room   3. 何 what?

4. 今 now   5. 船 ship, boat   6. 矢 arrow

7. 戸 door   8. 刀 sword, knife 9. 同 same

Kanji matching (answers)

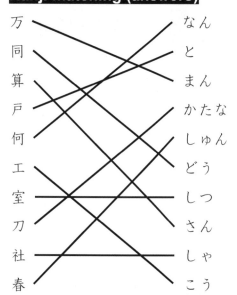

万	なん
同	と
算	まん
戸	かたな
何	しゅん
工	どう
室	しつ
刀	さん
社	しゃ
春	こう

Stroke order check (answers)

1. B   2. A   3. B   4. B   5. B   6. B

SR Super Review 8

SR8 | Kanji selection

Select the best kanji to fill in the blank in each sentence.

1. 今日は午後一時ごろ、＿＿＿食を とりました。
   A. 夜　　　　　　　B. 朝　　　　　　　C. 昼　　　　　　　D. 夕

2. わたしは＿＿＿学より図工のほうが すきです。
   A. 算　　　　　　　B. 科　　　　　　　C. 理　　　　　　　D. 社

3. 日本は＿＿＿車やバスが とてもべんり ですね。
   A. 自　　　　　　　B. 汽　　　　　　　C. 船　　　　　　　D. 電

4. 父は車を三＿＿＿、もっています。
   A. 組　　　　　　　B. 台　　　　　　　C. 点　　　　　　　D. 番

SR8 | Kanji reading

Select the best reading for the underlined kanji.

1. 夜中に外を歩く時は、気をつけて下さい。
   A. よる　　　　　　B. や　　　　　　　C. よ　　　　　　　D. ばん

2. 買いものは後回しにしないで、先に しましょう。
   A. ご　　　　　　　B. あと　　　　　　C. うしろ　　　　　D. のち

3. 今朝、何時ごろ会社に行きましたか。
   A. いま　　　　　　B. こん　　　　　　C. きん　　　　　　D. け

4. この人形は、子どもの時から家に ありますよ。
   A. かた　　　　　　B. かたち　　　　　C. けい　　　　　　D. ぎょう

SR8	**Compound kanji word puzzle**

Fill in the correct kanji based on the list below the puzzle.

1)		2)	3)
4)		5)	
6)	7)	8)	
		9)	

Down ↓

1) arts and crafts

3) wooden sword

5) classroom

6) captain

7) steam train

Left to Right →

1) figure

4) factory

8) inside the room

9) telephone

Right to Left ←

2) doll

7) steamship

9) electric train

SR8 | Answer Key 答え合わせ

Kanji selection (answers)

1. C – 昼食 (ちゅうしょく)

   I had lunch around 1 o'clock in the afternoon today.

2. B – 科学 (かがく)

   I like science more than arts and crafts.

3. D – 電車 (でんしゃ)

   Japanese buses and trains are very convenient.

4. B – 三台 (さんだい)

   My father owns three cars.

Kanji reading (answers)

1. C – 夜中 (よなか)

   Be careful when walking outside in the middle of the night.

2. B – 後回し (あとまわ)

   Let's not put off the shopping and do it first.

3. D – 今朝 (けさ)

   Around what time did you go to work (company) this morning?

4. D – 人形 (にんぎょう)

   This doll has been in my house since I was a child.

Compound kanji word puzzle (answers)

図	形	人	木
工	場	教	刀
船	汽	室	内
長	車	電	話

Glossary A:

Search by Reading

あ

あ(あき)	空	87
あ(う)	会	207
あ(う)	合	229
あ(かす)	明	158
あ(から)	空	87
あ(かり)	明	158
あ(がる)	上	46
あ(く)	明	158
あ(く)	空	87
あ(くる)	明	158
あ(ける)	明	158
あ(げる)	上	46
あ(たる)	当	230
あ(てる)	当	230
あ(わす)	合	229
あ(わせる)	合	229
あい	合	229
あいだ	間	362
あお	青	108
あか	赤	108
あか(らむ)	明	158
あか(るい)	明	158
あか(るむ)	明	158
あき	秋	361
あき(らか)	明	158
あさ	朝	373
あざ	字	129
あし	足	70
あたま	頭	257
あたら(しい)	新	156
あに	兄	248
あね	姉	248
あま	天	87
あま	雨	88
あめ	天	87
あめ	雨	88
あゆ(む)	歩	182
あら(た)	新	156
あら(にい)	新	156
ある(く)	歩	182

い

い(う)	言	198
い(かす)	生	79
い(きる)	生	79
い(く)	行	182
い(こと)	言	198
い(れる)	入	120
いえ	家	320
いけ	池	332
いし	石	98
イチ	一	16
いち	市	339
イツ	一	16
いつ (つ)	五	17
いと	糸	138
いぬ	犬	98
いま	今	375
いもうと	妹	249
いろ	色	349
いわ	岩	309
イン	引	220
イン	音	138

う

ウ	右	47
ウ	羽	288
ウ	雨	88
う(まれる)	生	79
う(む)	生	79
う(る)	売	191
う(れる)	売	191
うえ	上	46
うお	魚	269
うし	牛	268
うし(あと)	後	374
うし(ろ)	後	374
うた(う)	歌	191
うち	内	340
うち	家	320
うま	馬	268
うみ	海	308
うわ	上	46
ウン	雲	308

え

エ	会	207
エ	回	221
エ	絵	351
エン	円	57
エン	園	321
エン	遠	147

お

お	下	47
オウ	王	131
オウ	黄	349
おお(い)	多	157
おお(きい)	大	56
おおやけ	公	340
おく(れる)	後	374
おこな(う)	行	182
おし(える)	教	190
おそ(わる)	教	190
おと	音	138
おとうと	弟	248
おとこ	男	78
おな(じ)	同	404
おも(う)	思	190
おや	親	156
オン	音	138
おんな	女	79

か

カ	下	47
カ	何	403
カ	夏	360
カ	家	320
か	日	36
カ	歌	191
カ	火	37
カ	科	385
カ	花	98
か(う)	交	219
か(う)	買	192
か(く)	書	208
か(わす)	交	219
カイ	会	207
カイ	回	221
カイ	海	308
カイ	絵	351
かい	貝	139
かえ(す)	帰	183
かえ(る)	帰	183
かお	顔	256
カク	画	279
カク	角	299
かざ	風	307
かしら	頭	257
かず	数	191
かぜ	風	307
かぞ(える)	数	191
かた	形	395
かた	方	298

Glossary B:

Search by

Stroke Count

1 stroke

一	16

2 strokes

七	25
九	26
二	16
人	57
入	120
八	25
刀	403
力	70
十	26

3 strokes

万	402
三	17
上	46
下	47
丸	171
千	27
口	69
土	38
夕	108
大	56
女	79
子	79
小	57
山	88
川	89
工	383
弓	394
才	289

4 strokes

中	56
五	17
今	375
元	172
公	340
六	18
内	340
円	57
分	220
切	220
午	375
友	238
天	87
太	170
少	157
引	220
心	239
戸	402
手	70
文	122
方	298
日	36
月	36
木	37
止	229
毛	257
水	37
火	37
父	247
牛	268
犬	98
王	131

5 strokes

兄	248
冬	361
出	120
北	298
半	290
古	157
台	278
右	47
四	17
外	341
左	47
市	339
広	170
本	121
正	130
母	247
玉	139
生	79
用	230
田	107
白	109
目	58
矢	394
石	98
立	78

6 strokes

交	219
休	46
会	207
先	121
光	230
合	229
同	404
名	129
回	221
地	331
多	157
字	129
寺	320
年	131
当	230
早	121
毎	289
気	88
池	332
百	26
竹	140
米	269
糸	138
羽	288
考	208
耳	69
肉	258
自	238
色	349
虫	99
行	182
西	297

7 strokes

体	256
何	403
作	219
図	384
声	239
売	191
弟	248
形	395
村	107
来	182
汽	394
男	78
町	99
社	384
花	98
見	109
角	299
言	198
谷	309
貝	139
赤	108
走	181
足	70
車	139
近	147
里	330
麦	270

8 strokes

京	340
国	339
夜	374
妹	249
姉	248
学	130
岩	309
店	321
明	158
東	297
林	97
画	182
歩	279
直	237
知	238
空	87
金	38
長	171
門	321
雨	88
青	108

9 strokes

前	374
南	298
室	403
後	374
思	190
星	308
春	360
昼	373
活	231
海	308
点	279
秋	361
科	385
茶	350
草	140
計	200
音	138
風	307
食	207
首	257

10 strokes

原	330
夏	360
家	320
帰	183
弱	148
時	361
書	208
校	130
紙	350
記	199
通	181
馬	268
高	148

11 strokes

強	148
教	190
理	383
細	171
組	278
船	393
週	288
野	331
雪	307
魚	269
鳥	269
黄	349
黒	350

12 strokes

場	322
晴	237
朝	373
森	97
番	279
答	208
絵	351
買	192
道	331

間	362
雲	308

13 strokes

園	321
数	191
新	156
楽	149
話	199
遠	147
電	393

14 strokes

歌	191
算	384
聞	198
語	280
読	199
鳴	209

15 strokes

線	351

16 strokes

親	156
頭	257

18 strokes

曜	289
顔	256

Glossary C:

Search by English Meaning

A

ability	才	289
above	上	46
after	後	374
age	年	131
ahead	先	121
angle	角	299
answer	答	208
approach	近	147
arrow	矢	394
artisan	工	383
ask	聞	198
autumn	秋	361

B

ball	丸	171
ball	玉	139
bamboo	竹	140
barley	麦	270
basis	台	278
before	前	374
behind	後	374
below	下	47
big	大	56
big	太	170
bird	鳥	269
black	黒	350
blade	刀	403
blue	青	108
boat	船	393
body	体	256
book	書	208
book	本	121
bow	弓	394
bow-shaped	弓	394
boy	男	78
breeze	風	307
bright	明	158
brilliance	光	230
broad	広	170
bug	虫	99
business	用	230
buy	買	192

C

calculation	算	384
capital	京	340

car	車	139
cause	元	172
character	字	129
chief	長	171
chief	首	257
child	子	79
chronicle	記	199
circle	円	57
city	市	339
clear	明	158
clear	晴	237
cloud	雲	308
color	色	349
combine	合	229
come	来	182
come out	出	120
comfort	楽	149
company	社	384
conduct	行	182
consider	考	208
conversation	話	199
corner	角	299
correct	正	130
count	数	191
count	算	384
count	計	200
country	国	339
cow	牛	268
craft	工	383
cry	鳴	209
cut	切	220

D

day	日	36
day of the week	曜	289
day off	休	46
daytime	昼	373
direct	直	237
direction	方	298
do	行	182
dog	犬	98
door	戸	402
dot	点	279
down	下	47
drawing	図	384
duke	公	340

E

each	毎	289
ear	耳	69
early	早	121
earth	土	38
ease	楽	149
east	東	297
eat	食	207
eight	八	25
elder brother	兄	248
elder sister	姉	248
electricity	電	393
empty	空	87
energy	力	70
enjoyable	楽	149
enter	入	120
errand	用	230
evening	夕	108
every	毎	289
exchange	交	219
eye	目	58

F

face (person)	顔	256
fall	秋	361
far	遠	147
far	長	171
fast	早	121
fat	太	170
father	父	247
feather	羽	288
few	少	157
field	原	330
field	田	107
field	野	331
figure	図	384
figure	形	395
fine	細	171
fire	火	37
first	首	257
fish	魚	269
fit	合	229
five	五	17
flower	花	98
foot (leg 脚)	足	70
forest; woods	森	97
form	形	395
four	四	17
fresh	新	156
friend	友	238
front	前	374

plan	計	200
points	点	279
pond	池	332
portion	分	220
power	力	70
previous	先	121
prior	先	121
production	作	219
pull	引	220

R

rain	雨	88
rate	歩	182
raw	生	79
read	読	199
reason	理	383
recent	近	147
red	赤	108
reply	答	208
reputation	声	239
rest	休	46
return	帰	183
rice	米	269
rice paddy	田	107
right	右	47
rise	立	78
river	川	89
road	道	331
rock	岩	309
room	室	403
round	丸	171
round	円	57
run	走	181

S

same	同	404
say	言	198
school	校	130
scribe	記	199
segment	分	220
sell	売	191
sentence	文	122
seven	七	25
shape	形	395
shell	貝	139
shine	光	230
ship	船	393
shop	店	321
shrine	社	384

side	方	298
similar	同	404
since	来	182
sing	鳴	209
six	六	18
sky	空	87
small	小	57
snow	雪	307
society	社	384
soil	土	38
soil	地	331
song	歌	191
soon	直	237
sound	音	138
source	原	330
south	南	298
space	間	362
speak	言	198
speak	語	280
spirit	気	88
spread	広	170
spring	春	360
stand	台	278
stand up	立	78
star	星	308
steam	汽	394
step	歩	182
stone	石	98
stop	止	229
store	店	321
story	話	199
street	道	331
strengthen	強	148
string	糸	138
stroke	画	279
stroke	行	182
strong	強	148
study of	学	130
style	体	256
subject	科	385
summer	夏	360
sword	刀	403

T

talent	才	289
talk	話	199
tea	茶	350
teach	教	190
team	組	278
temple	寺	320

ten	十	26
ten quadrillion	京	340
ten thousand	万	402
the current	当	230
the origin	元	172
the public	公	340
thick	太	170
thin	細	171
think	思	190
think	考	208
thought	思	190
thousand (1000)	千	27
thread	糸	138
three	三	17
time	時	361
tiny amount	毛	257
to live	生	79
to look	見	109
town	町	99
tree	木	37
turn	回	221
turn	番	279
two	二	16
type	形	395

U

union	合	229
up	上	46
use	用	230

V

vacant	空	87
valley	谷	309
vapor	汽	394
village	村	107
village	里	330
voice	声	239

W

walk	歩	182
watch	番	279
water	水	37
way	道	331
weak	弱	148
week	週	288
west	西	297
what?	何	403

Other From Zero! Books

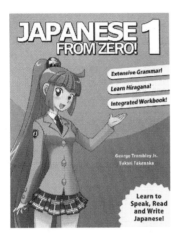

Chinese From Zero! Coming in 2017 (we hope)!

Made in United States
Orlando, FL
21 September 2024